LET'S STUDY
MATTHEW

In the same series:

Series Editor: SINCLAIR B. FERGUSON

Let's Study

MATTHEW

Mark E. Ross

THE BANNER OF TRUTH TRUST

THE BANNER OF TRUTH TRUST
3 Murrayfield Road, Edinburgh EH12 6EL, UK
P.O. Box 621, Carlisle, PA 17013, USA

*

© Mark E. Ross 2009
ISBN: 978 1 84871 007 8

*

Typeset in 11/12.5 pt Ehrhardt MT at the
Banner of Truth Trust, Edinburgh

Printed in the U.S.A. by
Versa Press, Inc.,
East Peoria, IL

FOR MY MOTHER,

BETTY JANE (BROWNFIELD) ROSS

whose Hannah-like prayer at my troubled birth
offered me to the service of the Lord
for the preservation of my life

(I SAMUEL 1:10–11)

Contents

Contents

Publisher's Preface

*L*et's *Study Matthew* is part of a series of books which explain and apply the message of Scripture. The series is designed to meet a specific and important need in the church. While not technical commentaries, the volumes comment on the text of a biblical book; and, without being merely lists of practical applications, they are concerned with the ways in which the teaching of Scripture can affect and transform our lives today. Understanding the Bible's message and applying its teaching are the aims.

Like other volumes in the series, *Let's Study Matthew* seeks to combine explanation and application. Its concern is to be helpful to ordinary Christian people by encouraging them to understand the message of the Bible and apply it to their own lives. The reader in view is not the person who is interested in all the detailed questions which fascinate the scholar, although behind the writing of each study lies an appreciation for careful and detailed scholarship. The aim is exposition of Scripture written in the language of a friend, seated alongside you with an open Bible.

Let's Study Matthew is designed to be used in various contexts. It can be used simply as an aid for individual Bible study. Some may find it helpful to use in their devotions with husband or wife, or to read in the context of the whole family.

In order to make these studies more useful, not only for individual use but also for group study in Sunday School classes and home, church or college, study guide material will be found on pp. 298–328. Sometimes we come away frustrated rather than helped by group discussions. Frequently that is because we have been encouraged to discuss a passage of Scripture which we do not understand very well in the first place. Understanding must always be the foundation for enriching discussion and for thought-ful, practical application. Thus, in addition to the exposition of *Matthew*, the additional material provides questions to encourage personal thought and study, or to be used as discussion starters. The Group Study Guide divides the material into twenty-six sec-tions and provides direction for leading and participating in group study and discussion.

Author's Preface

I am very conscious that in presenting this study I stand in debt to many who have laboured before me, and that I have entered into their labour. Acknowledgement of some of the most helpful written sources is given in the back of the book, and the reader is directed there for further study. I would also like to express my sincere and deep thanks to the trustees and editors of the Banner of Truth Trust for the privilege given me to undertake this study. The labour has been an immense blessing in my own life, and if readers should receive even half the benefit I have gained they will count themselves blessed as well.

One of the themes for which the *Gospel according to Matthew* is noted is the church. Church fathers from Cyprian to Augustine to Calvin and beyond have taught us that those who have God for their Father also have the Church for their mother. My life has certainly borne sustained witness to this truth. I was born, baptized, and nurtured in the Christian faith in the Third Presbyterian Church in Uniontown, Pennsylvania. The session and congregation of that church provided steady and generous support for me and my family through the many years of seminary and postgraduate education. The Bellefield Presbyterian Church of Pittsburgh, Pennsylvania, became my home during the years at university and seminary. There I first sensed a calling to the gospel ministry and was mentored by the ministers for service in the kingdom of God. While a postgraduate student in England, the Newcastle Baptist Church in Newcastle-under-Lyme, Staffordshire, welcomed and nurtured me and my family, and gave much encouragement toward the ministry.

I give special thanks to the session and congregation of the First Presbyterian Church of Columbia, South Carolina, where I was ordained to the gospel ministry. During twenty years of service there I enjoyed the opportunity of devoting myself to teaching and preaching the Holy Scriptures to a degree rarely enjoyed by associate pastors. I am particularly grateful to the members of the Men's Friday Morning Bible Study and the Berean Sunday School Class where these lessons were first presented. Their eager reception of the expositions as well as their comments and questions prompted me to dig deeply in my studies. Above all others, my enduring thanks and love go to my wife, Connie, for her constant support and spiritual help. I sincerely and justly say of her, as John Calvin said of Idelette, that she has been 'the best companion of my life . . . (and) the faithful helper of my ministry'. God alone knows how great has been the impact of her prayers and love upon my life.

As a commentary on 'the first gospel', from which the church has been so deeply and constantly nurtured, I dedicate this book to my mother, Mrs Ralph G. (Betty Jane Brownfield) Ross. It was her prayers and love that were first in my life, and from her I first learned the things of God. I still remember her helping me as a small boy to memorize the 'beatitudes' of Matthew's Gospel. Her example of persevering godliness has been an inspiration to me. As the dedication reveals, it was with her loving prayers that both my life and my ministry began and have since been sustained.

Reading the Gospel
according to Matthew

As we open the New Testament, the first book that we meet is the *Gospel according to Matthew*. It is followed by the other three gospels, *Mark, Luke,* and *John.* They occur in this order because among the early church fathers it was generally believed that this was the order in which they were written. *Matthew* was something of a favourite Gospel for them, for they quote it more often than any of the others. In their minds it was indeed 'the first Gospel', not only first in time but in a way first also in importance. Not that they thought the other Gospels were somehow less the Word of God, or less authoritative. It was just that Matthew was pre-eminent, a *primus inter pares,* 'first among equals'.

THE GOSPEL

Like the other Gospels, *Matthew* provides us with a collection of the words and deeds of Jesus. Speaking very generally, the collection is ordered chronologically, though comparison of this Gospel with the others will reveal that topical considerations are also at work. A first glance, therefore, might suggest that this is a biography. However, when we look closer, we will see that, if so, it is a biography of a rather unusual type. Of the approximately thirty-three years of Jesus' life, perhaps twenty-five or so are passed over in silence. We are told just a little of his birth in Bethlehem and his family's sojourn in Egypt before they finally settled in Nazareth (*Matt.* 1–2). Then we are told nothing of his life until the beginning of his public ministry in the days of John the Baptist (*Matt.* 3:17–23), when Luke tells us he was about thirty years of age (*Luke* 3:23). From that point the story concentrates on Jesus' ministry in Galilee (unlike *John*, which has much to say about his ministry in Jerusalem), before nearly a fourth of the book details just the last week of Jesus' life in Jerusalem. The other Gospels treat his life in much the same manner.

While of necessity all biographies are selective, the Gospels seem to be peculiarly so. We will perhaps understand them best if we think of them less as biographies of Jesus than as revelations of God through the words and deeds of Jesus, focused on the making of the new covenant (thus the special emphasis on the last week of Jesus' life). The Gospel writers have chosen from among all that Jesus said and did (*John* 20:30–31) according to their own special interests and leading from the Holy Spirit, and they have presented it to us in their own distinctive way. Thus, what we are given in the Gospels are perhaps best described as 'literary portraits' drawn from the words and deeds of Jesus Christ, in which we see 'the light of the knowledge of the glory of God in the face of Jesus Christ' (*2 Cor.* 4:6).

ACCORDING TO . . .

Each of the four Gospels has come down to us in manuscripts titled and identified by a short phrase, 'The Gospel according to . . .' or sometimes more simply, 'According to . . .' In these titles the little phrase, 'according to . . .', indicates authorship. It marks for us an important characteristic of the Gospels, but one which can easily be misunderstood by modern readers. For it might suggest that what we have before us are just the opinions and views of the named writer, all of which are subject to the fallibility and biases of other human writers. Many scholars have said as much, and the impression has become widespread. However, if you were to accept this way of thinking you would make a very big mistake, 'because you know neither the Scriptures nor the power of God' (*Matt.* 22:29). Understanding and overcoming this mistake will take a little bit of history, a measure of theology, some careful thinking, and much faithful praying, but the effort will put us in the right position to begin reading and studying the *Gospel according to Matthew*, 'not as the word of men but as what it really is, the word of God, which is at work in you believers' (*I Thess.* 2:13).

1. A little bit of history. With the advent of the scientific revolution and the rise of historical criticism in Western civilization, many scholars began to view and read the Bible in a new way. Success in explaining more of the world according to naturalistic laws and powers encouraged some to draw the completely unfounded conclusion that all things could be explained naturalistically. In keeping with this new way of thinking, a growing number of scholars placed greater emphasis on the human character of the Bible, treating it as they would just any other book. In many cases the human character was all that survived—no word from God remained. This 'higher critical view' of the Bible, as it came to be called, brought with it destructive effects both for the church and for the world. It has created 'a famine . . . of hearing the words of the LORD' (*Amos* 8:11), leaving us with just human words—none of which can be known to be more reliable than another.

2. A measure of theology. In attempting to make their case, these critical scholars suggested that just as the white light from the sun which enters a church is coloured by the stained glass windows through which it passes, so the white light of God's revelation was coloured or tainted as it passed through the human messengers who spoke or wrote it. For many of these scholars, if not all, light from God was indeed to be found in the Bible, but not purely, for the Bible also contained the biases and errors of the authors who gave us this word. B. B. Warfield accurately diagnosed the error in this thinking long ago. He pointed out that those who think this way have forgotten that the God of revelation and inspiration, who sends his white light of revelation down out of heaven, is also the God of providence and grace, who forms the human messengers through which he gives his revelation. As the light of revelation passes through these human stained glass windows, the light is neither tainted, distorted, nor corrupted with things not present at its origin. Rather, the light is refracted into the many colours which constitute the white light of revelation. The light entering the church passes through stained glass windows 'whose designer and builder is God' (*Heb.* 11:10), and it is bent and refracted to give to the church just the illumination intended by the architect. Thus, the distinctive emphases and messages to be found in the individual books of the Bible are not mere human perspectives (more or less accurate) of the revelation given to us by God; they are the distinct and many-splendoured elements that make up the full spectrum of divine revelation. We can therefore say of Matthew, as he himself said of Isaiah: in this book is 'what the Lord had spoken by the prophet' (*Matt.* 1:22), for in Matthew's case too he 'spoke from God . . . being carried along by the Holy Spirit' (*2 Pet.* 1:21).

3. Some careful thinking. Because the Bible is a collection of human literary products which are also sacred writings 'breathed out' from God (*2 Tim.* 3:16), it should be read and studied with both these features in view. The words and deeds of Jesus recorded in this book were not mechanically dictated and simply pieced together in a more or less chronological arrangement. What is written, how it is expressed, and how it is arranged are all functions of human literary art, for no aspect of the human personality formed by God for this task has been suppressed by the Holy Spirit in producing the Scriptures. We should not be surprised to find features in Matthew's presentation of the words and deeds of Jesus, which vary from Mark's, or Luke's, or John's. Recognizing that this book is a work of human literary art, we should seek to understand how these distinctive features form and shape the message we are given. In addition, we should not only pay attention to what is said in a given passage we are reading at the moment; but also consider what has come before and after it, and how the passage fits into the overall plan of the book.

We need to gain both the bird's eye view of the book (its overall development) and the worm's eye view of the passages (what each one says). Our reading and study should take in both, so that the whole and its parts may be understood clearly. While this study is arranged in a piecemeal manner suitable for daily reading and study, an effort will be made to keep the reader apprised of Matthew's overall story development as we go along.

But understanding *Matthew*, as with all the Scriptures, will take repeated readings of the whole book, as of the rest of the Scriptures. Each time through will give us a better bird's eye view of the whole, and this will give us a richer worm's eye view as we concentrate our meditations upon particular passages.

4. *Much faithful praying.* Above all else, if we would understand the truths given to us in the Scriptures and see them in harmony with one another, our study must be spiritual, that is, aided by the Spirit of God. Human intellect, however diligent and gifted, is not sufficient for grasping the truth of God by its own power. Spiritual insight comes only as a gift from God (see *Matt.* 16:17), so our study must be prayerful above all else. If we were just dealing with understanding Matthew as a human author, there might be some hope of comprehending him in a purely natural way, for he is a man with a nature like ours. Yet even at this level we face serious limitations: 'For who knows a person's thoughts except the spirit of that person which is in him?' How much more then, if we are to understand the things of God, must we receive that knowledge from God himself: 'So also no one comprehends the thoughts of God except the Spirit of God' (*1 Cor.* 2:11). Spiritual truth must be Spiritually discerned. If in the sacred writings we would be wise for salvation (*2 Tim.* 3:15), let us pray for God the Holy Spirit to open our eyes, so that we 'may turn from darkness to light and from the power of Satan to God, that (we) might receive forgiveness of sins and a place among those who are sanctified by faith in (Jesus Christ)' (*Acts* 26:18).

MATTHEW

The early church fathers (for example, Papias, Irenaeus, Origen, Eusebius, Chrysostom, Jerome, Augustine, and others) tell us that our first Gospel was written by Matthew, the tax-collector who became an apostle of Jesus Christ (*Matt.* 9:9–13, 10:1–4). They say he wrote it for Hebrews who had believed in Jesus. There is a distinctively Jewish quality to this book, for one of its chief themes is to show that the Old Testament promises of God are fulfilled in Jesus Christ. Numerous quotations from the Old Testament are included, and many more allusions made. In all this we can perceive in Matthew, as we do in Paul,

> *(his) insight into the mystery of Christ, which was not made known to the sons of men in other generations as it has now been revealed to his holy apostles and prophets by the Spirit.*

This mystery is that the Gentiles are fellow heirs, members of the same body, and partakers of the promise in Christ Jesus through the gospel (Eph. 3:4–6).

The *Gospel according to Matthew* thus bears striking witness to the divine principle of salvation noted elsewhere in the New Testament, ' . . . to the Jew first and also to the Greek' (*Rom.* 1:16, 2:9–10; see also *Acts* 3:25-26, 13:46). It is thus most appropriately our doorway into the New Testament from the Old, standing perhaps both nearest in time and in thought to the Old Testament, providing us with a bridge between the time of anticipation and the time of fulfillment. Long before Augustine said it, Matthew demonstrated it: 'The New Testament is in the Old concealed, and in the New the Old revealed.'

In keeping with his themes of fulfilment and of salvation to Gentiles as well as Jews, Matthew highlights the theme of Jesus as King over all. He begins the Gospel with Jesus' royal genealogy running down the line of Davidic kings. He shows that Jesus is hailed in his birth as 'the born king of Israel' by Gentile wise men that have come from afar. His ministry is introduced by John the Baptist with the proclamation that 'the kingdom of heaven is at hand' (*Matt.* 3:2). Jesus goes about preaching 'the gospel of the kingdom' and demonstrates its power in healing 'every disease and every affliction' (*Matt.* 4:23); ruling over all the powers of the earth so that 'even winds and sea obey him' (*Matt.* 8:27); binding 'the strong man', Satan, that he might plunder his house (*Matt.* 12:22–29), in order to build his church against which the gates of hell will not prevail (*Matt.* 16:18).

In support of all this Matthew shows us that Jesus is the Son of Man (*Matt.* 16:13, 28; 20:28; 23:30; 24:27; 26:64), the messianic Son of David (*Matt.* 1:1, 9:27, 12:23, 15:22, 20:30–31, 22:41–46), and supremely the Son of God (*Matt.* 3:17, 8:29, 14:33, 16:16, 17:5, 27:54). In the great Olivet Discourse before his death, Jesus commands that his gospel of the kingdom be preached in the whole world as a testimony to all the nations (*Matt.* 24:14), before he comes again in all his and his Father's glory (*Matt.* 16:27, 24:30, 25:31, 26:64). Then Jesus is given over to death, for the one who is the Christ, the Messiah, the Son of Man, the Son of

David, and the Son of God, is also the Suffering Servant of Israel (*Matt.* 12:17–21), who must be cut off from among his people in order to win redemption for them (*Isa.* 52:13—53:12). At the end of the book the King stands victorious over sin and death, high upon a mountain in 'Galilee of the Gentiles', with *all* authority in heaven and earth given to him, sending forth his disciples to make disciples of *all* the nations, teaching them to obey *all* that Jesus has commanded, with the promise that Jesus will be with them *all* the days to the end of the age (*Matt.* 28:16–20). What a message this is—what drama, what pathos, what love, what glory, what longing fulfilled, what hope and promise for us today!

As Matthew shared Paul's insight into the mystery of Christ, so he shared his burden for their kinsmen according to the flesh, the Israelites, to whom belonged 'the adoption, the glory, the covenants, the giving of the law, the worship, and the promises'. To them also belonged 'the patriarchs, and from their race, according to the flesh, is the Christ, who is God over all, blessed forever. Amen' (*Rom.* 9:4—5). But a veil was and is over the eyes of many Israelites according to the flesh at the reading of the old covenant, because only through Christ is the veil taken away (*2 Cor.* 3:14). May there be no veil over our eyes in the reading of the new covenant. May the Lord who is the Spirit open our eyes so that we might understand fully the things that have been given us by God. May the Lord feed us in abundance from his Scriptures that we may live.

> *How precious is your steadfast love, O God! The children of mankind take refuge in the shadow of your wings. They feast on the abundance of your house, and you give them drink from the river of your delights. For with you is the fountain of life; in your light do we see light* (Psa. 36:7–9).

I

The New Beginning

The book of the genealogy of Jesus Christ, the son of David, the son of Abraham (Matt. 1:1).

The Gospel according to Matthew, and with it our New Testament, begins with a title (all of verse 1) rooting its message deeply and firmly in the Old Testament. The very first words of the book in its original Greek text, *Biblos geneseos* (literally, 'book of genesis'), are reminiscent of the first book of the Bible. In the Greek version of the Old Testament, so familiar to Matthew's readers, the exact phrase is found in the first two of the ten sections which organize the book of Genesis according to the generations from Adam to Jacob (*Gen.* 2:4; 5:1). The remaining eight sections then echo this phrase in part. This imitation of Genesis suggests that Matthew (like John, see *John* 1:1) is announcing a new Genesis, a new beginning, a new creation. The Old Testament had promised this (see *Isa.* 65:17–25). The New Testament will close with the same announcement: 'Behold, I am making all things new' (*Rev.* 21:5). As we shall see, Matthew builds his message on both the pattern and the substance of the Old Testament. What was promised long ago is now being fulfilled. This is the good news that Matthew brings to us. Oh, what a message is before us! Is it really possible that all things can be made new? Can our lives be made new? Can the world be made new? Matthew and the New Testament answer these questions with an unequivocal 'Yes!'

THE PROMISED MESSIAH

This message of the new beginning is centred in Jesus Christ. We

[1]

are so familiar with the name Jesus Christ that we might fail to appreciate how bold a claim Matthew and the New Testament make when using it. Christ is a title applied to Jesus. It is not his last name. It is the New Testament equivalent of the Old Testament word *mashiah* ('Anointed One', the Messiah). So from the very first sentence of the book, Matthew is claiming that Jesus is the Messiah, Yahweh's Anointed One, the One promised from ancient days to be God's Saviour for his people. Then Matthew extends this bold claim with two others, saying that Jesus Christ is 'the son of David, the son of Abraham'.

THE SON OF DAVID

As the son of David, or rather, as the *Son* of David, Jesus the Christ is that Son promised to David whose throne and kingdom God would establish forever (*2 Sam.* 7:13). The Old Testament prophets had much to say about this Son. For instance, Jeremiah had predicted:

> *Behold, the days are coming, declares the* LORD, *when I will raise up for David a righteous Branch, and he shall reign as king and deal wisely, and shall execute justice and righteousness in the land. In his days Judah will be saved, and Israel will dwell securely. And this is the name by which he will be called: 'The* LORD *is our righteousness'* (Jer. 23:5–6).

Likewise Isaiah spoke, saying:

> *For to us a child is born,*
> *to us a son is given;*
> *and the government shall be upon his shoulder,*
> *and his name shall be called*
> > *Wonderful Counsellor, Mighty God,*
> > *Everlasting Father, Prince of Peace.*
> *Of the increase of his government and of peace*
> *there will be no end,*
> *on the throne of David and over his kingdom,*
> *to establish it and to uphold it*
> *with justice and with righteousness*
> *from this time forth and forevermore.*
> *The zeal of the* LORD *of hosts will do this* (Isa. 9:6–7).

Son of David is a title for Jesus found frequently in Matthew's Gospel (cf. 9:27; 12:23; 15:22; 20:30-31; 21:9; 21:15; 22:42; 22:45). Matthew never wants us to lose sight of the fact that Jesus is the one whose kingdom will never end. He sounds this note in the opening sentence, and he holds it throughout the book. If it is the promised Son of David who makes all things new, they shall be new forever. For his kingdom will never pass away.

THE SON OF ABRAHAM

As the 'son of Abraham' Jesus is also the promised seed in whom all the nations (see *Matt.* 28:18) are to be blessed (*Gen.* 22:18). Jewish readers in Jesus' days would not normally have thought of the promise to Abraham in terms of a singular seed. As a collective noun the singular word 'seed' could and did stand for the whole people of God, and God's promise certainly did guarantee that Abraham's seed would be as numerous as the stars in the sky (*Gen.* 15:5) or the sand on the seashore (*Gen.* 22:17). Yet Paul tells us that when God made a covenant with Abraham and his seed, there was a special reason for using the singular term 'seed' (not 'seeds', see *Gal.* 3:16). Paul explains that the blessing was most especially promised to one particular seed, Jesus the Christ. In him the covenant would be established, for in him alone the conditions of the covenant would be fully and perfectly kept. By his perfect life of obedience, he would fulfil the demands and obligations of the covenant for his people, thus guaranteeing that the blessings of the covenant would be theirs. By his death he would bear the curse of the covenant in their place, thus freeing them from that condemnation and death that otherwise would have prevented their receiving of the inheritance.

SUMMARY

Matthew's title promises much, and his book will deliver on that promise. In it Matthew will paint for us a portrait of Jesus using his words and deeds, and in most cases his colours will be taken from the Old Testament. In that portrait we will see 'the light of the knowledge of the glory of God in the face of Jesus Christ' (*2 Cor.* 4:6). Our own faith will grow and prosper the more we fill our souls with the blessed truth in this book. We will see the grand unity of the whole Bible. The record Matthew gives us provides abundant proof that Jesus is indeed the Christ, the promised Son of David and Seed of Abraham, in whom all the promises of God will find their *Yes* and *Amen* to the glory of God (*2 Cor.* 1:20). Blessed be his glorious name!

2

Messiah's Family Tree

*A*braham was the father of Isaac, and Isaac the father of Jacob, and Jacob the father of Judah and his brothers, *3* and Judah the father of Perez and Zerah by Tamar, and Perez the father of Hezron, and Hezron the father of Ram, *4* and Ram the father of Amminadab, and Amminadab the father of Nahshon, and Nahshon the father of Salmon, *5* and Salmon the father of Boaz by Rahab, and Boaz the father of Obed by Ruth, and Obed the father of Jesse, *6* and Jesse the father of David the king.

And David was the father of Solomon by the wife of Uriah, *7* and Solomon the father of Rehoboam, and Rehoboam the father of Abijah, and Abijah the father of Asaph, *8* and Asaph the father of Jehoshaphat, and Jehoshaphat the father of Joram, and Joram the father of Uzziah, *9* and Uzziah the father of Jotham, and Jotham the father of Ahaz, and Ahaz the father of Hezekiah, *10* and Hezekiah the father of Manasseh, and Manasseh the father of Amos, and Amos the father of Josiah, *11* and Josiah the father of Jechoniah and his brothers, at the time of the deportation to Babylon.

12 And after the deportation to Babylon: Jechoniah was the father of Shealtiel, and Shealtiel the father of Zerubbabel, *13* and Zerubbabel the father of Abiud, and Abiud the father of Eliakim, and Eliakim the father of Azor, *14* and Azor the father of Zadok, and Zadok the father of Achim, and Achim the father of Eliud, *15* and Eliud the father of Eleazar, and Eleazar the father of Matthan, and Matthan the father of Jacob, *16* and Jacob the father of Joseph the husband of Mary, of whom Jesus was born, who is called Christ.

17 So all the generations from Abraham to David were fourteen generations, and from David to the deportation to Babylon fourteen generations, and from the deportation to Babylon to the Christ fourteen generations (Matt. 1:2–17).

S tarting a book with a lengthy genealogy might seem to modern readers a very big mistake. 'Give us something that will grab our attention!' There is, however, good biblical precedent for this (see, for example, Exodus and 1 Chronicles), and Matthew is certainly one to follow biblical precedent. Furthermore, if you study this passage carefully, it is far from boring. It is a spring of life-giving water to thirsty souls. Let us drink deeply from it.

THE ROYAL HEIR

This genealogy moves directly to establish the claims made in the title. Primarily, it serves to show that Jesus is the Son of David, the promised king and rightful heir to the Davidic throne. So it starts from Abraham and moves to David. After David, the line of descent moves right down the list of succeeding kings (though skipping some: three in verse 8 – see *1 Chron.* 3:10–11) to the time when the monarchy and the nation were cut off, the deportation to Babylon. After the deportation, the genealogy continues and concludes with Jesus, who is indeed the Son of David. Once Matthew has made his point, his Gospel will make frequent use of the term Son of David, and will in other ways identify Jesus as the promised king (see *Matt.* 2:2, 6; 21:1-9; 27:11, 29, 37, 42).

The three stages of the genealogy also serve to emphasize God's faithfulness to his promises. In the movement of God's plan from Abraham to David, the highest point of fulfilment for the Old Testament is reached in the time of David (*1 Kings* 8:56) and Solomon. But after Solomon there is a decline, till at last the monarchy is cut off and the people exiled in the deportation to Babylon—no king, no land.

This might have suggested an end to the covenant promises of God. Yet the covenant demands a fulfilment, because God's own name was sworn to it (*Gen.* 15; 22:15; *Heb.* 6:17–18). So the Old Testament prophets spoke of a return from exile and of an everlasting fulfilment to the promises of God (*Ezek.* 39:25-29; see also *Isa.* 40-66; *Jer.* 30-33). By continuing the genealogy after the deportation, Matthew is showing that God remains faithful to his covenant promises, despite the sins of his people. 'Great David's greater Son' has come at last to establish the greater and everlasting kingdom. Thanks be to God!

FOURTEEN, FOURTEEN, FOURTEEN

The genealogy is presented in a carefully organized manner, divided into three stages with fourteen generations in each. Matthew wants us to notice this pattern, for he draws our attention to it (verse 17). Why is this important?

Since we are not given the explanation, we must be careful in speculating about it. To begin, however, we can be sure that he was not trying to give us the exact number of generations. We have already seen that in verse 8 three generations are skipped. Furthermore, if we compare Matthew's genealogy with Luke's (*Luke* 3:23–38), or with others in the Old Testament, we will find that there are many more generations from Abraham to Christ than 3 x 14. This cannot be a careless mistake on Matthew's part. Like the prophets of old, he 'spoke from God being moved by the Holy Spirit' (*2 Pet.* 1:21). He has then quite deliberately organized the genealogy in this way. He must want his readers to see and appreciate some special, symbolic significance in the number fourteen.

Several suggestions have been made. The number 7 is a very important number in Jewish culture (symbolizing completeness and fullness), so multiples of seven are sometimes used to put added emphasis on a grouping (see *Matt.* 18:22, not 'seven times, but up to seventy times seven'). Perhaps the three groupings of fourteen are intended to tell us that the working of God has now reached its fullness and completion in Jesus Christ. Matthew certainly makes this point elsewhere.

It has also been proposed that three groupings of fourteen indicate the arrival of the sabbath fulfilment. Three groups of fourteen are the same as six groups of seven, so if six groups of seven have been completed by the time of Jesus, then Jesus begins the seventh seven, or the time of fulfilment and rest. The marking of time by sevens is found elsewhere in Scripture (see *Lev.* 25:8–9; *2 Chron.* 36:20–21; *Dan.* 9:24–27). But Matthew stresses the number fourteen, not seven, so there must be something more here.

In the ancient Hebrew language the letters of the alphabet were also used for numbers, so each Hebrew word can have a numerical value. David's name in Hebrew has three letters (*dwd*), which are the fourth, the sixth, and again the fourth letters of the Hebrew alphabet, yielding the sum of fourteen (4 + 6 + 4 = 14). David's name is also the fourteenth member in the list from Abraham to the Christ. Perhaps, by his three-fold repetition of fourteen, Matthew is shouting to us, 'David! David! David!' Possibly, the other two ideas are also included, indicating that in Jesus, the promised Son of David, the time of fulfilment, and Sabbath rest have come. Whether it is one or all of the ideas, it is Matthew's way of putting his message in flashing neon lights, making sure that (at least his thoughtful, diligent) readers, do not miss his point.

SKELETONS IN THE CLOSET

Besides highlighting the exile, Matthew has another way of showing that Jesus has come to save his sinful people. Moving down through the genealogy, we observe a rather striking feature: the inclusion of four women, who are not the ones we might have expected. Sarah, for instance, that paragon of faith highlighted in Hebrews 11, is not mentioned. Of those who are, three were Gentiles (two were Canaanites, one was a Moabite) and the fourth, though Jewish, had married a Hittite (and she is left unnamed, described only as 'the wife of Uriah', to stress her Gentile connection). Three of these women were known for immoral sexual relations (*Gen.* 38; *Josh.* 2; *2 Sam.* 11). Is this the sort of family tree one normally puts out for public notice? What are we to make of this?

Again, Matthew does not explain his purpose, but whatever else he might be saying he is certainly making it clear that Jesus is not ashamed to call us brethren (*Heb.* 2:11). If our Christ is willing to enter the world through the line of sinful human beings, we should have no trouble believing that this man would 'eat with the tax-gatherers and sinners' (*Matt.* 9:11). As a tax-gatherer himself, Matthew would be especially grateful for this, and so should we. As we shall see, Matthew is also very eager to show that Gentiles are to be included among the people of God. Possibly, he has yet another purpose in mind, but we shall postpone that consideration until we discuss the virgin birth.

SUMMARY

Verses 1–17 of chapter 1 give us a prologue to Matthew's 'book of the genealogy of Jesus Christ, the son of David, the son of

Abraham'. In just 17 verses he has already told us a great deal. We know that Jesus is the Christ. We know that in him God has kept his covenant promises to Abraham and to David. We know that in him God's covenant faithfulness triumphs over human sin. We know that Jesus will come among sinners and receive them. Finally, we know that he is indeed the one whose kingdom will last forever, and who will keep his people in safety and security all their days. What good news is given to us in this great book! May our hearts ever be lifted with its glorious message.

3

God with Us

*N*ow *the birth of Jesus Christ took place in this way. When his mother Mary had been betrothed to Joseph, before they came together she was found to be with child from the Holy Spirit. ¹⁹And her husband Joseph, being a just man and unwilling to put her to shame, resolved to divorce her quietly. ²⁰ But as he considered these things, behold, an angel of the Lord appeared to him in a dream, saying, 'Joseph, son of David, do not fear to take Mary as your wife, for that which is conceived in her is from the Holy Spirit. ²¹ She will bear a son, and you shall call his name Jesus, for he will save his people from their sins.' ²² All this took place to fulfil what the Lord had spoken by the prophet: ²³ 'Behold, the virgin shall conceive and bear a son, and they shall call his name Immanuel' (which means, God with us). ²⁴ When Joseph woke from sleep, he did as the angel of the Lord commanded him: he took his wife, ²⁵ but knew her not until she had given birth to a son. And he called his name Jesus* (Matt. 1:18–25).

We have not gone far in Matthew's Gospel, but we have already learned a great deal about Jesus. The Old Testament gives us a line drawing of the Messiah; Matthew is putting in the colour, virtually painting by numbers. Our Lord Jesus is the Christ, the Messiah, and the Anointed One of God. He is the Son of David, the heir to the throne of an everlasting kingdom. He is the son of Abraham, the seed in which all the nations shall be blessed. There is still much more to learn about him, so very much more.

CONCEIVED BY THE HOLY SPIRIT

The Apostles' Creed teaches that Jesus was 'conceived by the Holy Spirit'. This passage gives proof for the claim. During the time of Mary's betrothal to Joseph, she was 'found to be with child from the Holy Spirit'. That was not the way Joseph saw it in the beginning. No doubt he supposed that she had been guilty of adultery, so he resolved to divorce her quietly. 'But as he considered these things, behold, an angel of the Lord appeared to him in a dream.'

This is the first occurrence of the word 'behold' (Greek, *idou*) in Matthew. It is one of his favourites. Of the 212 uses of the word in the New Testament, 62 of them are by Matthew, nearly a third. He often uses it to draw our attention to important points. This is certainly one of them. Jesus' conception in the womb of Mary was not a natural occurrence. He had no human father. He was 'conceived by the Holy Spirit'. Such an explanation could only be accepted on the strongest evidence. An angelic visitation provided that evidence: 'Behold, an angel of the Lord appeared to him . . .'

BORN OF THE VIRGIN MARY

Both Matthew and Luke stress that Mary was a virgin at the time of Jesus' conception (*Matt.* 1:23; *Luke* 1:27, 34). As we have seen, this initially caused quite a problem for Joseph. No doubt it would be a problem for others! Possibly John 8:41 is an indication that this problem continued with Jesus throughout his life. If so, some might think that God the Father would never have allowed his Son to be born under circumstances which left his legitimacy in doubt. The virgin birth is thus questioned on moral grounds. Matthew's skilful inclusion of the 'questionable' women in the genealogy perhaps anticipates this objection, for the God who is willing to welcome these immoral women into his covenant family, is not a God who considers his glory to be tarnished by drawing near to actual sinners, let alone to people merely suspected of sin.

Others have questioned the doctrine on scientific grounds, but we need not delay over this concern. Unless one knows that there is no God, and thus no power in the universe capable of performing a miracle, the possibility of miracles cannot be ruled out in advance. A virgin birth is simply no problem for an omnipotent God. Mary's virginity serves to highlight that Jesus' conception was indeed supernatural and from the Holy Spirit. This point is important for understanding who Jesus really is. He is truly a human being, but not merely a human being. While he was born from a woman like every other human since the beginning of time, his conception was not his beginning. The name he is given will explain more of this.

CALL HIS NAME JESUS

The angel tells Joseph that he must not fear to take Mary as his wife, for the child she now carries is 'from the Holy Spirit'. Mary will have a son and Joseph is to call his name Jesus. The angel also provides the explanation for the name: 'For he will save his people from their sins'.

The name Jesus is the Greek equivalent of the Hebrew name Joshua or Jehoshua, which means 'Yah(weh) is salvation'. Jesus will bear this name because 'he will save his people from their sins'. The people are his, and he is their Saviour, their Redeemer. Both his name and the explanation echo Psalm 130:7–8:

> *O Israel, hope in the LORD!*
> *For with the LORD there is steadfast love,*
> *And with him is plentiful redemption.*
> *And he will redeem Israel from all his iniquities.*

THE FULFILMENT OF PROPHECY

When the angel's speech is concluded, Matthew tells us that all this took place to fulfil what the Lord had spoken by the prophet (*Isa.* 7:14). Notice the comment on how the Scriptures came to be: ' . . . spoken by the Lord through the prophet' (see also *Matt.* 4:4; 19:4–5). For Matthew and the other New Testament writers, the writings of the Bible are the very words of God, given through human authors, but no less God's words for that reason.

Note here also another distinctive feature of Matthew's Gospel, his use of what are called the 'fulfilment formulas'. There are ten of these in Matthew's Gospel (1:22f.; 2:15; 2:17f.; 2:23; 4:14ff.; 8:17; 12:17ff.; 13:35; 21:4f.; 27:9f.), but his interest in the idea of fulfilment is found in other places besides (e.g., 2:5f.; 3:15; 5:17; 26:54–56). Part of the proof for Christianity is found in these fulfilled prophecies. It is one way in which God shows himself to be God, and in control of the history of world. He proves that he is God by telling us what will happen before it does (see *Isa.* 41:23; 44:7; 45:21; 46:10).

It also indicates that God's sovereign control over the events of history is for the accomplishment of his purposes. History is not a haphazard sequence of events, but the unfolding of a plan determined by the Most High God before the foundation of the world. History moves toward a goal. It is 'his story'. Events don't just happen willy-nilly; they come to pass in fulfilment of God's plan. Our God has been pleased to reveal what that plan is and some of the steps to be taken in reaching that goal. Matthew's fulfilment formulas draw our attention to some of these, and they remind us that God is in control. They assure us that God will faithfully perform what he has promised.

IMMANUEL

Matthew's first fulfilment formula comes from the prophet Isaiah, who prophesied about 800 years before Christ, 'Behold, the virgin shall conceive and bear a son, and they shall call his name Immanuel.' No one should be concerned by the difference between the angel's instructions that Joseph should name the child Jesus and the prophecy that his name would be called Immanuel. In biblical terms the calling of a name is not simply or even primarily a matter of telling us how someone is to be addressed. It is much more a matter of telling us who that person is, for the person's name reveals the person. Mary's child is to be called Jesus ('Yah is salvation') because he is Yahweh and will save his people from their sins. Likewise, his name will be called Immanuel because he is God with us. Matthew translates this Hebrew name to emphasize the point it makes: Mary's child is God himself who has come to be with us. The story of Jesus' birth is thus the story of God coming down from heaven to enter into our humanity and to dwell among us, to be with us, and to save his people from their sins.

The presence of God with us is a very important point for Matthew. He stresses it here at the beginning of his Gospel, and he comes back to it at the very end: 'And, behold, I am with you always, even to the end of the age' (*Matt.* 28:20). The Old Testament makes this message very prominent by referring to it over 100 times (for examples, see *Exod.* 3:12; *Josh.* 1:5; *Psa.* 23:4; 46:7,11; *Isa.* 43:2, 5; *Jer.* 1:8). Now, in Jesus Christ, all these promises of God are *Yes* and *Amen* (see *2 Cor.* 1:20).

[13]

SUMMARY

The supernatural conception of Jesus and his birth from the womb of the virgin Mary, in fulfilment of a prophecy made 800 years before his birth, assure us that Mary's child and Joseph's legal son is indeed God come down from heaven, to be with us, and to save us from our sins.

> *O come, let us adore him.*
> *O come, let us adore him.*
> *O come, let us adore him,*
>   *Christ, the Lord.*

4

A Light to the Gentiles

*N*ow *after Jesus was born in Bethlehem of Judea in the days of Herod the king, behold, wise men from the east came to Jeru-salem, ² saying, 'Where is he who has been born king of the Jews? For we saw his star when it rose and have come to worship him.' ³ When Herod the king heard this, he was troubled, and all Jerusalem with him; ⁴ and assembling all the chief priests and scribes of the people, he inquired of them where the Christ was to be born. ⁵ They told him, 'In Bethlehem of Judea, for so it is written by the prophet: ⁶ "And you, O Bethlehem, in the land of Judah, are by no means least among the rulers of Judah; for from you shall come a ruler who will shepherd my people Israel."' ⁷ Then Herod summoned the wise men secretly and ascertained from them what time the star had appeared. ⁸ And he sent them to Bethlehem, saying, 'Go and search diligently for the child, and when you have found him, bring me word, that I too may come and worship him.' ⁹ After listening to the king, they went on their way. And behold, the star that they had seen when it rose went before them until it came to rest over the place where the child was. ¹⁰ When they saw the star, they rejoiced exceedingly with great joy. ¹¹ And going into the house they saw the child with Mary his mother, and they fell down and worshipped him. Then, opening their treas-ures, they offered him gifts, gold and frankincense and myrrh. ¹² And being warned in a dream not to return to Herod, they departed to their own country by another way* (Matt. 2:1–12).

His name would be called Jesus, for he would 'save his people from their sins'. Who are his people? It is one of the special concerns of Matthew to show that the grace of God given in Jesus Christ to fulfil the promise made to Abraham is for Gentiles as well as Jews. The Gentile women of the genealogy have already suggested this. More examples will follow. Now, at the birth of the

Messiah, God summons Gentiles through a special star, and they come to worship him.

THE NATIONS COME TO THE LIGHT

Much legend and tradition has grown up around these mysterious visitors from the east, though we know very little about them. Matthew calls them *magoi* in the Greek text (usually 'Magi' in English), a word first used by the Medes and Persians for diviners of various sorts. By astrology, interpretation of dreams, and other means, they were supposed to be able to uncover hidden truth. The word is used several times in the book of Daniel (1:20; 2:2; 4:7; 5:7) for the magicians, astrologers or conjurers who served King Nebuchadnezzar. Possibly it was from Daniel that the members of this caste first learned the Jewish Scriptures and their prophecies of the promised King of the Jews. The prophecies of Balaam (*Num.* 23, 24), himself a man from the east (*Num.* 22:5) foretold that '. . . a star shall come out of Jacob, and a sceptre shall rise out of Israel . . .' (*Num.* 24:17). The reference here is to the Messiah himself, not to a star marking his birth, but one can easily imagine how these star-gazers from the east might have been intrigued by the prophecy. Yet why any star, however sudden its appearance and however regal its light, should have been understood by them to be a harbinger of the Messiah's birth we simply do not know. Whatever reasons they had for their conclusion, they were in fact right. God had sent the star to bring them to the Messiah.

We must read this event in the light of Psalm 72 and Isaiah 60. The glorious kingdom of the Messiah is to be worldwide (*Psa.* 72:8–11), and the nations or Gentiles will come to its light (*Isa.* 60:1–3). These texts speak of the consummation of the kingdom, but it is the way of the Bible to show us the end even at the beginning, giving us samples in part of what the whole will be like. Here we have a few token representatives of the nations; eventually there shall be a multitude which no man can number or count (*Gen.* 15:5; *Rev.* 7:9). Jesus understood the coming of the Greeks to him just before his crucifixion in the same way as Matthew presents the Magi (*John* 12:20–24)—as evidence that God is now at work to fulfil his ancient promise to Abraham, and bring the Gentiles to the Messiah.

[16]

'THE BORN KING OF THE JEWS'

The Magi came seeking (literally translated) 'the born King of the Jews'. Kingship belongs to him from birth. When Herod heard these words, he was troubled, and all Jerusalem was troubled with him (verse 3). Herod of course was troubled over the prospect of a rival to the throne. Jerusalem (probably) was troubled over what Herod might do in response. Already he had killed a wife and at least two of his sons, as well as many others, in his paranoia over power. Herod had become king of the Jews by a grant from the Romans, but he was not a Jew and he was bitterly resented by the Jewish people. Now there is news of one who has claim upon the title by right of birth. What might Herod do now?

Herod was right to be troubled by this news. For 'the earth is the LORD'S, and the fullness thereof, the world and those who dwell therein' (*Psa.* 24:1). It was revealed to Nebuchadnezzar long before that 'the Most High rules the kingdom of men and gives it to whom he will . . .' (*Dan.* 4:17). Herod might suppose that he has gained the title of king by his own wisdom and might. In more honest moments he might allow that he rules by the permission of Rome. But it is the Most High God who has put him where he is and God will remove him when he desires. Herod's kingdom, and all kingdoms like it, are not simply threatened by the advent of the Messiah; they are doomed. The kingdoms of this world will become the kingdom of our Lord and of his Christ, and he shall reign forever and ever (*Rev.* 11:15).

> *I saw in the night visions, and behold, with the clouds of heaven there came one like a son of man, and he came to the Ancient of Days, and was presented before him. And to him was given dominion and glory and a kingdom, that all peoples, nations, and languages should serve him; his dominion is an everlasting dominion, which shall not pass away, and his kingdom one which shall not be destroyed* (Dan. 7:13–14).

THE SHEPHERD KING

The Magi came to Jerusalem seeking where the born king might be found. Herod summoned the chief priests and scribes to inquire of them where the Messiah's birthplace was to be. They told him the Christ would be born in Bethlehem, for so it was written by the prophet,

And you, O Bethlehem, in the land of Judah; are by no means least among the rulers of Judah; for out of you shall come a ruler, who will shepherd my people Israel (Matt. 2:6; see Micah 5:2).

The last part of this quotation contains an addition taken from 2 Samuel 5:2 ('who will shepherd my people Israel'). Such composite quotations occur elsewhere in the New Testament (see *Mark* 1:2–3). One scripture is used to illuminate another. Here the concept of the shepherd is used to interpret the concept of ruler. The promised ruler is to come as the shepherd of God's people. He will not be a tyrant like Herod. He will not be like many earlier rulers of the house of David, who fed themselves and not the sheep (*Ezek.* 34). He will care for the sheep and deliver them; feed them, heal them, and lead them to rest (see *Ezek.* 34:11–16). Such is the character of 'the born King of the Jews'. He is the Chief Shepherd (*1 Pet.* 5:4), the Good Shepherd (*John* 10:11–16), the Shepherd and Overseer of our souls (*1 Pet.* 2:25), the great Shepherd of the sheep (*Heb.* 13:20). Because the Lord is our shepherd, we shall have all that we need (*Psa.* 23:1).

SUMMARY

If like Herod we are more concerned to rule our own lives, then we too should be troubled at the news that the Christ has come. But if like the Magi we will acknowledge him as King, bow down before him and give him our costliest treasures, then just as they 'rejoiced exceedingly with great joy' (verse 10), so shall we. The Star has come out of Jacob; a Sceptre has come out of Israel. To him shall be the obedience of the peoples (*Gen.* 49:10).

All the nations you have made shall come and worship before you, O Lord; and shall glorify your name. For you are great and do wondrous things; you alone are God (Psa. 86:9–10).

5

Biblical Déjà Vu

Now when they had departed, behold, an angel of the Lord appeared to Joseph in a dream and said, 'Rise, take the child and his mother, and flee to Egypt, and remain there until I tell you, for Herod is about to search for the child, to destroy him.' [14] And he rose and took the child and his mother by night and departed to Egypt [15] and remained there until the death of Herod. This was to fulfil what the Lord had spoken by the prophet, 'Out of Egypt I called my son.' [16] Then Herod, when he saw that he had been tricked by the wise men, became furious, and he sent and killed all the male children in Bethlehem and in all that region who were two years old or under, according to the time that he had ascertained from the wise men. [17] Then was fulfilled what was spoken by the prophet Jeremiah: [18] 'A voice was heard in Ramah, weeping and loud lamentation, Rachel weeping for her children; she refused to be comforted, because they are no more.' [19] But when Herod died, behold, an angel of the Lord appeared in a dream to Joseph in Egypt, [20] saying, 'Rise, take the child and his mother and go to the land of Israel, for those who sought the child's life are dead.' [21] And he rose and took the child and his mother and went to the land of Israel. [22] But when he heard that Archelaus was reigning over Judea in place of his father Herod, he was afraid to go there, and being warned in a dream he withdrew to the district of Galilee. [23] And he went and lived in a city called Nazareth, that what was spoken by the prophets might be fulfilled: 'He shall be called a Nazarene' (Matt. 2:13–23).

This section includes three more of the fulfilment formulas (verses 15, 18, 23). Normally we think of fulfilment as a prediction that comes true, as in Matthew 2:5–6. The prophet Micah predicted that the Messiah would be born in Bethlehem of Judea, as indeed he was. The events of this chapter are not fulfilments in this way. To see just how they are fulfilments will require our close attention.

A NEW EXODUS

Because Herod wanted to destroy the child, an angel appeared to Joseph in a dream and ordered him to flee to Egypt. Like Israel of old, sheltered in Egypt when threatened with death by famine, Jesus was sheltered in Egypt when threatened with death by the wrath of Herod. Similarly, as Moses was saved from the murderous plot of Pharaoh, in order that later he might save the people of God, so Jesus must be saved from the murderous plot of Herod.

When the danger had passed, Jesus was recalled from Egypt. Matthew indicates that this is a fulfilment of what the Lord had spoken by the prophet (*Hos.* 11:1), 'Out of Egypt I called my son.' Reading this verse in its context, we are somewhat puzzled. For the prophet Hosea in that place is looking back to the Exodus, when God called Israel out of Egypt, not forward to the calling of Jesus out of Egypt. 'When Israel was a child, I loved him, and out of Egypt I called my son' (*Hos.* 11:1). How can the return of Jesus to the land of Israel be a fulfilment of God's words through Hosea?

The answer lies in seeing that the calling of Israel out of Egypt and the calling of Jesus out of Egypt are very closely related to one another, in a way much more significant than just two separate events that are similar to one another. Israel was called out of Egypt because of God's determination to fulfil his promise to Abraham and to bring his people into blessing. Jesus is called out of Egypt for exactly the same reason. Indeed, so closely are these two events in purpose and nature that one can see that the first Exodus anticipated the second. Since the first Exodus did not accomplish all that God had planned for his people—that is, did not bring them into the fullness of salvation with everlasting rest, but only into a shadow or copy of it—the later and greater Exodus becomes necessary in order to fulfil the purposes of God revealed in the first Exodus.

The technical term for this type of relation between two events (or two people) in the Scriptures is *typology*. The first Exodus is a *type* (or copy) of the second, the second being called the *antitype* (the original). We might say that typologies create for us a sense of

[20]

biblical *déjà vu*. Psychologists define *déjà vu* as an illusion or feeling that something which is being experienced for the first time has happened before. What I am calling biblical *déjà vu* is not an illusion or a feeling; but like *déjà vu* in the ordinary sense, it does involve the sense that a new and distinct event has somehow happened before. That is precisely what we have in this case. Jesus' exodus from Egypt reminds us of Israel's exodus, and it should. That is because the two events are really manifestations of the same saving purpose of God, the first having anticipated the second, even demanded it, since the first was only a shadow of the second.

RACHEL WEEPING FOR HER CHILDREN

Another example of typology can be found in the next fulfilment (verses 17–18). In his furious rage Herod sought to destroy the Christ child; but since he did not know which child was the royal seed, he ordered the massacre of all the male children in Bethlehem two years old and under. Pharaoh in Egypt also sought to kill the male babies of Israel (*Exod.* 1:15–22). Just noting Herod's killing of the male children is enough to remind us of Pharaoh's deed, but Matthew also reminds us of another parallel found in the prophet Jeremiah (verse 18, see *Jer.* 31:15):

> *A voice was heard in Ramah,*
> *weeping and loud lamentation,*
> *Rachel weeping for her children;*
> *she refused to be comforted,*
> *because they are no more.*

Again, as we consider the verse in Jeremiah, we are struck by the fact that the prophet is not looking ahead to Jesus' day, but commenting on the past, when the northern kingdom of Israel was overthrown by the Assyrians, and many of her people were killed or carried away into exile. Yet here too there is a strong connection between the two events. At the time Jeremiah makes this prophecy, Rachel (whose grave is situated near Ramah) weeps for her children. In the days of Jesus, mothers weep for their children. But the story in Jeremiah does not end there. Jeremiah promised that one day Rachel's tears would be wiped away, for the exiles would come back from the land of the enemy (*Jer.* 31:10–20). Matthew

[21]

is silently suggesting the same for the people of his day. Their sorrow will be turned to joy. He cites only the one text from Jeremiah, but he has in mind the context of that verse also. It is found in the 'book of comfort', the prophecies of the future day of blessing (*Jer.* 30–33), when the new covenant will be fulfilled (*Jer.* 31:31–34). As the first Exodus was marked by Pharaoh's destruction of the Israelite children, and a later exodus was marked by the slaughter of Israelites at the hands of the Assyrians and Babylonians, so the final exodus begins with Herod's destruction of Israelite children. As the first two were followed by deliverance and blessing, so will the final one. Thanks be to God!

HE SHALL BE CALLED A NAZARENE

The third fulfilment statement (verse 23) in this section is the most curious of them all. No verse in the Bible says anything close to what Matthew claims the prophets foretold about Jesus. Notice, however, that Matthew cites this statement from the prophets; not one prophet, but many. The statement is intended as a summary of what several prophets taught, not an exact quote from just one of them. Another curious thing about the saying is that it refers to Jesus as a Nazarene (because he lived in Nazareth), though the Old Testament never uses the name or ever mentions the town of Nazareth. How then could the prophets have said that he would be called a Nazarene?

Several suggestions have been made. The one which this writer finds most compelling is this: Though the Old Testament never uses the word Nazarene, it does tell us that Jesus will be one who fits that description as it was understood by Matthew and his readers. Some idea of what the term meant in Matthew's day can be gained from John's Gospel (*John* 1:46), when Nathanael asks, 'Can anything good come out of Nazareth?' Nazareth was a town of no distinction: a nothing-town where nobody (of any consequence) lived. People from there would be regarded as insignificant. The Pharisees consider him of no account, because (they thought) he came from Galilee (*John* 7:52). Isaiah foretold that he would be despised in just this way (*Isa.* 53:2, 3):

> . . . *like a root out of dry ground; he had no form or majesty that we should look at him, and no beauty that we should desire him. He was*

despised and rejected by men, a man of sorrows and acquainted with grief; and as one from whom men hide their faces he was despised, and we esteemed him not.

SUMMARY

As Matthew continues to paint his portrait of Jesus, dark colours of exile, weeping, and rejection are starting to appear. Later they will become more pronounced. Though he was the born king of Israel, heir to David's throne, worthy of the worship from all the nations, and 'God with us', Jesus was indeed a Nazarene, for our sake. He came among us in lowliness and humility, to lead us in a new exodus, out of our bondage to sin and death, into the glorious liberty of the children of God, wiping every tear from our eyes. All these things took place to fulfil what had been spoken by the prophets. Thanks be to God!

6

Hear Ye! Hear Ye!

In those days John the Baptist came preaching in the wilderness of Judea, [2] *'Repent, for the kingdom of heaven is at hand.'* [3] *For this is he who was spoken of by the prophet Isaiah when he said, 'The voice of one crying in the wilderness: "Prepare the way of the Lord; make his paths straight."'* [4] *Now John wore a garment of camel's hair and a leather belt around his waist, and his food was locusts and wild honey.* [5] *Then Jerusalem and all Judea and all the region about the Jordan were going out to him,* [6] *and they were baptized by him in the river Jordan, confessing their sins.* [7] *But when he saw many of the Pharisees and Sadducees coming for baptism, he said to them, 'You brood of vipers! Who warned you to flee from the wrath to come?* [8] *Bear fruit in keeping with repentance.* [9] *And do not presume to say to yourselves, "We have Abraham as our father", for I tell you, God is able from these stones to raise up children for Abraham.* [10] *Even now the axe is laid to the root of the trees. Every tree therefore that does not bear good fruit is cut down and thrown into the fire.* [11] *I baptize you with water for repentance, but he who is coming after me is mightier than I, whose sandals I am not worthy to carry. He will baptize you with the Holy Spirit and with fire.* [12] *His winnowing fork is in his hand, and he will clear his threshing floor and gather his wheat into the barn, but the chaff he will burn with unquenchable fire'* (Matt. 3:1–12).

From Jesus' childhood home in Nazareth we are transported quickly to the wilderness of Judea, where John the Baptist is preaching. The sudden change of setting and time (skipping over about 25 years of Jesus' life) might seem abrupt; but that is only if we suppose that Matthew aims to give us a biography of Jesus. His purpose is rather to present and explain Jesus as the Saviour of his people, and this movement precisely fits his purpose. For this is not the first time in history that deliverance from Egypt is followed by a movement to the wilderness (*Exod.* 15:22), with a passage through the waters sandwiched in between. The ancient pattern is used again to structure the story. As the saying goes, 'It's (biblical) *déjà vu* all over again.'

REPENT!

The first thing we are told about John is that he came preaching. His message is succinctly summarized, 'Repent, for the kingdom of heaven is at hand.' Significantly, when Jesus begins his public preaching, his message is exactly the same (see 4:17). This indicates a strong continuity between John and Jesus, and tells us what is most fundamental to their preaching.

The message begins with a call to action, 'Repent!' This is a demand for change: change in what people do, what they think, and what they value. A reason is then given for this call, 'for the kingdom of heaven is at hand'. Much has been written on what is meant by 'the kingdom of heaven', but for our present purposes we can summarize the idea briefly in terms of 'the reign and rule of God'. (Jews of that time typically avoided direct mention of the name of God, so Matthew generally uses the phrase 'kingdom of heaven' where the other Gospels use 'kingdom of God', but the meaning is the same; see *Matt.* 19:23–24 where the two are used interchangeably).

John's announcement is that God is now entering human history in a decisive way, one which demands our conformity to his purposes lest we perish in his judgment. Paul preached the same message to the Athenians:

> *The times of ignorance God overlooked, but now he commands all people everywhere to repent, because he has fixed a day on which he will judge the world in righteousness by a man whom he has appointed; and of this he has given assurance to all by raising him from the dead* (Acts 17:30–31).

So much of modern preaching overlooks this fundamental point. If there is any urgency to our appeals, it is to receive, not to repent. Concerns about righteousness are not a high priority for us; but they were for John, and they were for Jesus, and they were for the

[25]

apostles (see *Luke* 24:47; *Acts* 2:38). As we shall see, there is also a message about receiving, of what can be gained and enjoyed. But all of that must never be separated from this fundamental call to repentance. For blessing does not fall upon all indiscriminately. It is those who repent that receive. There is something very strange about our preaching if we find no place in it for what was first in the preaching of John, of Jesus, and of the apostles.

THE WILDERNESS

Great emphasis is placed upon the setting of John's ministry. It is the wilderness. Matthew tells us this, and then shows that it fulfils prophecy. A text from Isaiah is cited (verse 3, see *Isa.* 40:3), 'The voice of one crying in the wilderness: Prepare the way of the Lord; make his paths straight.'

Why is John's message and baptism identified with the wilderness? The wilderness has special meaning in the Old Testament, having both positive and negative connotations. Israel was taken to the wilderness immediately following the deliverance from Egypt. There she met God in a series of dramatic encounters. He provided water and bread in the wilderness. He met them on Mount Sinai and gave them his law and established his covenant with them. But the wilderness was also the setting for Israel's rebellion against God, her refusal to trust God. The wilderness then became the place of judgment, with many falling in the wilderness (*Psa.* 95:8–11).

When the prophets looked to the future renewal of the people of God following the exile, they foresaw a return to the wilderness for Israel. Hosea speaks of God taking Israel again into the wilderness, that there he might 'allure' her back to himself (*Hos.* 2:14). Ezekiel also predicts that God will again bring his people into the wilderness, there to judge them: purifying them of all that is unclean and establishing them in his covenant.

> *I will bring you out from the peoples and gather you out of the countries where you are scattered, with a mighty hand and an outstretched arm and with wrath poured out. And I will bring you into the wilderness of the peoples, and there I will enter into judgment with you face to face. As I entered into judgment with your fathers in the wilderness of the*

land of Egypt, so I will enter into judgment with you, declares the Lord
GOD. I will make you pass under the rod, and I will bring you into the
bond of the covenant. I will purge out the rebels from among you, and
those who transgress against me . . . (Ezek. 20:34–38a).

Isaiah sees the wilderness as the place where God will return to
his people, so that a way for him must be prepared (*Isa.* 40:3). For
these reasons the Qumran sect of John's day went to live in the
wilderness near the Dead Sea, in expectation that there the Lord
would come to his people again.

Matthew presents John's ministry as the fulfilment of the
prophets' expectation. Hence, the people must go out to John in
the wilderness; he does not preach in their cities. They must come
to him, submit to his baptism of repentance, and consecrate their
lives anew to God. The time for action is now; John's demand is
urgent. Already the axe is laid to the root of the tree. The kingdom
of heaven is at hand.

John's baptism is a ritual judgment, a symbolic trial by ordeal,
anticipating the real baptism and judgment of Jesus that will follow. Paul identified the passage of Israel through the sea as a baptism into Moses (*1 Cor.* 10:2). Israel entered the sea by faith in the
Lord who led them; they emerged victorious on the other side.
Egypt went into the sea in rebellion against God; they perished in
the way. So John warns those who come for his baptism that they
must bring forth fruit in keeping with their repentance, else they
will not escape the wrath which is to come (verses 7–10).

SUMMARY

With the appearance of John the Baptist, Ezekiel's wilderness
judgment has begun. God is calling his people from the nations
and bringing them into the wilderness. The kingdom of heaven is
at hand. The times of ignorance God has overlooked. Now he commands all people everywhere to repent.

7

The Baptism of Jesus

Then Jesus came from Galilee to the Jordan to John, to be bap-tized by him. [14] John would have prevented him, saying, 'I need to be baptized by you, and do you come to me?' [15] But Jesus answered him, 'Let it be so now, for thus it is fitting for us to fulfil all righteous-ness.' Then he consented. [16] And when Jesus was baptized, immediate-ly he went up from the water, and behold, the heavens were opened to him, and he saw the Spirit of God descending like a dove and coming to rest on him; [17] and behold, a voice from heaven said, 'This is my beloved Son, with whom I am well pleased' (Matt. 3:13–17).

Once we understand the nature and significance of the baptism ritual conducted by John, we will be as shocked as he was to see Jesus emerging from the crowd seeking to be baptized. How inappropriate it all seems! Yet Jesus makes no mistakes, and his being there is both necessary and important. We will find much comfort in it.

FULFILLING ALL RIGHTEOUSNESS

Matthew tells us that when Jesus presents himself for baptism, John shrinks from the idea. Rather, he says, 'I need to be baptized by you' (verse 14). Jesus replies, 'Let it be so now, for thus it is fit-ting for us to fulfil all righteousness' (verse 15).

How does this baptism of Jesus fulfil all righteousness? Surely he does not need to repent and he has no sins that must be for-given? Indeed he does not. But his people do. In repentance one turns from his sinful ways and turns to the ways of God. Jesus does not perform the first of these for himself, but only for his people. He does perform the second, both for himself and for his people.

[28]

He must act for them, consecrating himself to the service of God, fulfilling all that the law demands. As we have seen, John's appearance marks the advent of the kingdom of heaven. His preaching issues an urgent demand: 'Repent!' God is now demanding of his people that they come forth in repentance and consecration. The time is at hand.

Now there were many coming to John, some in sincerity and some not. John urges them to bring forth fruit in keeping with their repentance, in order that their sincerity might be proven. As only God can look on the heart, neither John nor anyone else can tell the sincerity and truth of someone coming forward to receive baptism. But God can look on the heart, and in the case of Jesus we are not left in doubt about the verdict: 'This is my beloved Son, in whom I am well pleased.' Having symbolically passed through the waters of judgment, Jesus is vindicated as a true son of God, indeed as the Son of God, by the voice from heaven and by the anointing with the Holy Spirit.

SON OF GOD

The title *Son of God* is especially rich. Most readers today will understand it as a title of deity, marking Jesus as the second Person of the Trinity. All that is included. Matthew has already anticipated it. Jesus' conception from the Holy Spirit, his name Jesus, the angel's explanation for his name with its echo of Psalm 130, the name Immanuel from Isaiah 7:14, and the Magi's journey to worship him have already pointed toward direct identification of Jesus with Yahweh, now come in our flesh. More of this identification will come in the chapters to follow.

But there is another side to the title *Son of God*. Matthew has already linked this idea with Israel in the return of Jesus from Egypt (*Matt.* 2:15). 'Out of Egypt have I called my son.' Israel was also God's son, his 'first-born' (*Exod.* 4:22–23). Of the many uses of 'Father' for God in this Gospel, half of them are in connection with Jesus, and the other half for the disciples and the people of God. God is our Father too. As the Son of God, then, Jesus is God, to be sure. He is also the true son of God. He is everything we were meant to be. Having become one with us in our humanity, he has now revealed perfectly what we were meant to be: a people wholly consecrated to God, being his very image in the world, in all that we are and all that we do. The declaration made from heaven at the baptism of Jesus carries all of this with it. Jesus is everything that God is, and he is also everything that we were meant to be, and will be when our redemption is complete. So as we hear the words that vindicate Jesus as the perfectly consecrated Son of God, and as we hear of the Father's perfect delight in him, we must also hear the Father's verdict for and delight in all his sons and daughters who are his in Jesus Christ. In Jesus we too may be true sons of God, and find that his delight is in us.

KING AND SUFFERING SERVANT

The words from heaven tell us still more. The statement echoes a combination of words from Psalm 2:7, *'You are my Son,* today I have begotten you', and Isaiah 42:1, 'Behold my servant, whom I uphold, my chosen, *in whom my soul delights.'* The words from Psalm 2 indicate that Jesus is the promised Messiah-King of Israel, begotten of the Father, who will have the ends of the earth as his possession (verse 8). This Son of God must be 'kissed' by the rulers of the earth, or they will perish before him (verses 10–12). The words from Isaiah 42, however, remind us that this victorious king will suffer much before his triumph. Anointed with God's Spirit (*Isa.* 42:1), as indeed Jesus was at his baptism, he will not faint nor be discouraged until he has established justice in the earth (*Isa.* 42:4). The suffering which is only implicit in this chapter is made prominent in the portrait of the Servant in Isaiah 52:14–53:12:

> *His appearance was so marred, beyond human semblance, and his form beyond that of the children of mankind . . . he was despised and rejected of men; a man of sorrows and acquainted with grief . . . by oppression and judgment he was taken away . . . cut off out of the land of the living.*

This Messianic combination of unimaginable suffering, even seeming defeat in death, together with ultimate triumph and glorification proved too much to grasp for even Peter and the disciples (*Matt.* 16:22; 17:22–23). Yet this is precisely the combination we must have if we are to understand Jesus accurately, and if we are to understand our own life and calling in the world. For as Jesus will make very clear, the path of suffering awaits us all in this world if we would be his disciples (see *Matt.* 16:24–28).

Jesus' baptism foreshadows all of this. His submission to John's baptism of judgment points to his own baptism of judgment at the cross (see *Mark* 10:39 and *Luke* 12:50 where the sufferings of the cross are identified as a baptism for Jesus). The declaration from heaven (*Matt.* 3:17, with *Isa.* 42) points to the fact that he will emerge victorious from this ordeal of judgment. In this the salvation of God's people is achieved. In this also the glory of God is revealed. The participation of each member of the Trinity is in the whole work of salvation, as the Father sends, the Son suffers, and the Holy Spirit anoints and sustains. Hence each member of the Trinity is presented to us in Jesus' baptism, as the Father speaks from heaven, the Spirit descends as a dove, and the Son is identified.

SUMMARY

Understood in the light of its Old Testament background, the baptism of Jesus tells us much about himself and his calling, and about ourselves and our calling. He comes to be among us, and to take our place, both in the obedient consecration of his whole life and in his willing embrace of suffering for us. His life marks out the pattern of our own, for though we will not suffer the punishment for our sins, we will endure hardship and affliction for his sake, and we too must be wholly consecrated to God. But thanks be to God, for his victory also signals ours!

8

Testing in the Wilderness

Then Jesus was led up by the Spirit into the wilderness to be tempted by the devil. ² And after fasting forty days and forty nights, he was hungry. ³ And the tempter came and said to him, 'If you are the Son of God, command these stones to become loaves of bread.' ⁴ But he answered, 'It is written, "Man shall not live by bread alone, but by every word that comes from the mouth of God."' ⁵ Then the devil took him to the holy city and set him on the pinnacle of the temple ⁶ and said to him, 'If you are the Son of God, throw yourself down, for it is written, "He will command his angels concerning you", and "On their hands they will bear you up, lest you strike your foot against a stone."' ⁷ Jesus said to him, 'Again it is written, "You shall not put the Lord your God to the test."' ⁸ Again, the devil took him to a very high mountain and showed him all the kingdoms of the world and their glory. ⁹ And he said to him, 'All these I will give you, if you will fall down and worship me.' ¹⁰ Then Jesus said to him, 'Be gone, Satan! For it is written, "You shall worship the Lord your God and him only shall you serve."' ¹¹ Then the devil left him, and behold, angels came and were ministering to him (Matt. 4:1–11).

The movement of Jesus away from the crowds surrounding John in the Jordan valley into the solitary wilderness might suggest a change of focus for Matthew. The chapter division made at this point probably encourages readers in that view. However, this passage is closely linked with Jesus' baptism in chapter 3. The setting is still the wilderness (*Matt.* 3:1,3; 4:1), with all its prophetic significance (*Isa.* 40:3–5; *Ezek.* 20:34–38). Both passages centre on Jesus as the Son of God (*Matt.* 3:17; 4:3,6). Both passages emphasize the work of the Spirit (*Matt.* 3:16; 4:1).

HE WAS HUNGRY

Forty days and forty nights without food is surely a long time. Matthew's simple statement that 'he was hungry' will seem a colossal understatement. One could, however, easily underestimate the severity of this trial for Jesus by supposing that his deity kept him from experiencing this trial as we would have experienced it. That would be a big mistake, both in understanding Jesus in his two natures, and in what his sufferings and temptations mean for us. Matthew, like most of the New Testament, simply presents Jesus to us as both God and man. Little is said to try to explain the mystery created by these affirmations. Yet enough is told us to keep us from mistakes. As his death was a real death, so his hunger was real hunger, and his temptations were real temptations. The joining of the two natures in one Person was not a blending of the two into one nature. His human nature was distinct from his divine nature, though not separated from it, because joined in one person. Possibly, the creed of the Council of Chalcedon (AD 451) has put it all together as well as it can be briefly stated:

> *We, then, following the holy Fathers, all with one consent, teach men to confess one and the same Son, our Lord Jesus Christ, the same perfect in Godhead and also perfect in manhood; truly God and truly Man . . . in all things like unto us without sin . . . to be acknowledged in two natures, inconfusedly [i.e, without blending them together], unchangeably, indivisibly, inseparably; the distinction of natures being by no means taken away by the union, but rather the property of each nature being preserved, and concurring in one Person and one Subsistence, not parted or divided into two persons, but one and the same Son, and only begotten, God the Word, the Lord Jesus Christ.*

The real hunger of Jesus is an indication of his true humanity, his oneness with us. His experiences in Gethsemane and at Calvary tell us more. In the garden we see the potential conflict between the will of Jesus in his human nature—desiring to avoid the horror of the cross (*Matt.* 26:36–44)—and the will of his Father (which is also his own will in his divine nature). In his human nature he can thirst on the cross (*John* 19:28), as he can grow hungry in the wilderness. As he bears the punishment due to sinners while suffering on the cross, he knows in his human nature and consciousness true alienation from his Father (*Matt.* 27:46). It is in his humanity that

[33]

he must secure our salvation, obeying and suffering in our place. Thus his hunger teaches us that he is surely able to sympathize with our weaknesses (*Heb.* 4:15).

LIVING BY EVERY WORD

Understanding the true humanity of Jesus is crucial for this passage, not only for appreciating the reality of his suffering and temptations, but also for understanding their purpose. Immediately following his baptism, then (or, as Mark would say, *immediately*) Jesus is led by the Spirit into the wilderness. Like Israel of old after passing through the sea (*Exod.* 15:22), Jesus is led by the Spirit into a wilderness where there is no bread. Can this really be the plan of God? Does the Spirit actually lead us into a wilderness?

Israel found all this too much to bear, so she grumbled against God and turned away in disobedience. Jesus must succeed where Israel failed. He must continue to trust God and the leading of the Spirit, even when he is led into difficult circumstances where temptation abounds. Indeed, it is precisely so that he can be tempted by the devil that he is being led into the wilderness by the Spirit (*Matt.* 4:1). And in those temptations, what is at stake is whether he is a true Son of God, an obedient and faithful Son of God who will follow his Father's will and leading, whatever the circumstances might be. So the devil comes to him, 'If you are the Son of God, command these stones to become loaves of bread.' Jesus makes his reply out of the book of Deuteronomy, saying, 'Man shall not live by bread alone, but by every word that comes from the mouth of God.'

This statement is found in Deuteronomy 8:3, in the very chapter where Moses explained to the people why they had been led into the wilderness, 'That [the LORD] might humble you, testing you to know what was in your heart, whether you would keep his commandments or not' (verse 2). For if they would live in the promised land given to them, they must obey the commandments of the Lord (*Deut.* 8:11–20). Only true and faithful sons may live in God's promised land. So, where Israel failed, Jesus must succeed. He must be tested and tried as we are tried, but he must succeed where we have failed. It is in this way that he secures for us a place in the promised land of everlasting peace, joy and righteousness.

SUMMARY

Acting on our behalf, Jesus takes his place among us, leading us in repentance and consecration of life, then going forth in the wilderness to prove what is in his heart, whether he will obey God or not. Following the Spirit, he is tempted in all things as we are, yet without sin. Therefore he secures for himself and for his people the right to enter into God's rest (*Psa.* 95:7–11; *Heb.* 3:7–4:16).

9

The Time Has Come

N̄ow when he heard that John had been arrested, he withdrew into Galilee. ¹³ *And leaving Nazareth he went and lived in Capernaum by the sea, in the territory of Zebulun and Naphtali,* ¹⁴ *so that what was spoken by the prophet Isaiah might be fulfilled:* ¹⁵ *'The land of Zebulun and the land of Naphtali, the way of the sea, beyond the Jordan, Galilee of the Gentiles—* ¹⁶ *the people dwelling in darkness have seen a great light, and for those dwelling in the region and shadow of death, on them a light has dawned.'* ¹⁷ *From that time Jesus began to preach, saying, 'Repent, for the kingdom of heaven is at hand.'* ¹⁸ *While walking by the Sea of Galilee, he saw two brothers, Simon (who is called Peter) and Andrew his brother, casting a net into the sea, for they were fishermen.* ¹⁹ *And he said to them, 'Follow me, and I will make you fishers of men.'* ²⁰ *Immediately they left their nets and followed him.* ²¹ *And going on from there he saw two other brothers, James the son of Zebedee and John his brother, in the boat with Zebedee their father, mending their nets, and he called them.* ²² *Immediately they left the boat and their father and followed him.* ²³ *And he went throughout all Galilee, teaching in their synagogues and proclaiming the gospel of the kingdom and healing every disease and every affliction among the people.* ²⁴ *So his fame spread throughout all Syria, and they brought him all the sick, those afflicted with various diseases and pains, those oppressed by demons, epileptics, and paralytics, and he healed them.* ²⁵ *And great crowds followed him from Galilee and the Decapolis, and from Jerusalem and Judea, and from beyond the Jordan* (Matt. 4:12–25).

The arrest of John marks the moment when Jesus is to begin his public ministry. The forerunner has completed his work, and he must decrease. The one who is mightier than he must now increase (*John* 3:30). Jesus 'withdrew' into Galilee. While this might suggest a retreat from danger, Matthew provides another reason for the move to Galilee: 'That what was spoken by the prophet Isaiah might be fulfilled'. This is the fifth of Matthew's fulfilment sayings, and it marks a theme which will be very important for the whole of his Gospel.

GALILEE OF THE GENTILES

Place names abound in the opening verses of this section: 'he withdrew into Galilee. And leaving Nazareth he went and lived in Capernaum by the sea, in the territory of Zebulun and Naphtali.' We do not wait long to find out why they are mentioned. The withdrawal into Galilee puts Jesus in the place prophesied by Isaiah for the dawning of the light of the gospel:

> *The land of Zebulun and the land of Naphtali,*
> *the way of the sea, beyond the Jordan, Galilee of the Gentiles—*
> *The people dwelling in darkness have seen a great light,*
> *and for those dwelling in the region and shadow of death,*
> *on them a light has dawned* (Matt. 4:15–16; Isa. 9:1–2).

Modern politicians usually choose carefully the place where they announce their campaign for office. If they seek to run on a platform of education, they might choose a school or a university. If they seek to run on a platform of attracting commerce, they might choose a noted place of business. If they seek to run on a platform of job creation, they might choose a place where unemployment is high. The beginning of Jesus' ministry is also chosen with a purpose in mind. The good news he brings is for all people, Jews and Gentiles alike. So he chooses Galilee, Galilee of the Gentiles. This region of mixed population serves well as the place where the light of the gospel will be revealed. Here Jesus takes up the urgent message of John the Baptist: 'Repent, for the kingdom of heaven is at hand.'

CALLING DISCIPLES

Walking by the Sea of Galilee, Jesus calls his first disciples, two fishermen brothers by the names of Simon and Andrew. 'Follow me', says Jesus, 'and I will make you fishers of men.' Immediately they left their nets and followed him. Going on from there, he calls two more brothers, James and John, the sons of Zebedee. They are also fishermen, and with their father are now mending their nets. Immediately they left the boat and their father and followed him. The only other disciple whose call is recorded for us is Matthew himself (*Matt*. 9:9). He too is called to follow Jesus, and though the word 'immediately' is not used there, the impression given is that he too responded without delay: 'And he rose and followed him.'

Surely examples are being given to us here. When Jesus calls, we are to obey and follow immediately. So it was with Abraham, the father of all who believe (*Rom*. 4:11,16). When he was called to leave his country, his kindred, and his father's house, to go out to a land that God would show him, Abraham obeyed (*Heb*. 11:8). When he was tested, he offered up Isaac, his only son (*Heb*. 11:17). So it must be with the children of Abraham. When Jesus calls, we must obey. His demand is urgent: 'Repent, for the kingdom of heaven is at hand.' Our response must be without delay. Let us immediately leave what we must, and follow him.

WORD AND DEED

As the ministry in Galilee begins, Matthew summarizes it for us in a way that will prove to be very important later on (see *Matt*. 9:35; 10:5–8). Jesus was teaching in their synagogues and proclaiming the gospel of the kingdom. He was also healing every disease and every affliction among the people. For Matthew, it is not enough simply to say that he was healing every disease and affliction. This is a matter of great importance to him: Jesus heals every disease and every affliction. Nothing can withstand his power.

There is great hope for us in these words. The good news of the consummated kingdom is that he will make all things new and wipe away every tear from our eyes (*Rev*. 21:4). The kingdom which Jesus brings removes everything that hinders our joy and comfort. His healing ministry gives demonstration of this. Though for now only some will taste of his healing, yet when the kingdom comes in all its fullness all who are saved will know it completely. Like the sample fruits of the promised land brought back by the spies (*Num*. 13), the healing miracles of Jesus speak to us of the healing which will come to all his children when the age is complete. Today, perhaps, we will be sorrowful, but our sorrow will be turned into joy (*John* 16:20). Thanks be to God!

[38]

SUMMARY

The beginning of the gospel shows us that its scope is to reach all the nations, and it will reach them in all their afflictions. It is truly a glorious kingdom which comes. Let us not delay our response, but immediately yield all that we have and are to Christ's supreme call.

New Testament Sinai

Seeing the crowds, he went up on the mountain, and when he sat down, his disciples came to him. ² And he opened his mouth and taught them, saying: ³ 'Blessed are the poor in spirit, for theirs is the kingdom of heaven. ⁴ Blessed are those who mourn, for they shall be comforted. ⁵ Blessed are the meek, for they shall inherit the earth. ⁶ Blessed are those who hunger and thirst for righteousness, for they shall be satisfied. ⁷ Blessed are the merciful, for they shall receive mercy. ⁸ Blessed are the pure in heart, for they shall see God. ⁹ Blessed are the peacemakers, for they shall be called sons of God. ¹⁰ Blessed are those who are persecuted for righteousness' sake, for theirs is the kingdom of heaven (Matt. 5:1–10).

The descent of Jesus into Egypt when threatened by death, his exodus from Egypt, his following of the Spirit into the wilderness, and his passage through the waters of baptism have reminded us of the ancient exodus from Egypt. When Israel had made her exodus, she met with God on Mount Sinai. Jesus, having gathered a people to himself from Galilee of the Gentiles, now takes them to a mountain. There he will expound his kingdom law for them. The ancient pattern continues to structure Matthew's presentation of Jesus.

BLESSED ARE YE . . .

The Sermon on the Mount opens with a series of formula-like sayings, each in two parts. The first part begins with 'Blessed are . . .' and the second with '. . . for theirs is . . .' or 'for they shall . . .' In the first part a spiritual description is given of those who are blessed, and in the second part a specific blessing is identified as belonging to those who meet that description. Effectively, the second part of the sentence explains how those identified in the first part are indeed blessed.

There are nine such sayings, but it is perhaps best to take the first eight together as a set (verses 3–10) and put the ninth (verse 11) with the following verses (verses 12–16). The first eight beatitudes (so-called from the Latin word for 'blessed' used in this place, since a large segment of the church used Latin for about 1000 years) belong in a set since the first and last members promise the same blessing, for theirs is the kingdom of heaven. This is a literary form called an inclusion, which serves to mark off a section. Notice too that the second part of the first and last beatitudes contains a present tense statement ('for theirs is . . .') whereas each of the ones in between contains a future tense statement ('for they shall . . .').

This way of tying the beatitudes together emphasizes for us that this is not a list of separate, spiritual qualities, from which one might choose one or more as a personal goal, in the hope of gaining the blessing assigned to it. Rather, this is the unified portrait of those blessed souls whose great privilege it is to possess already— now in the present time—the kingdom of heaven. It is therefore a 'package deal', as we might say. All of them come together. This is the portrait of kingdom citizens. Like members of one tribe or family, descended from one father, they share common features. Likewise, as members of one family, they all possess their Father's kingdom.

A PECULIAR PEOPLE

As we look closely at this spiritual description of kingdom heirs, we are surprised beyond words. Surely those who possess the kingdom should stand out above the rest, having accomplished great deeds, being noted for their virtues, and honoured by all. But what do we find? The citizens who possess the kingdom are:

• *the poor in spirit*—who know they have no righteousness of their own.

• *those who mourn*—who grieve over their lack of righteousness.

• *the meek*—who, being neither proud nor arrogant, humble themselves under the mighty hand of God and claim nothing for themselves.

• *those who hunger and thirst for righteousness*—who intensely long for that righteousness of life that is pleasing to God.

• *the merciful*—who show mercy to others, as they remember their own need for mercy from God.

• *the pure in heart*—who aim exclusively to please their one Master by doing his will.

• *the peacemakers*—who like their Father, the God of peace, work for peace between God and sinners, and between people.

• *those who are persecuted for righteousness' sake*—who while mourning over their own lack of righteousness, and hunger and thirst after that righteousness which is pleasing to God, find themselves hated in the world and persecuted for a righteousness they never knew they had.

What strange citizens they are, yet how like the Lord Jesus who saved them for himself. For he was 'meek and lowly in heart' (*Matt.* 11:29). Though the Son of God, he demanded nothing for himself, but trusted completely in his Father's provision, even after forty days and nights without food (*Matt.* 4:2–4). The 'food' for which he hungered was to do the Father's will (*John* 4:34). Even in the face of a death which descended into hell, his one aim was not his own (human) will, but his Father's (*Matt.* 26:39). Though he came as the friend of sinners, preaching peace, and showing mercy, he was despised and rejected of men, persecuted and afflicted, and at last delivered over to death. Kingdom citizens are like their King; sons of God are like their God.

NOW, AND NOT YET

As noted above, the middle six beatitudes all state their blessing in the future tense ('for they shall . . .'), while the first and last state their blessing in the present tense ('for theirs is . . .'). This highlights for us a most important feature about the life of kingdom citizens while they live in this world. Some of God's blessings are ours now, while others are not yet, but will be in the future. Right now, kingdom citizens possess the kingdom itself. Theirs is the kingdom of heaven. It has been graciously given to them by the Father's good pleasure (*Luke* 12:32). At the same time, many blessings of the kingdom have not yet been given, or have not yet been given in all their fullness. These are 'not yet'. The righteousness (to be understood here as holiness of life or perfect conformity to Christ) for which we hunger and thirst, the lack of which we now mourn, has not yet been given in all its fullness. We are not yet conformed to the image of Christ. Yet in part it is possessed, and for that part the sons of God are even now persecuted. Today we mourn over what we lack, but the day will come when we shall be comforted and satisfied. Today, we are meek, and claim nothing for ourselves, but the day will come when we shall inherit the earth.

SUMMARY

From the top of the New Testament Sinai, Jesus reveals the kingdom that in him now draws near. The ones who inherit this kingdom are indeed a peculiar people. In their own eyes they are noted more for what they lack than for what they have; yet mysteriously they already possess all things, either in whole or in part. While hated and persecuted in the world, they have the sure and certain hope that theirs is the kingdom of heaven. Truly they are a blessed people. Thanks be to God!

11

You Are . . .

'*B*lessed are you when others revile you and persecute you and utter all kinds of evil against you falsely on my account. [12] Rejoice and be glad, for your reward is great in heaven, for so they persecuted the prophets who were before you. [13] You are the salt of the earth, but if salt has lost its taste, how shall its saltiness be restored? It is no longer good for anything except to be thrown out and trampled under people's feet. [14] You are the light of the world. A city set on a hill cannot be hidden. [15] Nor do people light a lamp and put it under a basket, but on a stand, and it gives light to all in the house. [16] In the same way, let your light shine before others, so that they may see your good works and give glory to your Father who is in heaven'* (Matt. 5:11–16).

The set of eight beatitudes was completed by repeating the same blessing in the eighth as was promised in the first. In addition, this repetition marked a return to the present tense of the blessing promised in the first beatitude, instead of the future tense used in the second through seventh. These features suggest that the set is completed. Yet in verse 11 we again meet with the most distinctive feature of the beatitudes, the opening words 'Blessed are . . .' In addition, the theme of verse 11 is the same as in verse 10, the persecution of the righteous. Do not these two features argue for tying verse 11 to the previous verses? Are the reasons given in the previous chapter sufficient for separating this verse from verses 3–10 and joining them to those which follow? Does it really make much difference?

BLESSED ARE YOU

The unifying factor in verses 11–16 is the direct address of the second person plural: 'Blessed are you . . . You are . . . You are

[44]

. . .' Here the sermon moves from speaking in the abstract third person and speaks directly to people now hearing his words. Who are these people to whom he now speaks? The answer is most important, because it tells us who it is that inherits the blessings of the kingdom of heaven.

In the opening verse of this chapter we are told that when Jesus saw the crowds, he went up on the mountain and 'his disciples came to him'. In verse 2 we are told that Jesus opened his mouth and taught them. So Jesus is now speaking to his disciples, those who follow him. The crowds, apparently, are still within hearing distance, for when the sermon concludes we read that 'the crowds were astonished at his teaching' (*Matt.* 7:28). But the ones to whom he speaks are his disciples. They are the ones who receive his pronouncements of blessing.

The word disciples (Greek, *mathetai*) is from a verb which means 'to learn' or 'to be taught'. Those who follow Jesus are taught by him, and to follow Jesus is to follow his teaching also. It is not, however, just a matter of following a particular way of life. Later, Jesus will say, 'A disciple is not above his teacher, nor a servant above his master. It is enough for the disciple to be like his teacher, and the servant like his master' (*Matt.* 10:24–25). Being a disciple is as much about 'being' as 'doing'. Becoming like Christ is central. Consequently, it is both a matter of the heart and of the outward life.

THE SALT OF THE EARTH

Those who are Christ's disciples are 'the salt of the earth'. These words are so memorable that they have become a common saying in our own language today. The metaphor speaks of the preserving influence the disciples have on those around them, and on the world as a whole, hindering the rapid decay that would otherwise take place. It is, indeed, precisely this influence that makes them so hated by the world, when in fact the world should be grateful for them. The world's headlong rush toward the evils that it has called good is opposed by the presence of Christ's disciples in the world, just as salt impedes the process of decay in meat left exposed to the air. Their lives and their witness stand as a rebuke to society, provoking its opposition. It is just such opposition that is counted blessed, for it shows that these disciples bear the same nature as the prophets who came before them. Thus they receive the same treatment from the world, and the same treatment (blessing) from God.

THE LIGHT OF THE WORLD

It is also this transformed character that makes them 'the light of the world'. Once they were darkness, but now they are light in the Lord (*Eph.* 5:8). The true light that enlightens every man has shone upon their hearts, and as children of the light they walk in the light. Christ exhorts them to let their light shine. No one, he says, lights a lamp and then puts it under a basket. The lamp's purpose is to give light, so it is placed on a stand where it can give light to all in the house. In the same way, Christ has lighted his people with his own light, and we too are intended to shine in all the world, giving light to all in the house. There is, we see, an imperative that follows from the indicative descriptions that are given of the disciples. Who they are determines what they are to do. They are salt, so they must not lose their saltiness. They are light, so they are to let their light shine, in order that glory may be given to their Father in heaven.

SUMMARY

This section contains a great calling to the church. As salt in the earth we are to stand against the decay of the world around us. As the light of the world we are to shine in the darkness that all in the house might see. In part this happens automatically, for who we are as disciples means that our very being and nature stand opposed to the world around us. Jesus said, 'If you were of the world, the world would love you as one of its own; but because you are not of the world, but I chose you out of the world, therefore the world hates you' (*John* 15:19). Being the disciples of Christ who are becoming like him, the world hates us just as it hated him. 'If the world hates you, know that it has hated me before it hated you.' This is why our persecution is actually a great comfort to us. 'Rejoice and be glad, for your reward is great in heaven, for so they persecuted the prophets who were before you' (verse 12). But we must not allow the world's hatred to drive us from our calling in the world. We must not lose our saltiness by compromising our obedience and witness. We must let our light shine in such a way that others may see our good works and give glory to our Father who is in heaven. What you are must determine how you live. May God help us all to live to the honour and glory of his name.

12

Greatness in the Kingdom

'*D* *o not think that I have come to abolish the Law or the Proph-ets; I have not come to abolish them but to fulfil them. * [18] *For truly, I say to you, until heaven and earth pass away, not an iota, not a dot, will pass from the Law until all is accomplished. * [19] *Therefore whoever relaxes one of the least of these commandments and teaches others to do the same will be called least in the kingdom of heaven, but whoever does them and teaches them will be called great in the kingdom of heaven. * [20] *For I tell you, unless your righteousness exceeds that of the scribes and Pharisees, you will never enter the kingdom of heaven*' (Matt. 5:17–20).

With this section we move into the main body of the sermon on the mount (*Matt.* 5:17–7:12), and it provides us with the key to understanding it all. This section is also marked off by an inclusion, found in the words '. . . the Law and the Prophets' (see 5:17 and 7:12). A common theme runs throughout the section. Like the beatitudes of the opening section, the theme is the nature of Christian character, of kingdom righteousness. Now, however, it becomes clear that the exposition of this righteousness is point-edly directed as a contrast to the dominant, and erroneous, view of righteousness prevalent among the people—the righteousness of the scribes and Pharisees.

DO NOT THINK

There is a forcefulness to this exhortation that we must not miss. Whatever else people might think about Jesus Christ, it is imper-ative that they do not think that he has come to abolish the Law and the Prophets. As we move further into the book of Matthew, we will see that people did think this; at least the scribes and the Pharisees did. We see it in the accusations which come when his disciples are found to be plucking heads of wheat as they walked along the road on a Sabbath day (12:1–2). The accusations also come when Jesus heals on the Sabbath (12:9–14). They come again when his disciples are found not to be following 'the tradition of the elders', by not washing their hands in the ritually prescribed way (15:1–2).

People continue to think this way today. They rightly point out the New Testament teaching on salvation by grace, and not by works of the law; but then wrongly conclude that obedience to the law is of little or no consequence for the saved person. Jesus' teaching on the law in the Sermon on the Mount strikes a fatal blow against such teaching. As he concludes the sermon, he states emphatically that those who enter the kingdom of heaven are those who do the will of the Father (7:21). He rejects those who practise lawlessness (7:23). Here he states that those who keep and teach the law will be called great in the kingdom of heaven (5:19). Law-keeping, therefore, is central to the teaching of Jesus and to the Christian life.

There are, to be sure, some difficult questions on this topic. Some Old Testament laws are clearly set aside in the New Testament. Examples are the ceremonial laws of animal sacrifice (*Heb.* 9:1–10:18), and the dietary laws of ritual cleanliness (*Matt.* 15:1–20; see *Mark* 7:19; *Acts* 10). Likewise, the Old Testament Levitical priesthood, after the order of Aaron, is replaced by the New Testament priesthood of Christ, after the order of Melchizedek (*Heb.* 6:13–8:13). The Old Testament covenant sign of circumcision is replaced by the New Testament sign of baptism (*Matt.* 28:19; see *Acts* 2:38; 15:1–35; *Gal.* 2:11–21; 5:2–4; *Col.* 2:11–12). In addition, the civil penalties of the Sinai covenant (that is, the penalties to be applied by Israel's human government for the violations of law) do not seem to be binding in the New Testament. Jesus speaks of divorce being permitted in cases of adultery, whereas the law of Moses prescribed death for the adulterer (*Lev.* 20:10), and so 'divorce' would have been automatic, complete and final. This is clear from the New Testament. At the same time, however, it is equally clear that much of the Old Testament law is carried over into the New Testament without change: for example, the laws against idolatry, murder, adultery, stealing, bearing false witness, and coveting, etc. The Ten Commandments may conveniently serve as a summary of these laws.

NOT TO ABOLISH, BUT TO FULFIL

Jesus describes his purpose concerning the law in the profound and somewhat mysterious words 'I have not come to abolish, but to fulfil.' What does it mean to fulfil the law? In the case of the ceremonial laws, the meaning seems clear enough. These laws are described as 'a shadow of the good things to come instead of the true form of these realities' (*Heb.* 10:1). Animal sacrifices represented the shedding of human blood. The worshipper who presented an animal for his sacrifice became identified with that animal in such a way that the animal's death was accepted in the place of the worshipper. But justice was not truly served in this manner for, as the New Testament says, 'It is impossible for the blood of bulls and goats to take away sins' (*Heb.* 10:4). What the blood of bulls and goats could do, however, was represent the blood of Jesus, the true lamb of God, who would give his life as a ransom for many. By his death on the cross, therefore, Jesus fulfilled the ceremonial law.

The dietary laws, similarly, represented moral cleanliness. Those who are morally unclean can have no fellowship with God. Those who are ritually unclean (from eating foods, or touching what is dead, etc.) are treated as morally unclean; and ritual cleansing is treated as moral cleansing. But the ritual nature of these things is made clear in the New Testament, and Jesus brings this out (*Matt.* 15:1–20; see *Mark* 7:19; *Acts* 10). Jesus fulfils the ceremonial law by bringing out its true meaning, and providing for a true means of cleansing from moral corruption.

The moral law he fulfils by keeping it perfectly, even while tempted and tried in all things such as we are (*Heb.* 4:15). For Jesus, the law was not set aside, but had to be kept in every respect. He had to keep it because the law is not arbitrary. Rather, it is the expression of God's own character. For the whole law can be summed up in love, and God is love (*Rom.* 13:8–10; *1 John* 4:16). Hence the law expresses the very nature of love and thus the very nature of God. The law is therefore as eternal as God himself and cannot be set aside. It must be fulfilled. Jesus has come to do just that, and those who know his saving work will likewise seek to fulfil it, by his grace. Love so amazing, so divine, demands our soul, our life, our all.

A GREATER RIGHTEOUSNESS

It is precisely this kind of law fulfilment that must be found in disciples of Christ. Far from being indifferent to the law's demands, they hunger and thirst after this righteousness, and mourn over the shortfalls in their lives. They cannot be content with the righteousness of the scribes and Pharisees, which is satisfied by matters of ceremonial detail, but neglects the weightier matters of the law (*Matt.* 23:23); or which is satisfied with outward appearance, while neglecting the inner purity of the heart and mind (23:25–28). In short, the righteousness which is found in the Law and the Prophets, the righteousness taught by Jesus, is far broader and far deeper than what can be found in the scribes and Pharisees. It is broader because it embraces the weightier matters of the law without neglecting the lesser; and it is deeper because it aims at purity in the inner soul as well as in the outer appearance.

SUMMARY

The teaching of Jesus is indeed a challenge to the greatest mind. How does one hold in harmony the way of salvation by grace alone, apart from works of the law, and a refusal to lessen the law's demands for a life of faithful obedience? It is a hard thing to do. But it must be done, for while Jesus clearly has come to save his people from their sins, and while it is indeed the poor in spirit and not those with the righteousness of the scribes and Pharisees who go down to their homes justified, it is equally true that those who enter the kingdom of heaven are those who do the will of the Father. It is imperative, therefore, that we do not think that Christ has come to abolish the law. He did not. Rather, he came to fulfil it. Thanks be to God that he did!

[51]

13

Body and Soul

'You have heard that it was said to those of old, "You shall not murder; and whoever murders will be liable to judgment." [22] But I say to you that everyone who is angry with his brother will be liable to judgment; whoever insults his brother will be liable to the council; and whoever says, "You fool!" will be liable to the hell of fire. [23] So if you are offering your gift at the altar and there remember that your brother has something against you, [24] leave your gift there before the altar and go. First be reconciled to your brother, and then come and offer your gift. [25] Come to terms quickly with your accuser while you are going with him to court, lest your accuser hand you over to the judge, and the judge to the guard, and you be put in prison. [26] Truly, I say to you, you will never get out until you have paid the last penny. [27] You have heard that it was said, "You shall not commit adultery." [28] But I say to you that everyone who looks at a woman with lustful intent has already committed adultery with her in his heart. [29] If your right eye causes you to sin, tear it out and throw it away. For it is better that you lose one of your members than that your whole body be thrown into hell. [30] And if your right hand causes you to sin, cut it off and throw it away. For it is better that you lose one of your members than that your whole body go into hell. [31] It was also said, "Whoever divorces his wife, let him give her a certificate of divorce." [32] But I say to you that everyone who divorces his wife, except on the ground of sexual immorality, makes her commit adultery. And whoever marries a divorced woman commits adultery' (Matt. 5:21–32).

This section begins the exposition of the Law and the Prophets as Jesus understands them, which is the way we are to understand them too. The aim throughout is to clarify the true teaching of the Law and the Prophets, and to set it in contrast to the misunderstandings imposed by the scribes and Pharisees on the

[52]

people. According to the scribes and Pharisees, a righteousness of the outward body will suffice. But the kingdom of God requires a greater righteousness—one for both body and soul.

YOU HAVE HEARD

The remainder of Matthew 5 (verses 21–48) contains a series of teachings, each of which is introduced by the words, 'You have heard.' What is the significance of this?

In the light of the emphatic denial of Matthew 5:17, that we must not think that Jesus has come to abolish the Law, it is plain that these words serve to keep us from making that mistake. Jesus is going to contrast what the people have heard with what he will say to them. His teaching will be contrasted with what the people have heard from others, that is, from those who have taught them, their scribes and Pharisees.

Following the introductory words, a quotation is given of what the people have heard. In many of these cases, we have a quotation that seems to be taken directly from the Old Testament. It might appear, therefore, that Jesus is contrasting his own teaching with that of the Old Testament.

However, when Jesus quotes the Old Testament, he typically uses a phrase like 'It is written' (see *Matt.* 4:4,7,10). Indeed, the word 'Scripture' means 'what is written'. But here Jesus is referring to what the people have heard. We can see the difference when we examine the last example given in this chapter (5:43): 'You have heard that it was said, "You shall love your neighbour, and hate your enemy."' The first part of this quotation does indeed come from the Old Testament (*Lev.* 19:18). But the second part, '. . . and hate your enemy', is nowhere to be found in the written law of God.

It is, however, to be found in what the people have heard, in what they have been taught by the scribes and Pharisees. What Jesus does in this section is to present the true teaching of what is written, and to contrast it sharply with the misunderstandings and perversions of the law that were current among the scribes and Pharisees, and which were taught to the people in their synagogues.

THE NEGATIVE AND THE POSITIVE

In this section Jesus aims to clarify the meaning of the sixth and seventh commandments, prohibiting murder and adultery. In each case he shows that though the commandments are given in negative form, 'Thou shall not . . .', there is a positive requirement that belongs to them also. According to Jesus it is not enough, in our keeping of the law, if we simply avoid doing what the commandment explicitly prohibits—in this case, murder and adultery. We must also avoid those thoughts and deeds which tend toward murder and adultery. Thus, anger and angry words, which can tend toward the act of murder, are likewise prohibited by the law. Lust, which can lead toward the act of adultery, is likewise prohibited by the law.

The truly righteous person aims at purity of the heart as well as purity of words and deeds. In addition, not only does the righteous person look to the inner thoughts and motives as well as to the outer deeds and words, he also endeavours to take whatever steps are necessary to maintain that purity of heart and life.

Thus, if there is anything that causes another person to be angry with him, the righteous man will seek to be reconciled to that person (5:23–26). The anger in another person's heart is thus equally of concern to us, so far as we are able to do anything about it. Similarly, if there is anything in our life that moves us toward lustful thoughts or adulterous deeds (5:29–30), we aim to remove those stumbling blocks. Divorce, which Jesus will treat more fully later (19:1–12), comes up in this place too, for it can become the cause of adultery in our own lives or in the lives of others. That is because, when divorce occurs on grounds not approved in Scripture, any subsequent marriage of the divorced persons will be adulterous in its inception (see *Additonal Note* on pp. 299–300).

The disciple of Jesus is a law-keeper. We keep the law not so that we might justify ourselves before God (for that is the erroneous righteousness of the scribes and Pharisees), but in order that we might walk in the ways which are pleasing to God, to show him our love and gratitude. We also aim to walk in the way of blessing, and know the blessedness that comes to those whose way is blameless, who walk in the ways of the Lord (*Psa.* 119:1). We remember that the peacemakers are blessed, so we aim to be reconciled to all who have anything against us. We remember that the pure in heart are blessed, so we aim to keep our hearts and minds pure to desire only those things which the Lord would be pleased to give us.

DOES MUTILATION HELP?

The last two verses of this section are perhaps easy to misunderstand, for it would seem that plucking out one's eye or cutting off one's hand is required of those whose eyes or hands 'cause' them to sin. But a moment's thought here would save us from such a mistake. For in the context of the seventh commandment, it can readily be seen that a blind man or one with no hands could still commit adultery and lust.

As remedies for dealing with impure lust and sexual sin such mutilations would have no power to prevent sins of this kind. Jesus is here using hyperbole, indicating that whatever it takes to keep oneself in the way of righteousness and truth is worth the sacrifice. If plucking out one's eye could keep one from sinning, it would be far better to do that than to maintain the member and give oneself over to the sin and end up in hell. If cutting off one's hand could keep one from committing adultery, it would be far better to do so than to give in to the temptation and end up in hell. Typically, however, such remedies would have no power at all to keep us from such sins.

What Jesus is saying is that however great the sacrifice, and however painful the solution, whatever it takes to win the battle against sin in your life, we should spare no effort in it. The call to holiness is urgent. The blessing to be found is great. Do not dally with sin in your life.

SUMMARY

The teaching of the scribes and Pharisees is especially dangerous. It teaches men to trust in themselves for salvation. By reducing the law's demands to ceremonial acts like tithing garden herbs, people are left with the idea that diligence in such matters will save them. By ignoring the taming of the heart's desires, the scribes and Pharisees leave people enslaved to their own inner corruptions. Jesus calls us to a greater righteousness, one of such surpassing worth that if mutilation could help us, it would be worth the pain involved. Holiness, however, is not that easy! We shall need something much more powerful than self-abasement in dealing with the corruptions of our hearts and lives (see *Col.* 2:23). Indeed, as we shall see later, what we need is far beyond our natural strength, and can only be found in the supernatural grace of God.

14

The True Standard

'*A*gain you have heard that it was said to those of old, "You shall not swear falsely, but shall perform to the Lord what you have sworn." [34] But I say to you, Do not take an oath at all, either by heaven, for it is the throne of God, [35] or by the earth, for it is his footstool, or by Jerusalem, for it is the city of the great King. [36] And do not take an oath by your head, for you cannot make one hair white or black. [37] Let what you say be simply "Yes" or "No"; anything more than this comes from evil. [38] You have heard that it was said, "An eye for an eye and a tooth for a tooth." [39] But I say to you, Do not resist the one who is evil. But if anyone slaps you on the right cheek, turn to him the other also. [40] And if anyone would sue you and take your tunic, let him have your cloak as well. [41] And if anyone forces you to go one mile, go with him two miles. [42] Give to the one who begs from you, and do not refuse the one who would borrow from you. [43] You have heard that it was said, "You shall love your neighbour and hate your enemy." [44] But I say to you, Love your enemies and pray for those who persecute you, [45] so that you may be sons of your Father who is in heaven. For he makes his sun rise on the evil and on the good, and sends rain on the just and on the unjust. [46] For if you love those who love you, what reward do you have? Do not even the tax collectors do the same? [47] And if you greet only your brothers, what more are you doing than others? Do not even the Gentiles do the same? [48] You therefore must be perfect, as your heavenly Father is perfect'* (Matt. 5:33–48).

Jesus is exposing the righteousness of the scribes and Pharisees as a false righteousness. It is whitewash rather than true purity (*Matt.* 23:25–28). It is gold paint over a wax filling in cracked pottery, rather than a vessel of pure gold. It is lightweight, neglecting the weightier matters of the law. It is ceremonial rather than moral, tithing garden herbs rather than giving one's heart, soul, mind, and strength to the Lord. It is a masquerade rather than a true demonstration of piety. Three more examples of this are found in this next section of the Sermon on the Mount.

DOES YOUR 'YES' *MEAN* 'YES'?

The background needed to understand what Jesus says about vows and oaths in verses 33–37 can be found in Matthew 23:16–22. In the Judaism of Jesus' day, an elaborate system of qualifications had developed around the swearing of oaths and vows. In many cases, swearing by something, apparently to provide confirmation of the truth or sincerity of a vow, could in fact be a deception, not binding the one who vowed at all, and leaving the other person without grounds for the vindication of his claims. Thus, as Jesus reveals, one who swore by the temple of God was not bound to perform what he had vowed. But if he swore by the *gold* of the temple, then he was bound. In such a case, swearing by the temple of God— which invokes God's own dwelling place as the confirmation of one's vow—is being used as a deception. This is outrageous, and Jesus roundly condemns it. God's commandments bind us to truth-telling in all dealings with our neighbour. A person of true character should never need to make a vow, for his 'yes' is always a 'yes'. Of course, there are matters of great social consequence when additional confirmation is required. In such cases a vow may be made, but in all ordinary dealings, our word should be our bond, as the saying goes. Swearing oaths and making vows for the purpose of deception is altogether evil.

IS YOUR HEART FREE FROM MALICE?

The next example involves the abuse of the ancient principle of *lex talionis*, the 'law of retaliation'. As a principle of justice, 'an eye for an eye' is an eminently worthy principle. It prescribes that the punishment must fit the crime: no more, and no less. What could be more just and fair than that? It guides rulers and those in authority for the administration of justice, teaching them to apportion punishment to the crime so that there is equity, so far as that is possible in this life. It is explicitly cited in three places in the Old

Testament (*Exod.* 21:22–25; *Lev.* 24:17–20; *Deut.* 19:15–21), but the echo of it is heard in many other places too.

However, in the hands of the scribes and Pharisees, it became the justification for a vindictive spirit. In their view, it permitted retaliation in kind whenever one suffered a wrong—paying back the offender with everything he deserved (and perhaps more). Taken from its original context in social jurisprudence, where it served to moderate as well as legislate appropriate punishment, it became an aggressive principle for inter-personal relations, crushing forgiveness and generosity, turning the 'golden rule' on its head: Do unto others as they have done unto you! Not surprisingly, kingdom righteousness demands a very different spirit, the very spirit of the King himself, as we shall see.

LOVE YOUR ENEMIES

The final example of scribal and Pharisaical twisting of the Old Testament law concerns the second great commandment, Love your neighbour as yourself. We have already noticed how this commandment was corrupted in 'the righteousness of the scribes and Pharisees'. Their interpretation of the commandment allowed them to hate their enemies. Again, not surprisingly, kingdom righteousness is quite otherwise. Jesus says that his followers must love their enemies and pray for those who persecute them. He also gives a reason why it must be so: in order that you may be sons of your Father who is in heaven.

Kingdom righteousness is the righteousness of the King himself. God demonstrated his love for us while we were yet sinners, living in rebellion against his rule. It was while we were his enemies that God reconciled us to himself through the death of his Son. Having received such a love while we were God's enemies, he calls us to extend that same love toward our own enemies. As Jesus prayed for those who persecuted him, even while hanging on the cross (*Luke* 23:34), so we must pray for those who persecute us. Loving only those who love us requires nothing special of us. But loving those who persecute us, oppose us, slander us, and utter all manner of evil against us falsely, requires supernatural grace. Such grace is given to those who are the sons of God. His own gracious character is worked out in them, and as they have freely received they freely give.

SUMMARY

The final verse of this chapter makes clear the purpose of all this teaching: you are to be perfect, even as your heavenly Father is perfect. Being like our Father, conformed to the image of his Son—that is the goal! God aims to reveal himself in the very character of his children, the sons of the living God. The character of the King is the true standard of righteousness in his kingdom. Being like him in all our ways must be the goal of our lives. May God help us all so to live, that we may make known his gracious ways.

15

Practising Your Righteousness

'*Beware of practising your righteousness before other people in order to be seen by them, for then you will have no reward from your Father who is in heaven. ² Thus, when you give to the needy, sound no trumpet before you, as the hypocrites do in the synagogues and in the streets, that they may be praised by others. Truly, I say to you, they have received their reward. ³ But when you give to the needy, do not let your left hand know what your right hand is doing, ⁴ so that your giving may be in secret. And your Father who sees in secret will reward you. ⁵ And when you pray, you must not be like the hypocrites. For they love to stand and pray in the synagogues and at the street corners, that they may be seen by others. Truly, I say to you, they have received their reward. ⁶ But when you pray, go into your room and shut the door and pray to your Father who is in secret. And your Father who sees in secret will reward you. ⁷ And when you pray, do not heap up empty phrases as the Gentiles do, for they think that they will be heard for their many words. ⁸ Do not be like them, for your Father knows what you need before you ask him. ⁹ Pray then like this: "Our Father in heaven, hallowed be your name. ¹⁰ Your kingdom come, your will be done, on earth as it is in heaven. ¹¹ Give us this day our daily bread, ¹² and forgive us our debts, as we also have forgiven our debtors. ¹³ And lead us not into temptation, but deliver us from evil." ¹⁴ For if you forgive others their trespasses, your heavenly Father will also forgive you, ¹⁵ but if you do not forgive others their trespasses, neither will your Father forgive your trespasses. ¹⁶ And when you fast, do not look gloomy like the hypocrites, for they disfigure their faces that their fasting may be seen by others. Truly, I say to you, they have received their reward. ¹⁷ But when you fast, anoint your head and wash your face, ¹⁸ that your fasting may not be seen by others but by your Father who is in secret. And your Father who sees in secret will reward you*' (Matt. 6:1–18).

Three examples of common piety or religious expression are examined in the next section: *giving to the needy, praying, and fasting*. In each case, the way in which the scribes and Pharisees (here called hypocrites, see 23:13, 23, 25, 27, 29) practised their righteousness is exposed as corrupted by an evil motive. The approved way of kingdom righteousness is then explained. The major difference between the two forms of righteousness is revealed in the opening verse: 'Beware of practising your righteousness before other people in order to be seen by them, for then you will have no reward from your Father who is in heaven.' The remedy is to live your life not for the approval of others, but solely for the approval of God.

PRACTICE AND REWARD

Running throughout this section is a repeated emphasis on gaining reward for one's practice. The hypocrites practised their righteousness before other people in order to be seen by them. They give to the needy in order to be praised by them (verse 2). They stand and pray that they may be seen by others (verse 6). They fast and disfigure their faces that their fasting may be seen by others (verse 16). In each case, Jesus says they have gained their reward. Having aimed at being seen by others, they have succeeded in their goal; so they have their reward in full. But they have no reward from God.

In directing his disciples away from these hypocritical practices, Jesus seeks to motivate them toward a true practice of righteousness by warning them that those who practise their righteousness in order to be seen by others will have no reward from their Father in heaven. Is Jesus teaching us that we should be seeking a reward from God? Would not such a view suggest that the proper practice of righteousness will earn or merit a reward from God? Does this not lead us away from reliance on the grace of God into a legalistic mindset, where we seek to earn blessing and reward through the merit of good works? The concerns expressed here are proper concerns, for they raise questions about the proper motivation for righteous living. We must not, however, allow these concerns to blind us to a prominent emphasis in this passage. Each discussion of the three forms of piety concludes with a prescription for the proper practice, with the assurance that 'your Father who sees in secret will reward you' (see verses 4, 6, 16). Proper practice does gain reward, according to Jesus.

We must not think, however, that proper practice *merits* such a reward. One does not *deserve* or *earn* favour from God by the proper practice of righteousness. Even a perfect practice of righteousness would not gain one a right to be rewarded. As Jesus elsewhere taught, 'When you have done all that you were commanded, say, "We are unworthy servants; we have only done what was our duty"' (*Luke* 17:10). Any reward given for simply doing what is required will still be a gracious gift.

Such is the Father's way with his children. He does reward—graciously reward—their faithful practice of righteousness. The way of righteousness is indeed a blessed way. Great blessing comes to those who walk in the way of the Lord (*Psa.* 119:1). Those who give to others will also receive for themselves (*Luke* 6:38). Those who forgive others will themselves be forgiven (*Matt.* 6:14). Those who pray and fast in sincerity of heart will be heard and answered according to the good will of God (*Matt.* 7:7–11). God does not stand aloof and removed from his children, insensitive to their needs and heedless of their cries. Nor does he overlook their obedience and service to him. Indeed, every cup of cold water given in his name will have its reward (*Matt.* 10:42).

SECRET PIETY

The root error of the hypocrites discussed in this section is found in their motive to be seen by others when they practise their righteousness. The praise and admiration of others is what mainly concerns them. It must not be so for the disciples of Christ. For them, the approval of God is uppermost. His favour is worth more than all the praise earth can give. So the disciples of Christ make no effort to practise their righteousness before other people, in order to be seen by them. But does this mean that the practice of kingdom righteousness is entirely a secret matter, never to be seen by others? If so, how does this fit with the commandment given earlier in the sermon (5:16), 'Let your light shine before others, so that they may see your good works and give glory to your Father who is in heaven'?

[63]

The reconciliation of these two is not difficult in thought, but it can be difficult in practice. In *Matt.* 5:16 we are being told to live our life before God in such a way that when others see our good works, they will give glory to our Father who is in heaven. A disciple's whole life is to be lived for the honour and glory of God: his public life *and* his private life. The good deeds to which we are called by God, those 'prepared beforehand, that we should walk in them' (*Eph.* 2:10), are in many cases unavoidably public. Disciples are not called to forego doing good works just because others might see them. But one is to take care that in doing them the glory is given to God. One must not do them in such a way as to draw attention to oneself. Quiet, humble service is the norm. To be sure, for some deeds honour may indeed come to us, even though we have sought to avoid it. We should receive that as God's gift, for those who honour God will be honoured by God (*1 Sam.* 2:30). The issue is not whether we have received honour for our good works, but whether we have done them to receive honour. It is mainly a matter of one's motive, not whether the deed is public or private.

SUMMARY

The righteousness of the scribes and Pharisees is fundamentally self-centred, aiming to gain for oneself reward and praise. The disciples of Jesus Christ practise their righteousness for a very different reason. Those who pray, 'Hallowed be your name', also live that God's name may be hallowed. The praise and reward to be gained from others is not their concern. The praise and reward they seek is that which comes from above. May God enable us so to live.

16

Seeking the Kingdom

'Do not lay up for yourselves treasures on earth, where moth and rust destroy and where thieves break in and steal, [20] but lay up for yourselves treasures in heaven, where neither moth nor rust destroys and where thieves do not break in and steal. [21] For where your treasure is, there your heart will be also. [22] The eye is the lamp of the body. So, if your eye is healthy, your whole body will be full of light, [23] but if your eye is bad, your whole body will be full of darkness. If then the light in you is darkness, how great is the darkness! [24] No one can serve two masters, for either he will hate the one and love the other, or he will be devoted to the one and despise the other. You cannot serve God and money.

[25] 'Therefore I tell you, do not be anxious about your life, what you will eat or what you will drink, nor about your body, what you will put on. Is not life more than food, and the body more than clothing? [26] Look at the birds of the air: they neither sow nor reap nor gather into barns, and yet your heavenly Father feeds them. Are you not of more value than they? And which of you by being anxious can add a single hour to his span of life? [28] And why are you anxious about clothing? Consider the lilies of the field, how they grow: they neither toil nor spin, [29] yet I tell you, even Solomon in all his glory was not arrayed like one of these. [30] But if God so clothes the grass of the field, which today is alive and tomorrow is thrown into the oven, will he not much more clothe you, O you of little faith? [31] Therefore do not be anxious, saying, 'What shall we eat?' or 'What shall we drink?' or 'What shall we wear?' [32] For the Gentiles seek after all these things, and your heavenly Father knows that you need them all. [33] But seek first the kingdom of God and his righteousness, and all these things will be added to you. [34] Therefore do not be anxious about tomorrow, for tomorrow will be anxious for itself. Sufficient for the day is its own trouble' (Matt. 6:19–34).

The lesson pursued in the previous section is carried further in this one, driving us toward that singleness of heart wherein we live solely for the honour and glory of God, trusting him for all that we might need. As the saying goes, here is 'where the rubber meets the road'. The real test of faithful discipleship is not found so much in the public exercises of religion as in the daily life of obedience and service. The things which dominate our hearts and minds in the rush of our daily lives tell far more about us than what others might see by our attendance at religious services.

WHAT TREASURE ARE YOU SEEKING?

Verses 19–21 are used to open up our hearts and call us to a close inspection of what we find. What is our main concern in life? What do we really want to gain and possess? For many, it is the good things of this world, the treasures of this world, which they seek. Jesus exposes this as a foolish and tragic pursuit. For all that this world offers is corruptible and fading away. Whatever this world can provide us, forces in this world can take from us. Moths and rust consume them. Thieves break in and steal them. Large homes can be destroyed by large storms. Multiplied wealth can lose its value, and prove worthless against the ravages of disease and death. Where can one go to find a secure treasure?

Jesus says that the only secure treasure is to be found in heaven, though it can be enjoyed even on earth. These are the things which God has prepared for us and not the kind of things that can be eaten away by the decaying forces of this world. Indeed, the treasures of heaven remain with us even while we are suffering under the decaying forces of this world:

> So we do not lose heart. Though our outer nature is wasting away, our inner nature is being renewed day by day. For this slight momentary affliction is preparing for us an eternal weight of glory beyond all comparison, as we look not to the things that are seen but to the things which are unseen. For the things which are seen are transient, but the things that are unseen are eternal (2 Cor. 4:16–18).

What treasure are you seeking, a transient one or an eternal one? Look closely at it. Make sure that your eye is sound and able to tell the difference (verses 22–24), for if it is not, your whole life will be full of darkness. Make sure that the treasure you seek is really capable of standing up to the tests of time. It makes all the difference in the world, and in the world to come. 'Solid joys and lasting treasure, none but Zion's children know' (John Newton's hymn, *Glorious Things of Thee are Spoken*).

ARE YOU ANXIOUS ABOUT YOUR LIFE?

Because we are creatures of flesh and blood, and vulnerable to harm and injury, we are naturally concerned about our comfort and safety in this world. *What we shall eat, and what we shall drink, and what we shall put on* are matters which regularly concern us. But it is all too easy to give too much attention to such things. Fretting and worrying about these things can easily become an obsession. Seemingly, those living with an adequate measure of earthly comforts will be less threatened by these concerns than others, yet far too often those who do possess more than adequate provisions for this life are even more consumed with worry about them, always wanting more and more, and never having enough.

Jesus calls his disciples to a life focused on far greater things than the material necessities and comforts of life. He calls us to focus on the advancement of his kingdom, and its righteousness. We are called to focus on doing the will of God, trusting that he will provide for all that we need.

This does not mean that we do nothing toward meeting our own needs, for God has not called us to passivity and inactivity; and he is not encouraging us to live irresponsibly and look to others to do for us all that we need. No, that is not faithfulness in discipleship. We must live responsibly and work to provide for ourselves and others (*2 Thess.* 3:6–12). But we do so as people of faith, trusting God to provide all that we need through our labours. We must not be so concerned with daily provisions, or with future, earthly security, that the things which pertain to God's kingdom and righteousness are pushed from the centre of our lives. The God who clothes the grass of the field, and feeds the birds of the air, will care for the children who are of so much greater value to him than all the world of nature. 'He who did not spare his own Son but gave him up for us all, how will he not also with him graciously give us all things' (*Rom.* 8:32). Our heavenly Father knows full well—

indeed, much better than we ourselves know—what we need in this world. His love for us includes providing for us all that we need. So we can safely trust him to care for us, even when the decaying forces of this world threaten to leave us in need or deprivation. So trusting in his faithfulness to provide, we must seek first his kingdom and his righteousness, and all these things will be added to us (verse 34).

SUMMARY

Concerns about the things of this world can never be put entirely out of our minds, nor would it be right to do so. But they must be kept in check, and they must not be allowed to divert us from our main calling in life, seeking the kingdom of God and its righteousness. It is faith in the goodness and love of God that can keep us steady under all the threatening pressures of life. Knowing and trusting that God is loving, faithful, good, and able to do all things will keep us steady in faith and hope, whatever the pressures of life might be. Thanks be to God.

17

Summing Up the Whole

'*Judge not, that you be not judged. ² For with the judgment you pronounce you will be judged, and with the measure you use it will be measured to you. ³ Why do you see the speck that is in your brother's eye, but do not notice the log that is in your own eye? ⁴ Or how can you say to your brother, 'Let me take the speck out of your eye,' when there is the log in your own eye? ⁵ You hypocrite, first take the log out of your own eye, and then you will see clearly to take the speck out of your brother's eye. ⁶ Do not give dogs what is holy, and do not throw your pearls before pigs, lest they trample them underfoot and turn to attack you. ⁷ Ask, and it will be given to you; seek, and you will find; knock, and it will be opened to you. ⁸ For everyone who asks receives, and the one who seeks finds, and to the one who knocks it will be opened. ⁹ Or which one of you, if his son asks him for bread, will give him a stone? ¹⁰ Or if he asks for a fish, will give him a serpent? ¹¹ If you then, who are evil, know how to give good gifts to your children, how much more will your Father who is in heaven give good things to those who ask him! ¹² So whatever you wish that others would do to you, do also to them, for this is the Law and the Prophets'* (Matt. 7:1–12).

This section brings us to the conclusion of the main body of the sermon. We can see this by the closing of the inclusion in verse 12, 'So whatever you wish that others would do to you, do also to them, for this is the Law and the Prophets.' This verse provides a summation of all the Law and Prophets, and indicates that all that Jesus has been teaching from *Matt.* 5:17 onward has been expounding the Law and the Prophets. This summary statement is another way of saying 'Love your neighbour as yourself.'

JUDGE NOT, THAT YOU BE NOT JUDGED

Possibly this verse (*Matt.* 7:1) is the most quoted verse of the Sermon on the Mount. It might also be the most misunderstood. It is often quoted to support the idea that love for other people demands a tolerant and even an indulgent attitude toward them and their actions, leaving them free to choose for themselves what path in life they wish to follow without criticism or censure. Understood in this way, it seems to commend a 'live and let live' attitude toward others, a policy which seeks to maximize personal freedom of choice and minimize the criticisms we get from other people.

One cannot, however, read the New Testament and come away with the idea that this is what Jesus taught. In *Matt.* 18:15–20 Jesus says that when our brother sins, we should go to him, seeking to restore him to the path of faithfulness, just as a good shepherd seeks for a lost sheep (see *Matt.* 18:12–14). He outlines a series of gentle but firm efforts intended to restore the erring brother to the path of righteousness. So we cannot think that Jesus intended that we should never make moral judgments about the lives of others.

While it is important to be clear on what this 'judge not' does not mean, it is equally important that we understand what it does. The word *judge*, the English word, and the Greek word which it translates, have a fairly wide range of meaning. Various English words could be used to translate that Greek word (*krino*), depending on the context. Among the words which the ESV uses to translate this one word are *condemn* (*John* 3:17), *decide* (*Acts* 20:16), *go to law* (*1 Cor.* 6:1), and *conclude* (*2 Cor.* 5:14). Given this range of meaning, we should not be surprised to see that in one sense to judge might be a bad thing, while in another sense it could be a good or necessary thing. So, here we read, 'Judge not, that you be not judged,' while in *John* 7:24 we read, 'Do not judge by appearances, but judge with right judgment.'

So what is it precisely that Jesus is prohibiting in this context? From the verses which follow it is clear that Jesus is considering how we deal with other people. He speaks of seeing a speck in another's eye while having a log in our own (verse 3). There is moral evaluation here (seeing the speck in the other's eye) and there is moral blindness (not seeing the log that is in our own eye), making us hypocrites (verse 5). We see a harsh and censorious attitude toward others, criticizing and condemning them, while a more generous and patient approach is taken toward oneself. Using a harsh measure when dealing with others and a generous one with ourselves is certainly not doing to others as we would have them do to us.

The point is not that moral evaluation should never be made. This is clear from verse 6, which tells us we must not give what is holy to dogs, nor cast pearls before swine. One cannot obey such commandments without making some moral evaluation. But love demands that when we must make moral evaluations of others that it be done in love and humility. Love demands that we care for one another. Parents must do this for their children. Likewise, when we see our brother going astray, we should do all that we can to restore him to the right path. We are our brother's keeper (see *Gen.* 4:9). James says, 'Whoever brings back a sinner from his wandering will save his soul from death and will cover a multitude of sins' (*James* 5:20). The way of love demands moral evaluation, not turning a blind eye to the sins of others; but it also demands that the moral evaluation proceed from a heart of love, free from self-righteousness, and aimed at helping the other person, not condemning him.

THE GIVING FATHER

As indicated above, verse 12 represents the conclusion to the main body of the Sermon on the Mount. In verses 7–11 there is rapid movement toward that conclusion. Verse 7 is especially well known: 'Ask, and it will be given to you; seek, and you will find; knock, and it will be opened to you.' It looks like we have suddenly moved into a lesson on prayer. We have. But is it a general lesson about prayer, or is it a more focused lesson, aimed at something quite specific? Seen in context, it is quite specific in its aim. The demands of Jesus upon his disciples are very great. The true understanding of the Law and Prophets demands of us a righteousness far greater than that of the scribes and Pharisees. It demands of us not only clean hands but pure hearts (*Psa.* 24:4). And in the present context, it demands that we love our neighbour as ourselves, doing for him whatever we would have him do for us. How can such a demand ever be met? Not by our own strength to be sure. We can only live in this way by the grace of God and by the empowering of his Spirit. Thus we are encouraged to find this help in God: asking for it, seeking it, and knocking until he opens to us. The present tense imperative verbs used here indicate persistent effort in gaining from God what we need. We must pray with the great church father Augustine, 'My whole hope is in your exceeding great mercy and that alone. Give what you command and command what you will.' Jesus provides us abundant encouragement to pray for what we need, for it is to our heavenly Father that we pray, who gives good gifts to those who ask him.

SUMMARY

As Jesus concludes his exposition of the Law and the Prophets, we can see how high are the demands made of us. We are indeed to be perfect, even as our heavenly Father is perfect (*Matt.* 5:48). For that reason he concludes by warning against a condemning, judgmental mindset toward others, and by commending a humble spirit toward God whereby we continually seek the grace and help we need to live as his children. Those who know they are weak will seek their strength in God, and like Jacob, they will not let him go until he blesses them (see *Gen.* 32:26).

18

The Two Ways

'*E*nter *by the narrow gate. For the gate is wide and the way is easy that leads to destruction, and those who enter by it are many.* [14] *For the gate is narrow and the way is hard that leads to life, and those who find it are few.* [15] *Beware of false prophets, who come to you in sheep's clothing but inwardly are ravenous wolves.* [16] *You will recognize them by their fruits. Are grapes gathered from thornbushes, or figs from thistles?* [17] *So, every healthy tree bears good fruit, but the diseased tree bears bad fruit.* [18] *A healthy tree cannot bear bad fruit, nor can a diseased tree bear good fruit.* [19] *Every tree that does not bear good fruit is cut down and thrown into the fire.* [20] *Thus you will recognize them by their fruits.* [21] *Not everyone who says to me, "Lord, Lord," will enter the kingdom of heaven, but the one who does the will of my Father who is in heaven.* [22] *On that day many will say to me, "Lord, Lord, did we not prophesy in your name, and cast out demons in your name, and do many mighty works in your name?"* [23] *And then will I declare to them, "I never knew you; depart from me, you workers of lawlessness."* [24] *Everyone then who hears these words of mine and does them will be like a wise man who built his house on the rock.* [25] *And the rain fell, and the floods came, and the winds blew and beat on that house, but it did not fall, because it had been founded on the rock.* [26] *And everyone who hears these words of mine and does not do them will be like a foolish man who built his house on the sand.* [27] *And the rain fell, and the floods came, and the winds blew and beat against that house, and it fell, and great was the fall of it.'* [28] *And when Jesus finished these sayings, the crowds were astonished at his teaching,* [29] *for he was teaching them as one who had authority, and not as their scribes* (Matt. 7:13–29).

The exposition of the Law and the Prophets is now ended. Jesus concludes his sermon with a series of exhortations, calling his disciples to put in practice the teaching he has given. Four striking contrasts between true and false religion are used to drive his point home. This portion of the sermon closely parallels the wisdom literature of the Old Testament, where the theme of the 'two ways' in life is very prominent (see *Psa.* 1 and *Prov.* 9 on the way of wisdom and folly).

TWO GATES

In the first contrast two gates are set before us, the one wide and the other narrow. The way through the narrow gate is hard, so hard that there are few who find it. The way through the wide gate is easy, and many are those who enter by it. Only the way of the narrow gate leads to life; the way of the wide gate leads to destruction. The teaching of Jesus is represented by the narrow gate. It calls for a righteousness that exceeds that of the scribes and Pharisees (*Matt.* 5:20). It is more encompassing than their righteousness, for it includes the weightier matters of the law as well as the lesser ones (*Matt.* 23:23–24). It is also deeper, including not only the outward works of the body but the inward thoughts and intentions of the heart (Matt. 23:25–26). Jesus words are clear (7:13): 'Enter by the narrow gate.' Our aim in serving him must be to walk in all his ways, keeping even the least of his commandments (5:19). That will necessarily put us in a minority position in the world, among the few rather than the many. True discipleship requires that we take the unpopular path.

TWO TREES

Finding one's 'way' in life is often a matter of following the teaching of others. Jesus warns his disciples to beware of false prophets. Outwardly they come in sheep's clothing, so they appear to be sheep, to be true followers of Jesus. Inwardly, however, they are ravenous wolves. Their true aim is to kill and devour unsuspecting prey. Their path leads to destruction. How is one to know which prophets to follow? Jesus says (verse 16), 'You will recognize them by their fruits.' Jesus tells us that healthy trees produce good fruit, while diseased trees produce bad fruit. The false prophets are diseased trees, so the fruit they produce will be bad fruit. But what is the 'bad fruit' which they produce? The next contrast will make that clear.

SAYERS AND DOERS

In the next verses (7:21–23) Jesus takes us to the last day, to the judgment at the end of history. In that day, he says, there will be many who have called him 'Lord' that will not enter the kingdom of heaven. Why not? Two reasons are given. First, Jesus did not 'know' them. That is, there was no personal relationship between Jesus and these false followers. Though they called Jesus 'Lord', prophesied in his name, cast out demons in his name, and performed many mighty works in his name, he had no personal relationship with them. Second, they were workers of 'lawlessness'. That is, they did not follow the teaching of Jesus and they did not keep the law of God. Notice that as the sermon draws to a close Jesus has returned to the importance of keeping the law. He is not, of course, teaching that salvation is by keeping the law. But he is saying that those who are saved will be known by their fruits, and their fruits will include obedience to the law of God. Theirs will not be a religion of just saying that they follow Jesus, while doing some works in his name. No, their religion will be one of following Jesus, of doing all that he says and commands. They are not like those whom James tells us say they have faith, but they have no works. The true followers of Christ can be known because their works show that they have faith (*James* 2:14–26).

WISE AND FOOLISH BUILDERS

Who then will enter the kingdom of heaven? The last contrast sets two builders before us. One was wise and built his house upon a rock. This builder heard the words of Jesus, and did them. He put them into practice. The other builder was foolish and built his house upon the sand. He too heard the teaching of Jesus, but he did not put it into practice. Both houses were assaulted by a storm. Rain fell, floods came, and winds blew and beat on the houses. The house built upon the rock did not fall. But the house built upon the sand did fall. So it is with those who hear the words of Jesus. Those who put the words into practice will not fall in the storms of life. But those who hear the words of Jesus and do not put them into practice will fall in the storms of life. Their 'houses' will surely collapse, and great will be their fall. Here too the words of James are so much like his brother's (*Gal.* 1:19):

But be doers of the word, and not hearers only, deceiving yourselves. For if anyone is a hearer of the word and not a doer, he is like a man who looks intently at his natural face in a mirror. For he looks at himself and goes away and at once forgets what he was like. But the one who looks into the perfect law, the law of liberty, and perseveres, being no hearer who forgets but a doer who acts, he will be blessed in his doing (James 1:22–25).

SUMMARY

The life of discipleship is a life of obedience to the teaching of Jesus, of obedience to the law of God. Faith alone saves, but the faith which saves is never alone, but is ever accompanied by good works. Good works are those which God has commanded in his Word, and not simply those we offer as substitutes for obedience. If we would enter the kingdom of heaven, we must enter by the narrow gate, following the teaching that produces the good fruit of obedience, building our lives upon the rock of Jesus' words. None of this can be done in our own strength, but only by the grace and help we find in God.

19

Healing Every Disease

*W*hen he came down from the mountain, great crowds followed him.
² *And behold, a leper came to him and knelt before him, say-*
ing, 'Lord, if you will, you can make me clean.' ³ *And Jesus stretched*
out his hand and touched him, saying, 'I will; be clean.' And imme-
diately his leprosy was cleansed. ⁴ *And Jesus said to him, 'See that*
you say nothing to anyone, but go, show yourself to the priest and
offer the gift that Moses commanded, for a proof to them.' ⁵ *When*
he entered Capernaum, a centurion came forward to him, appeal-
ing to him, ⁶ *'Lord, my servant is lying paralysed at home, suffering*
terribly.' ⁷ *And he said to him, 'I will come and heal him.'* ⁸ *But the*
centurion replied, 'Lord, I am not worthy to have you come under my
roof, but only say the word, and my servant will be healed. ⁹ *For I*
too am a man under authority, with soldiers under me. And I say to
one, "Go," and he goes, and to another, "Come," and he comes, and
to my servant, "Do this," and he does it.' ¹⁰ *When Jesus heard this, he*
marvelled and said to those who followed him, 'Truly, I tell you, with
no one in Israel have I found such faith. ¹¹ *I tell you, many will come*
from east and west and recline at table with Abraham, Isaac, and
Jacob in the kingdom of heaven, ¹² *while the sons of the kingdom will*
be thrown into the outer darkness. In that place there will be weeping
and gnashing of teeth.' ¹³ *And to the centurion Jesus said, 'Go; let it*
be done for you as you have believed.' And the servant was healed at
that very moment. ¹⁴ *And when Jesus entered Peter's house, he saw*
his mother-in-law lying sick with a fever. ¹⁵ *He touched her hand,*
and the fever left her, and she rose and began to serve him. ¹⁶ *That*
evening they brought to him many who were oppressed by demons,
and he cast out the spirits with a word and healed all who were sick.
¹⁷ *This was to fulfil what was spoken by the prophet Isaiah: 'He took*
our illnesses and bore our diseases.' ¹⁸ *Now when Jesus saw a crowd*
around him, he gave orders to go over to the other side. ¹⁹ *And a*
scribe came up and said to him, 'Teacher, I will follow you wherever
you go.' ²⁰ *And Jesus said to him, 'Foxes have holes, and birds of the*

air have nests, but the Son of Man has nowhere to lay his head.'
²¹ Another of the disciples said to him, 'Lord, let me first go and bury
my father.' ²² And Jesus said to him, 'Follow me, and leave the dead
to bury their own dead' (Matt. 8:1–22).

Chapters 8 and 9 contain ten great miracles performed by Jesus. In *Matt.* 4:23 Jesus' ministry had been summarized as 'teaching in their synagogues and proclaiming the gospel of the kingdom and healing every disease and every affliction'. This summary will reappear at *Matt.* 9:35. For Matthew, Jesus' healing power knows no limits: he heals *every* disease and *every* affliction. Some commentators have wondered whether this collection of ten miracles is intended to parallel the ten plagues of Egypt. It is certainly possible that Matthew had this in mind, though it is hard to be certain. One thing is clear: by these wonders the kingdom of Satan is shown to be helpless against the onslaught of the kingdom of heaven, just as Egypt was overwhelmed by the ten plagues. Interestingly, just as the ten plagues are grouped in series of three (where the first, fourth, and seventh plagues are all announced 'in the morning', while the third, sixth, and ninth plagues all occur without announcement), so these great wonders are likewise grouped in threes (8:1–17, 8:23–9:8, 9:18–34), with teaching on discipleship inserted between the groupings (8:18–22, 9:9–17).

HE TOOK OUR ILLNESSES

While each of the three healings in this section has distinctive things to teach us, we should also see them as a whole, fulfilling Isaiah's prophecy, 'He took our illnesses and bore our diseases' (verse 17, *Isa.* 53:4). This helps us to see that these healings were not just for a select few, or limited to minor problems. Rather, they are examples intended to instruct and encourage us all, for they reveal the purpose of Messiah's coming. First, Jesus cleanses a leper, who suffered not only physically but socially, being cut off from the rest of society, including family and friends. Jesus shows that not only is he able to heal such people but also willing (verses 2–3). He is not only powerful, but full of mercy. With the centurion, Jesus shows that he is able and willing to do this for Gentiles as well as for Jews. So Jesus heals 'every disease and every affliction', and he does it for all kinds of people, Jews and Gentiles alike, indeed for all who believe.

The third healing story begins with Simon Peter's mother-in-law, who is sick with a fever. When she is healed, she quickly begins to serve him—an example that all should follow, and a lesson that soon will be taught. Before that, however, Matthew tells us of more healings. The people of Capernaum brought to Jesus 'many who were oppressed with demons, and he cast out the spirits with a word and healed all who were sick' (verse 16). It is interesting to observe Matthew's report of this in comparison with Mark. Mark tells us (*Mark* 1:29–34) that they brought to him 'all who were sick or oppressed by demons' (verse 32) and Jesus 'healed many . . . and cast out many demons' (verse 34). Matthew reverses this. He tells us that they brought to Jesus 'many who were oppressed by demons . . .' and he 'healed all who were sick'. The two reports are completely harmonious. Mark is not saying that some were healed while some were not. His point is simply that many were brought and many were healed. He emphasizes the large number who came and were healed. Matthew, however, wants to say more. He wants us to know not only that many were healed—a remarkable fact in itself—but that the healing power of Jesus has no limit, that 'every disease and every affliction' was healed by him. There is no power on earth that can withstand him, and therefore nothing will ever limit our enjoyment of the blessing he has for his people.

FOLLOW ME

After the series of three is complete, Matthew inserts a brief story about discipleship. As the great crowds continued to follow and press in on him, Jesus ordered his disciples to go to the other side of the sea. Then two would-be disciples approached him. The first is a scribe, and he professes that he will follow Jesus wherever he goes. But Jesus replies that following him will mean hardship, for though foxes have holes and birds have nests, the Son of Man has nowhere to lay his head. Nothing more is heard from this scribe. Presumably the demands of discipleship were more than he could bear. Then 'another of the disciples', that is, one who had been following Jesus, came volunteering, but begged that he might have leave first to go and bury his father. Jesus' rather curt reply,

'Follow me, and let the dead bury their own dead', might seem harsh to modern ears, but we must read this text according to its own time. Nothing indicates that the disciple's father was dead and awaiting burial, or that he was even near to death. The request could have been for an indefinite delay in responding to the call to follow Jesus, thus allowing the would-be disciple to postpone his response to Jesus to some future, more convenient time. The brief report that Matthew gives makes it hard to be certain just what the man's circumstances were at the time. But the point Matthew seeks to make is abundantly clear: no obligations of any sort, and no desires of any kind, can pre-empt one's response. Everything must yield to the demands of the kingdom. The disciple's real problem can be seen in his own words, 'Lord, let *me first* . . .' These are not the words of a true disciple, for 'first' place belongs to the Lord, not to 'me'. We must have no other gods before him, that is, in his presence. The one 'who loves father and mother' more than Jesus is not worthy of him (*Matt.* 10:37). True discipleship demands that the Lord be supreme.

SUMMARY

Coordinated with each other as they are, the three healings and the brief teaching on discipleship have much to say to us. The healings remind us that the salvation Jesus brings is a complete salvation, freeing us from all that afflicts us, and freeing all who come to him in faith. Once we are his, we must respond in giving back to him all that we are and all that we have. There can no longer be a 'Lord, let me first . . .' Rather, we must hereafter put him first in everything.

20

Authority to Forgive

*A*nd when he got into the boat, his disciples followed him. [24] *And behold, there arose a great storm on the sea, so that the boat was being swamped by the waves; but he was asleep.* [25] *And they went and woke him, saying, 'Save us, Lord; we are perishing.'* [26] *And he said to them, 'Why are you afraid, O you of little faith?' Then he rose and rebuked the winds and the sea, and there was a great calm.* [27] *And the men marvelled, saying, 'What sort of man is this, that even winds and sea obey him?'* [28] *And when he came to the other side, to the country of the Gadarenes, two demon-possessed men met him, coming out of the tombs, so fierce that no one could pass that way.* [29] *And behold, they cried out, 'What have you to do with us, O Son of God? Have you come here to torment us before the time?'* [30] *Now a herd of many pigs was feeding at some distance from them.* [31] *And the demons begged him, saying, 'If you cast us out, send us away into the herd of pigs.'* [32] *And he said to them, 'Go.' So they came out and went into the pigs, and behold, the whole herd rushed down the steep bank into the sea and drowned in the waters.* [33] *The herdsmen fled, and going into the city they told everything, especially what had happened to the demon-possessed men.* [34] *And behold, all the city came out to meet Jesus, and when they saw him, they begged him to leave their region.* [9:1] *And getting into a boat he crossed over and came to his own city.* [2] *And behold, some people brought to him a paralytic, lying on a bed. And when Jesus saw their faith, he said to the paralytic, 'Take heart, my son; your sins are forgiven.'* [3] *And behold, some of the scribes said to themselves, 'This man is blaspheming.'* [4] *But Jesus, knowing their thoughts, said, 'Why do you think evil in your hearts?* [5] *For which is easier, to say, "Your sins are forgiven," or to say, "Rise and walk"?* [6] *But that you may know that the Son of Man has authority on earth to forgive sins'* – *he then said to the paralytic* – *'Rise, pick up your bed and go home.'* [7] *And he rose and went home.* [8] *When the crowds saw it, they were afraid, and they glorified God, who had given such authority to men.* [9] *As Jesus passed on from there, he saw a man* *called Matthew sitting at the tax booth, and he said to him, 'Follow me.' And he rose and followed him. [10] And as Jesus reclined at table in the house, behold, many tax collectors and sinners came and were reclining with Jesus and his disciples. [11] And when the Pharisees saw this, they said to his disciples, 'Why does your teacher eat with tax collectors and sinners?' [12] But when he heard it, he said, 'Those who are well have no need of a physician, but those who are sick. [13] Go and learn what this means, "I desire mercy, and not sacrifice." For I came not to call the righteous, but sinners.' [14] Then the disciples of John came to him, saying, 'Why do we and the Pharisees fast, but your disciples do not fast?' [15] And Jesus said to them, 'Can the wedding guests mourn as long as the bridegroom is with them? The days will come when the bridegroom is taken away from them, and then they will fast. [16] No one puts a piece of unshrunk cloth on an old garment, for the patch tears away from the garment, and a worse tear is made. [17] Neither is new wine put into old wineskins. If it is, the skins burst and the wine is spilled and the skins are destroyed. But new wine is put into fresh wineskins, and so both are preserved'* (Matt. 8:23–9:17).

With the first three miracles of this series, Matthew gave us his main point in a summary statement at the end of the report of the third miracle: the healings of Jesus were the fulfilment of Isaiah's prophecy. The second group of three also concludes with a summary statement: the crowds 'glorified God, who had given such authority to men' (*Matt.* 9:8). Jesus' authority will be displayed over winds and waves, over legions of demons, and finally over sin itself. This will be followed by Matthew's own testimony of salvation, which dramatically shows that Jesus does forgive even the worst sinners.

EVEN WINDS AND WAVES OBEY HIM

When Jesus was with his disciples in the boat, a great storm arose on the sea, 'so that the boat was being swamped by the waves'. When experienced fishermen fear that they will perish, we can be sure that, as Luke might say, 'no small tempest' (*Acts* 27:20) had come up. Jesus, however, was asleep (verse 24). The disciples woke him, saying, 'Save us, Lord; we are perishing.' Jesus awakes and rebukes the disciples for their little faith, and rebukes the winds and the sea. The 'great storm' then yields to a 'great calm' (verse

26). The disciples marvel: 'What sort of man is this, that even winds and sea obey him?' The one who showed himself supreme over 'every disease and every affliction' is likewise supreme over all the forces of nature. In the scene to follow, he also shows himself supreme over all the forces of darkness.

THE TESTIMONY OF TWO WITNESSES

When they have arrived on the other side of the sea, another storm comes up, this one from two demon-possessed men who come out to meet Jesus. Mark and Luke also report on this incident, and both do so at great length (*Mark* 5:1–20, *Luke* 8:26–39). However, they tell us of only one demoniac, possessed by a legion of demons. Matthew's account is much simpler, though it is clear that a group of demons are present. Matthew's noting that there are two demoniacs, where the other evangelists mention only one, is a feature of his story-telling that is present elsewhere too: he tells of two blind men who are healed (indeed, gives two incidents where two blind men are healed, 9:27–31 and 20:29–34); and he tells of two donkeys used in the procession into Jerusalem (21:2–5). In each of these other stories, Mark and Luke only mention one where Matthew has two. Is he seeing double?

Matthew's reporting two where the other evangelists mention only one does not involve a contradiction and need not raise concerns about the divine origin or truthfulness of the Scriptures. Where there is a contradiction, both of two statements cannot be true at the same time. With these statements, however, it is not the case that if the one is true the other is false. For if there are *two* there is certainly *one*. The truth of the report giving two implies the truth of the other report. The other evangelists do not report that there was *only* one demoniac, or *only* one blind man, or *only* one donkey. They simply focus on one of the two and do not mention the other. But for Matthew, reporting on the two is important. Why might that be? Given his general orientation toward a Jewish audience, it would appear that he is providing us with what the Law requires, that every fact be established by two or more witnesses (*Matt.* 18:16, *Deut.* 19:15). These two demoniacs concur in giving testimony to Jesus as the Son of God with authority and power (verse 29).

Then a very surprising development took place. Rather than send the demons away into the abyss (*Luke* 8:31), Jesus acceded to their request to send them away into a nearby herd of pigs. The pigs rushed down a steep bank into the sea and drowned. The herdsmen then fled and went into he city, telling everything that they had seen, 'especially what had happened to the demon-possessed men'. The people of the city came out to meet Jesus and 'they begged him to leave their region' (verse 34). Shocking indeed, but true, the people of that region preferred their pigs and their demoniacs to the healing authority and presence of Jesus. Jesus likewise acceded to their request, and left their region.

HE EVENS FORGIVES SIN

When he returned to his own city, Capernaum, some people in the town brought a paralysed man to Jesus, carrying him on a bed. Jesus, seeing their faith, said to the man, 'Take heart, my son, your sins are forgiven.' This saying produced a great controversy among the scribes, who thought Jesus to be blaspheming. But Jesus knew their thoughts and asked whether it was easier to say, 'Your sins are forgiven,' or to say, 'Rise and walk.' In actual fact, both are easy to *say*, yet also beyond mere human powers to *effect*. Jesus is capable of both. So to prove that he could forgive sins, he commanded the man to pick up his bed and go home. The man immediately did as he was told. The crowds marvelled and glorified God for such authority given among men as they had now seen in Jesus.

In further demonstration of this power, Matthew recounts his own 'healing'. As Jesus passed by he saw Matthew sitting at his tax-booth, and called him to follow him. Matthew, as the other disciples before him had done, followed him immediately. Later, Jesus was eating with a group of tax-collectors and sinners. This caused the Pharisees to complain against him. Jesus replied that those who are well have no need of a physician, but those who are sick. He came not to call the righteous, but sinners. Then the disciples of John the Baptist complained that Jesus' disciples did not fast, as they and Pharisees did. Jesus replied that this was because the bridegroom was still with them. They would fast when the bridegroom was taken away. What all this reveals is that, while the deeds of Jesus clearly prove that he is the Messiah, a fact to which even the demons bear witness, many remain blind to his identity. Jesus is bringing a 'new wine' religion, and fresh wineskins will be required to contain it.

SUMMARY

The power of Jesus truly knows no bounds. Winds and waves obey him. Demons submit to him. Every disease and every affliction yield to his healing touch, and he has authority on earth to forgive sins. But if we demand that he leave us alone with our demons and our pigs, he will accede to our request. If we attempt to force him to conform to our old wineskins, we will fail. A great choice is before us. If we would follow him, it must be with total commitment. If we do not, our loss will be total.

21

Sheep without a Shepherd

*W*hile he was saying these things to them, behold, a ruler came
in and knelt before him, saying, 'My daughter has just died,
but come and lay your hand on her, and she will live.' [19] And Jesus
rose and followed him, with his disciples. [20] And behold, a woman
who had suffered from a discharge of blood for twelve years came
up behind him and touched the fringe of his garment, [21] for she said
to herself, 'If I only touch his garment, I will be made well.' [22] Jesus
turned, and seeing her he said, 'Take heart, daughter; your faith has
made you well.' And instantly the woman was made well. [23] And
when Jesus came to the ruler's house and saw the flute players and
the crowd making a commotion, [24] he said, 'Go away, for the girl
is not dead but sleeping.' And they laughed at him. [25] But when the
crowd had been put outside, he went in and took her by the hand, and
the girl arose. [26] And the report of this went through all that district.
[27] And as Jesus passed on from there, two blind men followed him,
crying aloud, 'Have mercy on us, Son of David.' [28] When he entered
the house, the blind men came to him, and Jesus said to them, 'Do
you believe that I am able to do this?' They said to him, 'Yes, Lord.'
[29] Then he touched their eyes, saying, 'According to your faith be it
done to you.' [30] And their eyes were opened. And Jesus sternly warned
them, 'See that no one knows about it.' [31] But they went away and
spread his fame through all that district. [32] As they were going away,
behold, a demon-oppressed man who was mute was brought to him.
[33] And when the demon had been cast out, the mute man spoke. And
the crowds marvelled, saying, 'Never was anything like this seen in
Israel.' [34] But the Pharisees said, 'He casts out demons by the prince
of demons.' [35] And Jesus went throughout all the cities and villages,
teaching in their synagogues and proclaiming the gospel of the kingdom and healing every disease and every affliction. [36] When he saw
the crowds, he had compassion for them, because they were harassed
and helpless, like sheep without a shepherd. [37] Then he said to his

disciples, 'The harvest is plentiful, but the labourers are few; [38] *there-*
fore pray earnestly to the Lord of the harvest to send out labourers
into his harvest' (Matt. 9:18–38).

The final series of miracles in chapters 8 and 9 actually con-
sists of four miracles, bringing the total to ten. Still, they are
arranged in three groups, for the second one is tucked inside the
first. In this group the evidence continues to mount that Jesus
is indeed the Son of God, the Saviour of the world. Paradoxically,
however, there are many who cannot see what is so very plain.
Indeed, those who prove to be most blind are those who should
have seen most clearly, and they claim that Jesus' power is of
demonic origin. This leads Jesus to the conclusion that the
people are as sheep without a shepherd. In the next chapter, he will
appoint new shepherds for the flock.

THE DEAD ARE RAISED

Those who came seeking healing from Jesus certainly comprise
a mixed multitude. We have had a leper, a Roman centurion, a
woman with a fever, many sick in unnamed ways, demoniacs, a
paralytic, and two blind men. Now we have a ruler, whom Mark
and Luke tell us is a synagogue ruler named Jairus. The daughter of the ruler has just died, yet the man has faith that Jesus can
restore her to life, if only he will come and lay his hand upon her.
As Jesus makes his way there, a woman who has suffered twelve
years from a discharge of blood touches Jesus from behind when
he passes through the crowd. Matthew tells us that she had said to
herself, 'If I only touch his garment, I will be made well.' Her faith
was not in vain. Jesus turned and said to her, 'Take heart, daughter; your faith has made you well.' Instantly she was healed. Continuing on to the synagogue ruler's house, Jesus enters the room
of the deceased child and restores her to life. The ruler's faith too
was not in vain. The healing power of Jesus knows no limits, as
the faith of these two witnesses confirms. The report of this soon
spreads throughout that entire district. As the proof mounts, one
would expect the whole of Israel to embrace him as their Messiah,
but strangely they do not.

THE BLIND CAN SEE

Passing on from there, Jesus is followed by two blind men. They call out to him, 'Have mercy on us, Son of David.' This is Matthew's first use of the title 'Son of David' for Jesus since the opening verse of the book. The title will appear eight more times, often in connection with the healing power of Jesus. It is a major point for Matthew. As we saw in the opening chapter of this book, the title is Messianic. The Lord had promised to David that a son of his would reign over a kingdom that would last forever. Yet David was not a healer. The prophets saw the coming Son of David as one much greater than his father, able not only to defeat hostile armies, but to overthrow every enemy, heal every disease, and conquer sin and death itself.

> Then the eyes of the blind shall be opened, and the ears of the deaf unstopped; then shall the lame man leap like a deer, and the tongue of the mute sing for joy (Isa. 35:5, 6).

So clear is the evidence that Jesus is the promised Messiah that even the blind acclaim him as the Son of David, yet those who should see most plainly will not acknowledge him.

THOSE WHO SEE BECOME BLIND

The final healing in the collection of ten is of a demon-oppressed man who cannot speak. Interestingly, Matthew does not narrate the healing but only its aftermath. That is his main concern. When the demon had been cast out the mute man spoke and the crowds marvelled. 'Never was anything like this seen in Israel,' they said. But the Pharisees said, 'He casts out demons by the prince of demons.' Matthew will come back to this absurd and wicked interpretation of the healing power of Jesus in chapter 12. There he will deal with it at length. For now it is simply noted, and is used to provide the basis for the next saying of Jesus in 9:35–38. In these verses Matthew again summarizes Jesus' ministry as going about in all the cities and villages, 'teaching in their synagogues and proclaiming the gospel of the kingdom and healing every disease and every affliction' (verse 35; see also 4:23–25). These works clearly prove that Jesus is the promised Son of David, the Messiah, who has come to save his people from all their enemies, all their afflictions, and all their sins. But the Pharisees, who should know this much better than all the rest of the people, will not acknowledge it. Instead, they attribute these miraculous powers to Satan.

> *For judgment I came into this world, that those who do not see may see, and those who see may become blind* (John 9:39).

The leaders of the Jews were proving to be blind guides (see *Matt.* 23:16, 17, 26), leaving the crowds of people without proper guidance and protection. Even the disciples of John seemed more concerned about observing the traditions of fasting than about the gospel of the kingdom preached by Jesus (9:14–17). With such failure of leadership among the people, Jesus had compassion for them, because they were harassed and helpless, like sheep without a shepherd. He urged his disciples to pray: 'The harvest is plentiful, but the labourers are few; therefore pray earnestly to the Lord of the harvest to send out labourers into his harvest' (verse 37–38). As in Ezekiel's day, the shepherds of the people have failed to care for the flock of God (see *Ezek.* 34). In the next chapter, Jesus will do the very thing for which he told the disciples to pray. They will thus become a part of the answer to their own prayers.

SUMMARY

In chapters 8–9 Matthew has given us a ten-fold sampling of the healing and saving power of Jesus, just as in chapters 5–7 he presented the preaching and teaching ministry of Jesus. All this fulfils the Old Testament prophecies and proves that Jesus is the Messiah. Yet the leaders of the people do not acknowledge him, and the crowds will also prove to be unreliable when the time comes for Jesus to be crucified. Truly the people are as sheep without a shepherd. New labourers must be sent into the harvest—new shepherds, who have the heart of their master (*Jer.* 3:15).

22

Multiplying the Ministry

*A*nd he called to him his twelve disciples and gave them authority over unclean spirits, to cast them out, and to heal every disease and every affliction. ² The names of the twelve apostles are these: first, Simon, who is called Peter, and Andrew his brother; James the son of Zebedee, and John his brother; ³ Philip and Bartholomew; Thomas and Matthew the tax collector; James the son of Alphaeus, and Thaddaeus; ⁴ Simon the Cananaean, and Judas Iscariot, who betrayed him. ⁵ These twelve Jesus sent out, instructing them, 'Go nowhere among the Gentiles and enter no town of the Samaritans, ⁶ but go rather to the lost sheep of the house of Israel. ⁷ And proclaim as you go, saying, "The kingdom of heaven is at hand." ⁸ Heal the sick, raise the dead, cleanse lepers, cast out demons. You received without paying; give without pay. ⁹ Acquire no gold nor silver nor copper for your belts, ¹⁰ no bag for your journey, nor two tunics nor sandals nor a staff, for the labourer deserves his food. ¹¹ And whatever town or village you enter, find out who is worthy in it and stay there until you depart. ¹² As you enter the house, greet it. ¹³ And if the house is worthy, let your peace come upon it, but if it is not worthy, let your peace return to you. ¹⁴ And if anyone will not receive you or listen to your words, shake off the dust from your feet when you leave that house or town. ¹⁵ Truly, I say to you, it will be more bearable on the day of judgment for the land of Sodom and Gomorrah than for that town' (Matt. 10:1–15).

*A*s we have seen, chapters 5–9 present us with an introductory picture of the ministry of Jesus. *Matt.* 4:23 and 9:35 summarize this ministry as 'teaching in their synagogues and proclaiming the gospel of the kingdom and healing every disease and every affliction'. Chapter 9 ended with Jesus urging his disciples to pray the Lord of the harvest to send out workers into his harvest. Now Jesus will make his disciples the answer to their own prayers.

THE TWELVE SENT OUT

In this section we are given the names of the twelve whom Jesus chose to be his special disciples (verses 2–4), among the others who followed him. Matthew has told us the stories of how five of Jesus' disciples were called—Peter and Andrew, James and John (4:18–22), and Matthew himself (9:9–13)—but of the others he says nothing until now. He says that Jesus called to him 'his twelve disciples'. No explanation is given for the number, but they are later told that they will judge the twelve tribes of Israel (19:28). This reference and others in the New Testament (for example, *Rev.* 21:14) tell us that their number is intended to represent the total number of the people of God. Now these disciples are being sent out 'to the lost sheep of the house of Israel' (verse 6).

They are sent out to preach the same message which Jesus had been preaching, 'The kingdom of heaven is at hand' (verse 7). They were also given authority to cast out unclean spirits and to heal 'every disease and every affliction' (verse 2), just as Jesus had been doing (4:23–25, 9:35). Notice how the ministry of Jesus is to be reproduced in the ministry of his disciples. They preach the same message and they perform the same mighty works (verse 8) as he does. In them, as in him, the message is embodied in the works, demonstrating the power and the nature of the kingdom which comes. It is a gracious kingdom, bringing deliverance and wholeness, forgiveness and reconciliation, to all who receive Christ.

A RESTRICTED MINISTRY

Already in Matthew we have seen his concern to emphasize that the kingdom of heaven will include Gentiles. Here they seem to be excluded, but that is only a temporary restriction. Jesus is sending the disciples on a short-term mission, limited primarily in its geographic focus: 'Go nowhere among the Gentiles and enter no town of the Samaritans.' The method of Jesus, followed also by the apostles (see *Acts* 3:26, 13:46, 18:5, 6; *Rom.* 1:16), will be to go first to the house of Israel. Later will come the worldwide mission (*Matt.* 28:18–20).

[91]

There is another temporary restriction imposed on the disciples: 'Acquire no gold nor silver nor copper for your belts, no bag for your journey, nor two tunics nor sandals nor a staff, for the labourer deserves his food' (verses 9, 10). As a permanent and universal prescription for missionary service, these would seem to be very severe limitations. Should missionaries take no provisions when travelling overseas for what might be life-long service? Is it always wrong for a Christian worker to have anything more than just the clothing that he or she is wearing? Is Jesus prescribing a mendicant ministry (one where the workers must beg for their livelihood) for all those who follow him? He is not. This is made perfectly clear in Luke's Gospel (*Luke* 22:35–38) where Jesus reminds the disciples of these restrictions and then lifts them for their future service.

What then is the point of these temporary restrictions? In part, it is to build their faith, requiring them to trust God for their provisions, in order that they might see God's faithfulness in caring for his people. Jesus stresses this point when he removes the restrictions, reminding the disciples that, though they had gone out with nothing, still they had lacked nothing (*Luke* 22:35). But there is another important lesson here. Jesus is sending out his missionaries with incredible power to heal the sick, raise the dead, cleanse lepers, and cast out demons (verse 9). They could easily be turned aside from preaching the good news of salvation and become consumed with their own prosperity, even selling their services for high rewards. Yet they have such power because it was freely given; hence they must freely give such benefits to others. Their ministry is to represent their Lord, and it is his beneficence that they are showing. The Lord gives freely, hence those who represent him must likewise give freely, from the bounty they have freely received from him.

WORTHY AND UNWORTHY RECEIVERS

The final section of our passage (verses 11–15) introduces the theme of suffering on the part of the disciples, which will be the focus of the next section. Made dependent as they are on others for the provision of food and shelter, they will likely be received by some and rejected by others. Jesus makes plain that the Lord will take notice of how the disciples are received (see also 10:40–42).

In the case of those who reject the good news of the kingdom and reject the messengers of the king, Jesus says it will be more tolerable on the day of judgment for Sodom and Gomorrah than for those towns. As a testimony of this, the disciples are to shake off the dust from their feet when they leave a house or a town that rejects the good news. Correspondingly, those who receive the good news and its messengers are to receive a blessing of peace from the apostles. In this way they will represent their Lord, or as we might better say, they will *pre*-present their Lord, giving anticipation to the Lord's own dealings with such people on the day of judgment.

SUMMARY

Christian missionary service, like the Christian life generally, means representing Christ to the world in all that we say and do. While the apostles had a special and unique role to play in this service, and thus were given special powers not given to others, every Christian is called to represent the Lord in speaking his word and doing his will. In word and deed we are to show to the world the purposes and character of our God. May God help us all to represent him well.

23

Sheep in the Midst of Wolves

'*B*ehold, I am sending you out as sheep in the midst of wolves, so be wise as serpents and innocent as doves. *17* Beware of men, for they will deliver you over to courts and flog you in their synagogues, *18* and you will be dragged before governors and kings for my sake, to bear witness before them and the Gentiles. *19* When they deliver you over, do not be anxious how you are to speak or what you are to say, for what you are to say will be given to you in that hour. *20* For it is not you who speak, but the Spirit of your Father speaking through you. *21* Brother will deliver brother over to death, and the father his child, and children will rise against parents and have them put to death, *22* and you will be hated by all for my name's sake. But the one who endures to the end will be saved. *23* When they persecute you in one town, flee to the next, for truly, I say to you, you will not have gone through all the towns of Israel before the Son of Man comes. *24* A disciple is not above his teacher, nor a servant above his master. *25* It is enough for the disciple to be like his teacher, and the servant like his master. If they have called the master of the house Beelzebul, how much more will they malign those of his household. *26* So have no fear of them, for nothing is covered that will not be revealed, or hidden that will not be known. *27* What I tell you in the dark, say in the light, and what you hear whispered, proclaim on the housetops. *28* And do not fear those who kill the body but cannot kill the soul. Rather fear him who can destroy both soul and body in hell. *29* Are not two sparrows sold for a penny? And not one of them will fall to the ground apart from your Father. *30* But even the hairs of your head are all numbered. *31* Fear not, therefore; you are of more value than many sparrows. *32* So everyone who acknowledges me before men, I also will acknowledge before my Father who is in heaven, *33* but whoever denies me before men, I also will deny before my Father who is in heaven. *34* Do not think that I have come to bring peace to the *earth. I have not come to bring peace, but a sword. [35] For I have come to set a man against his father, and a daughter against her mother, and a daughter-in-law against her mother-in-law. [36] And a person's enemies will be those of his own household. [37] Whoever loves father or mother more than me is not worthy of me, and whoever loves son or daughter more than me is not worthy of me. [38] And whoever does not take his cross and follow me is not worthy of me. [39] Whoever finds his life will lose it, and whoever loses his life for my sake will find it. [40] Whoever receives you receives me, and whoever receives me receives him who sent me. [41] The one who receives a prophet because he is a prophet will receive a prophet's reward, and the one who receives a righteous person because he is a righteous person will receive a righteous person's reward. [42] And whoever gives one of these little ones even a cup of cold water because he is a disciple, truly, I say to you, he will by no means lose his reward.' [11:1] When Jesus had finished instructing his twelve disciples, he went on from there to teach and preach in their cities* (Matt. 10:16–11:1).

In the previous section the possibility of a hostile reception for the messengers was anticipated. Now Jesus discusses it in graphic detail. The disciples are being sent out as sheep in the midst of wolves. They must expect that their mission will meet with opposition. Indeed, great persecutions are to be expected, demanding of them great perseverance. What Jesus says here applies not just to the short-term mission the disciples are about to undertake, but to all subsequent missionary service done in his name, including our own.

PERSECUTION IS SURE TO COME

Service to Christ will meet with persecution. 'In the world you will have tribulation' (*John* 16:33). Jesus speaks of being handed over to courts, being flogged in the synagogues, and dragged before governors and kings. He speaks of betrayal: brother will deliver brother over to death, a father his child, and children their parents. The disciples will be hated by all for his name's sake. Such strife belongs to the very nature of Jesus' mission, which is not to bring an indiscriminate peace to everyone, but to effect a separation between the righteous and the wicked, even within families (verses 34–39). John the Baptist said that this would be the nature of Christ's ministry: 'His winnowing fork is in his hand, and he will clear his threshing floor and gather his wheat into the barn, but the chaff he will burn with unquenchable fire' (*Matt.* 3:12). Afterwards there would indeed be peace, but not before.

If such persecution is to come, the disciples must be prepared. They must not be surprised when they met with opposition, trials, and persecutions. If Jesus himself met with such opposition, the disciples should expect no less. 'A disciple is not above his teacher, nor a servant above his master' (verse 24). As disciples are called to be like their master in the ministry, so they must expect to be treated like their master. 'If they have called the master of the house Beelzebul, how much more will they malign those of his household' (verse 25).

HOLD ON TO THE END

Turning back is no option. If the disciples would be saved, they must endure to the end (verse 22). Those who acknowledge Jesus before others will themselves be acknowledged by Jesus before the Father. Those who deny him, he will deny before his Father in heaven (verse 32). The one who would save his life, by turning back or denying Christ, will in fact lose his life and perish; but the one who loses his life for Christ's sake will find it (verse 39). The New Testament has much 'conditional' language like this, and it can lead to confusion about how we are saved. The New Testament makes plain that we are not saved by our works, but by faith in Jesus Christ (*Rom.* 3:24, 4:1–5; *Gal.* 2:16; *Eph.* 2:8, 9; *Phil.* 3:9). How do we reconcile such 'conditional' language (concerning our works) with salvation as a gracious gift received by faith?

As we have already seen, we are indeed saved by faith alone, or rather, saved by the grace of God in Christ, received by faith alone. But the salvation we receive is a transforming salvation. Though saved *apart from* works (*Rom.* 3:28), yet we are not saved by a faith that produces no works (*James* 2:17). We become new creatures in Christ, whose lives show forth the new life we have in Christ. As John the Baptist put it, we bear fruit in keeping with our repentance (*Matt.* 3:8). Perseverance is one of those fruits. Those who have new life in Christ will persevere to the end. Those who turn back from the faith they once professed show that they never possessed that faith (see *1 John* 2:19). Those who shrink back end up being destroyed; but those who have been born of God are those who have faith and preserve their souls (*Heb.* 10:39). Indeed, it is by our perseverance and growth in grace that we grow up to full assurance of our hope and salvation (*Heb.* 6:11–12, *2 Pet.* 1:3–10).

FEAR NOT

If persecution is inevitable, and perseverance in faith is necessary, a very heavy burden is made to rest upon the disciples. Knowing this, Jesus speaks to our need: 'So have no fear of them . . . do not fear those who kill the body but cannot kill the soul . . . even the hairs of your head are numbered . . . everyone who acknowledges me before men, I also will acknowledge before my Father who is in heaven . . . whoever loses his life for my sake will find it' (verses 26–39). The Lord guards and sustains his followers, upholding them and keeping them to the end. He never leaves them nor forsakes them (*Heb.* 13:5). The perseverance of the saints is due to their preservation by the Lord.

At the same time, such perseverance is also the product of the effort put forth by the saints. Jesus said, 'If you abide in my word, you are truly my disciples, and you will know the truth and the truth will set you free' (*John* 8:31). Similarly, 'Abide in me, and I in you. As the branch cannot bear fruit by itself, unless it abides in the vine, neither can you, unless you abide in me . . . If you keep my commandments, you will abide in my love, just as I have kept my Father's commandments and abide in his love' (*John* 15:4, 10). Here is a great paradox in the Christian faith: those who are indifferent to the duties of Christian discipleship cannot comfort themselves that it does not matter whether they obey or not, thinking they are saved by grace apart from works; while those who diligently obey safely rest knowing that they are kept in Christ, not by the diligence of their works, but by the sustaining grace of Christ.

SUMMARY

The disciples of Christ in every age are sent out to do their Master's will and to be his representatives in all they say and do.

They can expect to be persecuted for this. Yet their hope and confidence is that he will sustain and keep them, however fierce the enemy's attack might be:

> . . . for he has said, 'I will never leave you nor forsake you.' So we can confidently say, 'The Lord is my helper; I will not fear; what can man do to me?' (Heb. 13:5–6).

24

Before the Son of Man Comes

When they persecute you in one town, flee to the next, for truly, I say to you, you will not have gone through all the towns of Israel before the Son of Man comes (Matt. 10:23).

In our discussion of Matthew 10:16–11:1 we passed over verse 23 without comment. In a brief study like this one there will be many verses passed over; limitations on space simply do not permit commenting on every verse, or commenting extensively on difficult verses. Readers seeking further explanation on such verses must refer to the larger commentaries, and to specialized studies in journal articles and books. Recommendations on a few other commentaries can be found at the conclusion of this book. But verse 23 is one of several in Matthew (including 16:28, 24:29-35, 26:64) dealing with the 'coming of the Son of Man' which are difficult to understand, so that, while extensive discussion of them all cannot be given here, perhaps something brief but useful can be offered in viewing them together.

APPROACHING DIFFICULT PASSAGES

As we come upon passages in the Scriptures which are difficult to understand, it is well that we keep in mind the following:

> *All things in Scripture are not alike plain in themselves, nor alike clear to all; yet those things which are necessary to be known, believed, and observed for salvation, are so clearly propounded and opened in some place of Scripture or other, that not only the learned, but the unlearned, in a due use of the ordinary means, may attain unto a sufficient understanding of them* (Westminster Confession of Faith, I. 7).

[99]

We should not expect that everything in Scripture will be easy to understand, or understandable with just a little extra effort. As the parables make clear, the Lord will give some teaching that will challenge our understanding and demand of us long and patient study. What we *must* know for salvation is indeed clearly set forth, but some things in the Scriptures will prove much more difficult to understand. The passages about 'the coming of the Son of Man' in Matthew are among those passages. Even to this day, after more than two thousand years of study by the best minds in the church, there are still differences of opinion on exactly what these verses are telling us.

FOCUS ON WHAT YOU *DO* KNOW

When facing a difficult passage, we should not let what we don't know confuse us about what we do. In the case of *Matt.* 10:23, we must not suppose that Jesus was predicting his second coming within the lifetime of the disciples, indeed, within the time of their short-term mission to 'the lost sheep of the house of Israel'. Why not? Because we know from what is taught clearly, elsewhere in Scripture, that Jesus is indeed the incarnate Son of God who cannot possibly teach anything that is false. Jesus' second coming did not occur during the lifetime of the apostles, so clearly that is not what he was teaching.

Could he have meant some other type of 'coming' than the second coming? Many scholars have supposed that he did. Some have thought that in this verse he had in mind 'coming' to the disciples within a short period of time, that is, 'catching up to the disciples', before they finished visiting all the towns in Israel. Others have supposed he was talking about 'coming in (or into) his kingdom' (as in *Matt.* 16:28); that is, gaining victory over death in the resurrection and being exalted to the right hand of God. This is a very attractive solution since these sayings in Matthew are associated with the title 'Son of Man', whose background is *Dan.* 7:13–14. In that passage, the 'coming' of the Son of Man is *to* the Father to receive his kingdom, not *from* the Father to consummate his kingdom on the earth. Understood in this way, the 'coming of the Son of Man' to the Father occurred at the ascension, which was during the lifetime of the disciples. Finally, some have thought that Jesus meant 'coming' in judgment against the nation of Israel, as happened in AD 70 when the Romans destroyed Jerusalem and its temple, bringing an end to the Old Testament sacrificial system and priesthood. None of these suggestions is without some plausibility, though all face difficulties when applied to the various passages (some perhaps more than others).

Still, there are yet other scholars who suppose that it is the second coming that is in view in all these passages. They believe that other parts of the passages are being misunderstood and cause our difficulties in interpretation. Thus in *Matt.* 10:23, some have thought that Jesus was only saying that a complete evangelization of the towns of Israel would not be completed before he returned, and that in fact it has not and will not before he comes again. Some have thought that the 'generation' which would not pass away (*Matt.* 24:34) before all the signs given by Jesus were fulfilled was simply the generation of people on the earth, the 'evil and adulterous generation' which seeks after signs (*Matt.* 12:39, 16:4), meaning the whole human race in all ages. Again, each of these suggestions has some merit to it, but each also faces difficulties in supplying a completely persuasive interpretation.

HOW TO GO FORWARD

Confronted with difficult passages, sometimes we must be content to live with the mystery that is left to us after all our efforts to resolve it. That does not mean, however, that such passages are without benefit to us. Not understanding everything does not mean we do not understand anything. For if we pay close attention to the way in which the verses function in their context, we can generally find some help in the passage for living out our faith. So in this case, whatever type of coming or whatever time Jesus had in mind, we know that the enemies pursuing us will not defeat us before he comes. Jesus says that when we are persecuted in one town, we should flee to the next; then he comforts us by the assurance that we shall not have gone through all the towns of Israel (that is, we shall not have exhausted all our places of refuge) 'before the Son of Man comes'. Truly, he will never leave us nor forsake us, but will come to us, to save us and keep us for his everlasting kingdom. Thanks be to God.

25

John's Questions and Ours

*N*ow when John heard in prison about the deeds of the Christ, he sent word by his disciples ³ and said to him, 'Are you the one who is to come, or shall we look for another?' ⁴ And Jesus answered them, 'Go and tell John what you hear and see: ⁵ the blind receive their sight and the lame walk, lepers are cleansed and the deaf hear, and the dead are raised up, and the poor have good news preached to them. ⁶ And blessed is the one who is not offended by me.' ⁷ As they went away, Jesus began to speak to the crowds concerning John: 'What did you go out into the wilderness to see? A reed shaken by the wind? ⁸ What then did you go out to see? A man dressed in soft clothing? Behold, those who wear soft clothing are in kings' houses. ⁹ What then did you go out to see? A prophet? Yes, I tell you, and more than a prophet. ¹⁰ This is he of whom it is written, "Behold, I send my messenger before your face, who will prepare your way before you."' ¹¹ Truly, I say to you, among those born of women there has arisen no one greater than John the Baptist. Yet the one who is least in the kingdom of heaven is greater than he. ¹² From the days of John the Baptist until now the kingdom of heaven has suffered violence, and the violent take it by force. ¹³ For all the Prophets and the Law prophesied until John, ¹⁴ and if you are willing to accept it, he is Elijah who is to come. ¹⁵ He who has ears to hear, let him hear* (Matt. 11:2–15).

Chapters 11 and 12 are devoted to a narrative of events that shows how various people and groups responded to the ministry of Jesus. Each chapter shows a number of incorrect responses to the person and works of Christ, and each shows the correct response. Chapter 13 will also deal with responses to the kingdom by way of parables. These are searching chapters, calling us to examine our own response to Jesus. They encourage us to make the right response, assuring us of a most gracious acceptance with Jesus if we do.

JOHN'S QUESTIONS

In *Matt.* 4:12 we were told that John the Baptist was taken into custody. *Matt.* 14:1–12 gives us more of the story, telling us why he was arrested by Herod the tetrarch (Herod Antipas, son of Herod the Great) and also how he came to die. Here we read something about John while he was in prison. Though he had heard about the works of Christ, it seems that something was troubling him. He sent word to Jesus asking whether he really was the Coming One or should they look for someone else (verse 3). Why would he ask such a question? Despite all that John had seen and heard about Jesus (see *John* 1:29–34), he seems to have doubts. How can this be?

We must take note of John's circumstances. He was in prison. He had been arrested because he denounced Herod for taking his brother Philip's wife as his own (*Matt.* 14:3). Days passed, probably weeks and months. Surely he knew that he could be executed at any time, as eventually he was – all this for doing the will of God. Should not the coming of the kingdom of heaven put an end to such injustices? But what had happened since those days when Jesus came to be baptized by John at the Jordan River? Not enough to match what John expected. So he wondered. Had he been mistaken? Was Jesus the Coming One, or should they look for another? When we go through sustained periods of hardship, and God does not send relief, we can find that questions arise in our hearts.

JESUS' ANSWER

Jesus told the disciples of John to return to their master and report to him what they had seen and heard:

> . . . *the blind receive their sight and the lame walk, lepers are cleansed and the deaf hear, and the dead are raised up, and the poor have good news preached to them* (verse 5).

These are the very works the prophets had foretold concerning the coming of the kingdom (see *Isa.* 35:5–6, 61:1). Clearly therefore the kingdom was at hand—the works of Jesus proved that—but

[103]

the kingdom was not yet consummated. God was delaying the consummation of his kingdom. The patience of God was (and is to this day) still being manifested, giving opportunity for sinners to repent and for the gospel to be proclaimed throughout the whole world as a testimony to the nations (see *Matt.* 24:14). Similarly, time is being given for the iniquity of the wicked to ripen to its fullness (as in *Gen.* 15:16), before the end will come, before the chaff will be burned in the unquenchable fire (*Matt.* 3:12, see *Rom.* 2:5, *1 Thess.* 2:16). Until then, the children of the kingdom will suffer in this world, even as Jesus himself suffered.

> *From the days of John the Baptist until now the kingdom of heaven has suffered violence, and the violent take it by force* (verse 12).

These words of Jesus are difficult, both to translate and to interpret, as comparison between several English translations will show (compare, for example, NIV and ESV). Larger commentaries than this one should be consulted for explanations of the difficulties. This writer will simply state his conviction that Jesus is saying that from John's days until that time the kingdom of heaven, which was announced by John and came with Jesus, suffered violence from violent men like Herod (as indeed John now suffered) and like the Pharisees, who would shortly be seeking to kill Jesus (see *Matt.* 12:14).

OUR QUESTIONS

It is precisely this suffering of the kingdom of heaven that is so confusing to so many. The wicked become confused by it. Wicked people 'presume on the riches of his kindness and forbearance and patience, not knowing that God's kindness is meant to lead [them] to repentance' (*Rom.* 2:4). They suppose God's patience means that he never will come in judgment against them, that things will always continue just as they always have (see *2 Pet.* 3:3–7). This is a mistake of everlasting consequence.

The children of the kingdom can also be confused by God's patience toward the wicked. We wonder why God does not save and deliver us now, why he permits his own to suffer at the hands of those who do not believe. Even death does not rid us of such questions, for we are told that the martyred souls in heaven cried out with a loud voice, 'O Sovereign Lord, holy and true, how long before you will judge and avenge our blood on those who dwell on the earth?' (*Rev.* 6:10). They were told to rest a little while longer, until the full number of their fellow-servants, and their brethren who were to be killed even as they had been, should be completed also (*Rev.* 6:11). Jesus speaks a word to us all (verse 6):

> *. . . blessed is the one who is not offended by me.*

SUMMARY

God has his purposes. Not all of them are made known to us; hence, John's and our questions. But we must never let the things we *don't* understand confuse us about what we *do*. The works of Jesus bear witness that the Father has sent him, that he is the Christ, that his kingdom will endure forever, and that one day he will wipe every tear from our eyes. For reasons not fully revealed, the consummation of that kingdom is now delayed. But in the fullness of time the consummation of the kingdom will come, just as surely as the inauguration of the kingdom came. For now we wait, trusting him to do all that he has promised, in the time he has appointed.

> *Judge not the Lord by feeble sense, but trust him for his grace:*
> *Behind a frowning providence he hides a smiling face.*
> *His purposes will ripen fast, unfolding every hour;*
> *The bud may have a bitter taste, but sweet will be the flower.*

William Cowper,
God Moves in a Mysterious Way

26

Sober Warning, Gracious Invitation

'*B*ut to what shall I compare this generation? It is like children sitting in the marketplaces and calling to their playmates, *17* "We played the flute for you, and you did not dance; we sang a dirge, and you did not mourn." *18* For John came neither eating nor drinking, and they say, "He has a demon." *19* The Son of Man came eating and drinking, and they say, "Look at him! A glutton and a drunkard, a friend of tax collectors and sinners!" Yet wisdom is justified by her deeds.' *20* Then he began to denounce the cities where most of his mighty works had been done, because they did not repent. *21* 'Woe to you, Chorazin! Woe to you, Bethsaida! For if the mighty works done in you had been done in Tyre and Sidon, they would have repented long ago in sackcloth and ashes. *22* But I tell you, it will be more bearable on the day of judgment for Tyre and Sidon than for you. *23* And you, Capernaum, will you be exalted to heaven? You will be brought down to Hades. For if the mighty works done in you had been done in Sodom, it would have remained until this day. *24* But I tell you that it will be more tolerable on the day of judgment for the land of Sodom than for you.' *25* At that time Jesus declared, 'I thank you, Father, Lord of heaven and earth, that you have hidden these things from the wise and understanding and revealed them to little children; *26* Father, for such was your gracious will. *27* All things have been handed over to me by my Father, and no one knows the Son except the Father, and no one knows the Father except the Son and anyone to whom the Son chooses to reveal him. *28* Come to me, all who labour and are heavy laden, and I will give you rest. *29* Take my yoke upon you, and learn from me, for I am gentle and lowly in heart, and you will find rest for your souls. *30* For my yoke is easy, and my burden is light' (Matt. 11:16–30).

I n this section Jesus denounces the responses that have been made to him by the crowds, especially by the cities where most of his mighty works had been done. He reveals that a terrible fate awaits those who saw his good works and did not repent. At the same time, he extends a gracious hand and invites all to come to him.

A FICKLE GENERATION

Though John the Baptist and Jesus preached the same message (compare *Matt.* 3:2 and 4:17), yet there were differences between them in their social conduct. They were, in fact, opposites in some things. Strangely, however, the crowds found fault with both (verses 18–19):

> *For John came neither eating nor drinking, and they say, 'He has a demon.' The Son of Man came eating and drinking, and they say, 'Look at him! A glutton and a drunkard, a friend of tax collectors and sinners!'*

A response like this reveals a deep hypocrisy and hardness of heart. These are people who love the darkness rather than the light. Rejection like this was even found in the cities where most of his mighty works had been done. Jesus pronounces 'Woe' upon Chorazin and Bethsaida, saying that their judgment will be far worse than that of Tyre and Sidon, cities legendary in the Old Testament for what came upon them (see *Isa.* 23 and *Ezek.* 26–28). He also pronounces 'Woe' upon Capernaum, the city which he had made his own (4:13). The judgment awaiting it would be worse than Sodom. Why such great judgments against these cities? Because they had seen the mighty works of Jesus and did not repent!

Judgment is according to one's deeds, and the gravity of one's sins is determined by the light one has received (*Rom.* 2:12). The cities where Jesus had done his mighty works had received much greater light, so their sins were that much greater. Tyre, Sidon, and Sodom had only the light of nature, and perhaps a bit of special revelation given to them. But Chorazin, Bethsaida, and Capernaum not only had the full revelation of the Old Testament, but they had seen the Lord of glory himself, performing those deeds which the prophets had predicted would be the work of the Messiah (see *Isa.* 35:5–6). Yet still they did not repent. They could not plead an excuse.

THE GRACIOUS INVITATION

In the face of such wicked and foolish rejection, Jesus gives himself to prayer. He thanks his Father, the Lord of heaven and earth, for his 'gracious will' in revealing the mysteries of the kingdom to 'little children' like his disciples, while keeping them hidden from the 'wise and understanding'. His prayer teaches us that in our own natural condition we will never respond to Jesus in the right way. Apart from the working of God's Spirit, opening our hearts and our minds, we will never come to Jesus in repentance and humility. Our sins have darkened our understanding, leaving us in ignorance. We have become callous and have given up ourselves to sensuality, greedy to practise every kind of impurity (*Eph.* 4:18–19). New hearts must be given to us (*Ezek.* 36:26). The God who made light to shine out of darkness must shine in our hearts, that we might see the light of the knowledge of the glory of God in the face of Jesus Christ (*2 Cor.* 4:6).

As it is the Father's 'gracious will' to reveal himself to the lowly, the Son likewise reaches out to them in one of the most moving invitations to be found in all the Scriptures:

> *Come to me, all who labour and are heavy laden, and I will give you rest. Take my yoke upon you, and learn of me, for I am gentle and lowly in heart, and you will find rest for your souls. For my yoke is easy, and my burden is light* (verses 28–30).

The invitation goes out to 'all who labour and are heavy laden'. Those in view are those worn out and beaten down. They have carried heavy burdens in life, burdens of sin and guilt, and the burdens of trying to deal with that sin and guilt through useless means. Jesus extends to them his own gracious way of salvation: 'Take my yoke upon you . . .'

This seems quite paradoxical. How can people worn out and beaten down find rest by taking a yoke upon themselves?

The answer lies in the nature of the yoke, or rather, in the nature of the one whose yoke it is. It is the yoke of one who is gentle and lowly of heart. The gentleness of Christ is revealed in his lowliness of heart. Though he was rich, yet for our sake he became poor (*2 Cor.* 8:9). Though he was in the form of God (that is, though he was God, possessing all the attributes that make God, God), yet he

[108]

'made himself nothing', taking the form of a servant (*Phil.* 2:6–7). For our sake, he who knew no sin was made to be sin, in order that in him we might become the righteousness of God (*2 Cor.* 5:21). One with such abounding grace will not lay upon us a yoke to crush us. He invites us also to 'learn of him'. Finding rest for our souls begins with coming to Christ, but it is also something we grow into more fully as time goes on. We learn more of his grace as we walk with him and commune with him, and the more we know of him the more we find rest in him.

We come to him in our sin and guilt, claiming nothing for ourselves, calling upon his mercy. He receives us in grace and calls us to be his disciples. His law is indeed a heavy burden, one that would crush us, were it to fall with full force upon us, but as it is resting on his shoulders, and we are resting in him, it is a yoke that is easy and a burden that is light (see *Acts* 15:10–11).

SUMMARY

The more light we have from Christ, the greater our sin—if we do not repent. But if we come to him in humility and repentance, the more light we have, the greater our rest. Praise be to the God and Father of our Lord Jesus Christ, for such was his 'gracious will', to reveal these things to 'little children'. Oh that we might have the heart of such 'little children', that we too might find rest for our souls.

27

Kingdom Opposition

*A*t that time Jesus went through the grainfields on the Sabbath. His disciples were hungry, and they began to pluck heads of grain and to eat. ² But when the Pharisees saw it, they said to him, 'Look, your disciples are doing what is not lawful to do on the Sabbath.' ³ He said to them, 'Have you not read what David did when he was hungry, and those who were with him: ⁴ how he entered the house of God and ate the bread of the Presence, which it was not lawful for him to eat nor for those who were with him, but only for the priests? ⁵ Or have you not read in the Law how on the Sabbath the priests in the temple profane the Sabbath and are guiltless? ⁶ I tell you, something greater than the temple is here. ⁷ And if you had known what this means, "I desire mercy, and not sacrifice," you would not have condemned the guiltless. ⁸ For the Son of Man is lord of the Sabbath.' ⁹ He went on from there and entered their synagogue. ¹⁰ And a man was there with a withered hand. And they asked him, 'Is it lawful to heal on the Sabbath?'— so that they might accuse him. ¹¹ He said to them, 'Which one of you who has a sheep, if it falls into a pit on the Sabbath, will not take hold of it and lift it out? ¹² Of how much more value is a man than a sheep! So it is lawful to do good on the Sabbath.' ¹³ Then he said to the man, 'Stretch out your hand.' And the man stretched it out, and it was restored, healthy like the other. ¹⁴ But the Pharisees went out and conspired against him, how to destroy him. ¹⁵ Jesus, aware of this, withdrew from there. And many followed him, and he healed them all ¹⁶ and ordered them not to make him known. ¹⁷ This was to fulfil what was spoken by the prophet Isaiah: ¹⁸ 'Behold, my servant whom I have chosen, my beloved with whom my soul is well pleased. I will put my Spirit upon him, and he will proclaim justice to the Gentiles. ¹⁹ He will not quarrel or cry aloud, nor will anyone hear his voice in the streets; ²⁰ a bruised reed he will not break, and a smouldering wick he will not quench, until he brings justice to victory; ²¹ and in his name the Gentiles will hope' (Matt. 12:1–21).

In this section we have two controversies with the Pharisees. Both serve to throw into sharp relief the liberating yoke of Jesus over against the bondage brought by the Pharisees. Here we will learn that the Pharisees now conspired to kill him. This prompts Matthew to provide another of his fulfilment formulas.

LORD OF THE SABBATH

As Jesus' disciples walked along a road on the Sabbath, they were hungry and picked some grains of wheat. Some Pharisees saw this and accused the disciples of breaking the Sabbath laws. Jesus, however, showed that their understanding of the law was deficient. As we learned from Jesus' temptation in the wilderness, a right understanding and application of the Word of God comes from interpreting each verse of Scripture in the light of the whole. Just as the devil twisted and misapplied *Psa.* 91 (see *Matt.* 4:5–7) so the Pharisees twist and misapply the Sabbath laws. Jesus shows this from the incident when David and his companions were hungry. The priests gave to them the consecrated bread of the tabernacle, which only the priests could eat (*1 Sam.* 21:1–6). The Pharisees had failed to understand the true intent of the law, and thus misapplied it in the present case.

Jesus declared that they had not understood *Hos.* 6:6, which surprisingly says that God desires mercy (Hebrew: *hesed*) and not sacrifice. Since the law does command sacrifice, this is a puzzling comment; but it challenges us to think deeply about the law's intent. Sacrifice performed merely as an outward act is empty of religious value. The right frame of heart must also be found in religious acts. Indeed, it is that frame of heart which constitutes the main element in an act of worship; the outward ceremonial act is merely the means for expressing that frame of heart.

But the Pharisees treated the outward act as ultimate. They treated the Sabbath law against work as forbidding the simple act of picking a few grains of wheat to satisfy one's hunger, treating it as equivalent to harvesting. Yet if they had understood the mercy of God, they would not have condemned such innocent people as the disciples were in this case. Jesus, himself the Lord of the Sabbath, is the true guide for a right understanding of the Sabbath law, as of the whole law.

MAKING WHOLE ON THE SABBATH

The next issue reveals their hypocrisy. When Jesus and his disciples reach the synagogue, they find there a man with a withered hand. The Pharisees ask Jesus, 'Is it lawful to heal on the Sabbath?' Their aim is to accuse Jesus of breaking the Sabbath law (verse 10). Jesus points them to their own practices: if a sheep falls into a pit on the Sabbath, they will lift it out, and it would be right to do so. The Pharisees would do this with one of their own sheep, but if it served their purpose they would readily condemn someone else for doing the same thing. Since a man is clearly of much more value than a sheep, there should be no question at all about whether it is right to heal on the Sabbath day. Yet the Pharisees are seeking to accuse him, so any excuse will do. So blinded are they in their sin and hostility toward Jesus that they cannot see how inconsistent they are with their own principles, not to mention how far they have deviated from the mind and heart of God. Thus, after presenting themselves as defenders of the law, they go out and conspire how they might kill him. They are indeed blind guides of the sheep.

THE TRUE SERVANT OF GOD

With a conspiracy against him now launched, Jesus once again strategically withdraws from where the Pharisees might apprehend him. But there were many people who followed him, and Jesus healed them all. Notice again the contrast with Mark's report of this incident, *Mark* 3:10; Matthew loves to stress that Jesus heals all. He also ordered that no one should make him known (see *Matt.* 8:4, 9:30).

All this happened, Matthew tells us, that what was spoken by Isaiah might be fulfilled. This is the longest Old Testament passage brought forward by Matthew as being fulfilled in Jesus' ministry. Following upon the recent exchanges between Jesus and the Pharisees, it provides a powerful contrast between Jesus, the true servant of God, and false servants like the Pharisees. For special emphasis, Matthew inserts his characteristic word 'Behold' to introduce the quotation. He says in effect, 'See how different is God's true servant from all who hypocritically usurp this title for themselves!' God's true servant is one chosen and loved by God.

God is well pleased with him and puts his Spirit upon him (verse 18). Matthew's words remind us of Jesus' baptism (*Matt.* 3:13–17). God's servant does not quarrel or cry aloud (verse 19). Thus Jesus calmly withdraws from the Pharisees and works quietly among the people. 'A bruised reed he will not break, and a smouldering wick he will not quench . . .' (verse 20). He deals gently with the weak and helpless, whereas, by contrast, the Pharisees would allow the hungry to go without food and the infirm to go without healing, all for the sake of their self-made Sabbath regulations. Isaiah prophesies that the wonderful healing and salvation performed by this servant will also benefit the Gentiles (a point made twice in this quotation, verses 18 and 21). The difference between the true servant of God and the Pharisees is as sharp as it could possibly be.

SUMMARY

The more we learn about the scribes and Pharisees, the more we see why Jesus felt such compassion for the people. The people were indeed 'harassed and helpless, like sheep without a shepherd' (*Matt.* 9:36). How wonderful it is that the Lord looked down upon his flock and determined to rescue them from such shepherds. He sent us a true servant and a good shepherd, one who would lay down his life for the sheep. If we would find rest, we must indeed come to this shepherd and receive his yoke. The yoke of the impostors will leave us labouring and heavy laden.

28

Plundering the Strong Man's House

Then a demon-oppressed man who was blind and mute was brought to him, and he healed him, so that the man spoke and saw. ²³ And all the people were amazed, and said, 'Can this be the Son of David?' ²⁴ But when the Pharisees heard it, they said, 'It is only by Beelzebul, the prince of demons, that this man casts out demons.' ²⁵ Knowing their thoughts, he said to them, 'Every kingdom divided against itself is laid waste, and no city or house divided against itself will stand. ²⁶ And if Satan casts out Satan, he is divided against himself. How then will his kingdom stand? ²⁷ And if I cast out demons by Beelzebul, by whom do your sons cast them out? Therefore they will be your judges. ²⁸ But if it is by the Spirit of God that I cast out demons, then the kingdom of God has come upon you. ²⁹ Or how can someone enter a strong man's house and plunder his goods, unless he first binds the strong man? Then indeed he may plunder his house. ³⁰ Whoever is not with me is against me, and whoever does not gather with me scatters. ³¹ Therefore I tell you, every sin and blasphemy will be forgiven people, but the blasphemy against the Spirit will not be forgiven. ³² And whoever speaks a word against the Son of Man will be forgiven, but whoever speaks against the Holy Spirit will not be forgiven, either in this age or in the age to come. ³³ Either make the tree good and its fruit good, or make the tree bad and its fruit bad, for the tree is known by its fruit. ³⁴ You brood of vipers! How can you speak good, when you are evil? For out of the abundance of the heart the mouth speaks. ³⁵ The good person out of his good treasure brings forth good, and the evil person out of his evil treasure brings forth evil. ³⁶ I tell you, on the day of judgment people will give account for every careless word they speak, ³⁷ for by your words you will be justified, and by your words you will be condemned' (Matt. 12:22–37).

Matthew continues his presentation of how the Pharisees responded to the ministry of Jesus. Already they have plotted to kill him (verse 14). Now their guilt is aggravated by the absurd and most wicked act of attributing the mighty works of Jesus to the power of Satan. Nicodemus had spoken the real truth for this group when he said, 'Rabbi, we know that you are a teacher come from God, for no one could do these signs that you do unless God is with him' (*John* 3:2). But if that truth be admitted, then the Pharisees must repent and come to Christ. Most of them are not willing to do this (Nicodemus being a notable exception, see *John* 7:50–52, 19:39, 40 — observe his growth in grace!). Let it not be so with any reader. Come to him, and he will give you rest.

THE POWER OF THE KINGDOM

'The reason the Son of God appeared was to destroy the works of the devil' (*1 John* 3:8b). The exorcisms performed by Jesus point to this aspect of Messiah's work. The coming of the kingdom of God means that Satan's kingdom will be overthrown, and his house plundered. The elect children of God who have lived under his bondage and tyranny will be set free (*Heb.* 2:14–15). The decisive blow to Satan's kingdom was to occur at the cross (*John* 12:31, see also *Col.* 2:15), but Satan's downfall is already being indicated as Jesus casts out demons and plunders the strong man's house.

When Jesus heals the blind and mute, demon-possessed man, the multitudes ask in amazement, 'Can this be the Son of David?' Notice again how the title 'Son of David' occurs in a healing setting. Matthew is driving home the point that the promised Son of David, the Messiah, comes with power to heal every disease and every affliction (*Matt.* 4:23, 9:35, *Isa.* 53:5, *Mal.* 4:2). While in this life not all children of the kingdom are healed, for reasons not fully revealed to us, the kingdom in its final, everlasting form will have complete healing for all. The breaking in of this healing power now shows unmistakably the arrival of the kingdom, and its nature—it is a kingdom of wholeness for body and soul. In this healing we also see the dispossession of Satan. The strong man has been bound by the one who is stronger. Satan can no longer hold the elect people of God in his deceptions (*Rev.* 20:1–3). The Son of David has come to save His people from the house of bondage (see *Exod.* 20:2). He has come 'to open their eyes, so that they may turn from darkness to light and from the dominion of Satan to God, that they may receive forgiveness of sins and a place among those who are sanctified by faith in [him]' (*Acts* 26:18). The day of deliverance has come.

OPPOSITION TO THE KINGDOM

But, as we have seen, not all welcome the arrival of this kingdom. When the Pharisees hear what the people are saying, they assert that Jesus casts out demons by the power of Beelzebul, the ruler of the demons (verse 24). Rather than acknowledge that the kingdom of God is among them, they wickedly attribute the mighty works of the Son of David to Satan. The Pharisees know better, hence their sin is very great, and their judgment is just: 'And this is the judgment: the light has come into the world, and people loved the darkness rather than the light because their deeds were evil' (*John* 3:19).

Jesus' response to the Pharisees highlights the fact that their position is both absurd on its face, and blasphemous in its content. For on their view, if Jesus' power to cast out demons comes from Satan himself, then Satan is overthrowing his own house, and working contrary to his own purposes. This is surely absurd. Only one explanation can serve for what has just happened: 'But if it is by the Spirit of God that I cast out demons, then the kingdom of God has come upon you' (verse 28).

The error of the Pharisees is not due to ignorance, but to wickedness. As we have noted, they know better. Their attempt to promote this wicked absurdity as the true explanation for Jesus' power to cast out demons proves that their hearts are very hard indeed, for they blaspheme the Holy Spirit in doing so. What comes out of their mouth betrays a heart deep in sin: 'the evil person out of his evil treasure brings forth evil' (verse 35b).

UNFORGIVABLE SIN

The wicked response of the Pharisees to his mighty works moves Jesus to one of His sternest warnings, a warning against a sin which will not be forgiven. 'And whoever speaks a word against the Son of Man will be forgiven; but whoever speaks against the Holy Spirit, will not be forgiven, either in this age or in the age to come' (verse 32). These awesome words have caused much alarm, and with good reason. While God shows himself 'merciful and gracious, slow to anger, and abounding in steadfast love and faithfulness, keeping steadfast love for thousands, forgiving iniquity and transgression and sin . . .' (*Exod.* 34:6–7), yet his patience is not endless toward those who persist in hardness of heart and rebel against his ways. The Pharisees have had long training in the Scriptures and therefore know that God alone can do wonders (*Psa.* 72:18). For such people to speak out of their evil hearts and attribute to the devil what they know can only be the work of the Spirit of God brings them perilously close to the place where God will not forgive, if indeed they have not reached that place already.

Blasphemy against the Holy Spirit is an unforgivable sin, but it is not one most people are capable of committing. Most people do not know enough about what God alone can do to commit this sin, for it is attributing what is plainly the supernatural work of God to the power of Satan, on the part of someone who knows that what he is saying is a wicked lie. A person born again by the Spirit of God cannot commit this sin. God keeps us from such sinning, by his own almighty power and his most loving grace. Having delivered us from the domain of darkness, he has transferred us to the kingdom of his beloved Son (*Col.* 1:13), where no one is able to snatch us out of his hand (*John* 10:27–29).

CONCLUSION

In Jesus Christ, the light of God has truly come into the world. No one could do the works he did unless God was with him. Yet people do love darkness rather than the light because their deeds are evil. May it not be so with us. May God so work in us that we shall come to the light, and walk in the light, to the honour and glory of God.

29

Warning against Unbelief

*T*hen some of the scribes and Pharisees answered him, saying, *'Teacher, we wish to see a sign from you.'* [39] *But he answered them, 'An evil and adulterous generation seeks for a sign, but no sign will be given to it except the sign of the prophet Jonah.* [40] *For just as Jonah was three days and three nights in the belly of the great fish, so will the Son of Man be three days and three nights in the heart of the earth.* [41] *The men of Nineveh will rise up at the judgment with this generation and condemn it, for they repented at the preaching of Jonah, and behold, something greater than Jonah is here.* [42] *The queen of the South will rise up at the judgment with this generation and condemn it, for she came from the ends of the earth to hear the wisdom of Solomon, and behold, something greater than Solomon is here.* [43] *When the unclean spirit has gone out of a person, it passes through waterless places seeking rest, but finds none.* [44] *Then it says, "I will return to my house from which I came." And when it comes, it finds the house empty, swept, and put in order.* [45] *Then it goes and brings with it seven other spirits more evil than itself, and they enter and dwell there, and the last state of that person is worse than the first. So also will it be with this evil generation.'* [46] *While he was still speaking to the people, behold, his mother and his brothers stood outside, asking to speak to him.* [48] *But he replied to the man who told him, 'Who is my mother, and who are my brothers?'* [49] *And stretching out his hand toward his disciples, he said, 'Here are my mother and my brothers!* [50] *For whoever does the will of my Father in heaven is my brother and sister and mother'* (Matt. 12:38–50).

A further example of how the Pharisees and their 'evil and adulterous generation' responded to Jesus is now given. Matthew again warns that a true and proper response to the coming of the kingdom in Jesus is demanded. Failing that, the condition of the generation concerned will prove worse than it was before. The chapter concludes, as chapter 11 concluded, with a portrait of the response which the kingdom demands and deserves.

DEMANDING A SIGN

Coming as it does so quickly on the heels of the exorcism and healing recorded in Matthew 12:22–37, the healing of the man with the withered hand in 12:9–14, and of course all the miracles previously recorded (see *Matt.* 8 and 9; also *Matt.* 4:23–24, 9:35), the request for a sign by the Pharisees smacks of the most insincere hypocrisy. What greater sign could be given? Even the ordinary people could see this: 'Yet many of the people believed in him. They said, "When the Christ appears, will he do more signs than this man has done?"' (*John* 7:31). So what might look like a sincere request for more convincing evidence must really be understood as an insincere evasion of the truth already plain to them (recall the warnings against blaspheming the Holy Spirit in the previous section). Jesus simply refuses to play their game. Their problem is not a lack of evidence, but a lack of will to respond to the evidence. Further demonstration of power will not improve their situation; indeed, as Jesus will make clear, it will only make things worse—much worse!

While the controversy in this chapter is with the Pharisees in particular, they are not a class by themselves, distinct from every other group of people. In many ways, they are quite representative of the people at large. Note that Jesus repeatedly refers to 'this generation' from verse 39 on (verses 41, 42, 45; see also 11:16, 16:4, 17:17). This broad designation reaches even to our own day. We must be careful not to be found among them.

Jesus says that no sign will be given to this 'evil and adulterous generation' except the sign of Jonah. The crowning miracle of Jesus, the one that would put an end to all questions concerning his claims, his person, his power, and his authority, would be his resurrection from the dead. He will be 'declared to be the Son of God in power according to the Spirit of holiness by his resurrection from the dead' (*Rom.* 1:4). Yet already the works done by Jesus proved that he had been sent from the Father. What had already been accomplished in his miraculous deeds, as well as in

[119]

his teaching, proved that he was 'greater than the temple', 'greater than Jonah', 'greater than Solomon' (*Matt.* 12:6,41,42). Yet to all these demonstrations many, many people of that 'generation' closed their eyes, their minds, and their hearts. There are none so blind as those who will not see! Again, Jesus highlights the sin of his detractors by pointing to the response of heathens to lesser works of God than 'this generation' had seen: the men of Nineveh repented at the preaching of Jonah, and the queen of the South came from 'the ends of the earth' to hear the wisdom of Solomon.

MATTERS MADE WORSE

It is this crass indifference of the people to what they have seen which prompts Jesus to intensify his warnings against their unbelief. He describes the situation of a man from whom a demon has gone out for a time, only later to return and find his former dwelling empty, swept clean, and put in order. The demon then gathers seven other demons more wicked than himself and occupies the man once again. The man's latter state, says Jesus, is now worse than his first.

The point of this account is made clear in Jesus' concluding statement: 'So also will it be with this evil generation' (verse 45). As in the hypothetical case of the man in Jesus' story, something has happened which will make matters much worse for 'this evil generation'. What is that something? Has a demon been cast out from among them? In a sense, yes. Jesus has come among them and with him the kingdom of God. Jesus has bound the strong man and now is plundering his house, delivering people from demonic possession in demonstration of it. This has just been seen and, along with the other miracles of healing performed, it proves beyond doubt that the kingdom of God has come among them (*Matt.* 12:28).

If in the face of this, the Pharisees and 'this evil generation' harden their hearts and refuse to acknowledge Jesus and his kingdom, then surely their last state has become much worse than it was before. For now that Jesus has done his work among them, the guilt of their indifferent or hostile responses to Jesus is much greater than the guilt of the cities and generations which did not see his work (see again *Matt.* 10:5–15, 11:20–24).

THE TRUE RESPONSE

How then are we to respond to the message and works of Jesus? We are not left to wonder. Matthew next records how the very family of Jesus, his mother and his brothers, at this point come seeking to speak with him. Surprisingly, Jesus does not immediately go out to them. Indeed, it might even appear that he responds in a rude fashion, as if to disown them. He says, as if he did not even know them, 'Who is my mother, and who are my brothers?' Then stretching out his hand toward his disciples, he says, 'Here are my mother and my brothers! For whoever does the will of my Father in heaven is my brother and sister and mother.'

How are we to respond to the message and works of Jesus? Our first duty is to acknowledge him and believe in him, coming to him and finding rest for our souls. Then, like his first disciples, we must follow him, going out into the world to serve him, doing the will of his and our Father in heaven. So it is that we shall prove ourselves to be the children of God, shining as lights 'in the midst of a crooked and twisted generation, holding fast to the word of life . . .' (*Phil.* 2:15–16).

SUMMARY

Matthew Chapters 11 and 12 provide narrative presentations of the various responses, the true and the false, which people made then and still make to the ministry of Jesus. This is not intended just to satisfy our historical curiosity. Like all biblical history, it is written for our instruction, so that through endurance and the encouragement of the Scriptures we might have hope (*Rom.* 15:4). The principal force of these chapters is to warn us against failing to respond to Jesus as we should. But in the midst of it we do find this glorious hope: Come to Jesus, and 'you will find rest for your souls' (*Matt.* 11:29)!

30

Teaching in Parables

*T*hat same day Jesus went out of the house and sat beside the sea. *² And great crowds gathered about him, so that he got into a boat and sat down. And the whole crowd stood on the beach. ³ And he told them many things in parables, saying: 'A sower went out to sow. ⁴ And as he sowed, some seeds fell along the path, and the birds came and devoured them. ⁵ Other seeds fell on rocky ground, where they did not have much soil, and immediately they sprang up, since they had no depth of soil, ⁶ but when the sun rose they were scorched. And since they had no root, they withered away. ⁷ Other seeds fell among thorns, and the thorns grew up and choked them. ⁸ Other seeds fell on good soil and produced grain, some a hundredfold, some sixty, some thirty. ⁹ He who has ears, let him hear.' ¹⁰ Then the disciples came and said to him, 'Why do you speak to them in parables?' ¹¹ And he answered them, 'To you it has been given to know the secrets of the kingdom of heaven, but to them it has not been given. ¹² For to the one who has, more will be given, and he will have an abundance, but from the one who has not, even what he has will be taken away. ¹³ This is why I speak to them in parables, because seeing they do not see, and hearing they do not hear, nor do they understand. ¹⁴ Indeed, in their case the prophecy of Isaiah is fulfilled that says: "You will indeed hear but never understand, and you will indeed see but never perceive. ¹⁵ For this people's heart has grown dull, and with their ears they can barely hear, and their eyes they have closed, lest they should see with their eyes and hear with their ears and understand with their heart and turn, and I would heal them." ¹⁶ But blessed are your eyes, for they see, and your ears, for they hear. ¹⁷ For truly, I say to you, many prophets and righteous people longed to see what you see, and did not see it, and to hear what you hear, and did not hear it. ¹⁸ Hear then the parable of the sower: ¹⁹ When anyone hears the word of the kingdom and does not understand it, the evil one comes and snatches away what has been sown in his heart. This is what was sown along the path. ²⁰ As for what was sown on rocky ground, this is the one* *who hears the word and immediately receives it with joy, [21] yet he has no root in himself, but endures for a while, and when tribulation or persecution arises on account of the word, immediately he falls away. [22] As for what was sown among thorns, this is the one who hears the word, but the cares of the world and the deceitfulness of riches choke the word, and it proves unfruitful. [23] As for what was sown on good soil, this is the one who hears the word and understands it. He indeed bears fruit and yields, in one case a hundredfold, in another sixty, and in another thirty'* (Matt. 13:1–23).

W e come now to the third long discourse of Matthew's Gospel (Chapter 13), and its theme is the same as the preceding narrative section (Chapters 11 and 12): how people *do* and how they *should* respond to the kingdom of heaven. Eight parables are now given, together with explanations as to why Jesus chose to speak to the crowds in parables. As we shall see, his reasons are not what many have supposed.

THE PARABLE OF THE SOWER

The first and indeed the most basic parable is the well-known parable of the sower. Jesus said that if the disciples did not understand this parable they would not understand the rest (*Mark* 4:13). We are therefore most fortunate that Jesus has given us the explanation for this parable (see verses 18–23), and he does so in words which are quite easy to understand. The parable describes four different ways in which people respond to the preaching of the Word. In three of these cases, there is no fruit borne from the seed. Only in the fourth case is there a response which bears fruit. If we ourselves would be found among this fourth and prosperous group, we must pay close attention to why the first three groups failed in their response.

Some might suppose that the parable presents us with a very careless sower in that he allows his seed to fall in such unproductive places. We must remember that Jesus' parable was not designed to teach us farming or the best way to sow seeds. The apparent carelessness of the sower actually corresponds rather well with the indiscriminate way in which the kingdom of God is preached. The Word is preached wherever it may be, giving all the opportunity to hear, without prior thought being given to whether or how people will respond to it. When the Word is preached in such an indiscriminate manner, it is the response to the preaching which makes the fateful discrimination.

UNFRUITFUL HEARING

Only those in the fourth category benefit from the preaching of the Word and bear fruit for the kingdom. The seed sown among the others is wasted and perishes. For one reason or another, no fruit is borne, and no saving benefit is received. The sober truth set before us in the first three categories is not the sad story of fruitless Christians, but the deeply sorrowful story of lost souls.

Why were they lost? Three basic reasons are given. In the first case, the word preached was like seed falling along the hardened path. Jesus says they failed to understand the word (verse 19). As the parables will make clear, careful thought and consideration must be given to the Word which is preached, otherwise it will not remain with us. Like birds of the air, the evil one comes and takes away the Word from us. In the second case, the Word is heard and, it seems, understood. It is received with joy and enthusiasm (verse 20). However, like seed which falls upon rocky ground, the Word that is heard does not take deep root in the hearer's life. When affliction or persecution arise (as certainly they will!), the person falls away, just as a plant withers under the heat of the sun when its roots have not gone deep in the soil. In the third case, the Word is understood, takes root, and begins to grow. However, like seed sown among thorns, the sprouting seed is eventually choked out by other things. Jesus says that the 'cares of the world and the deceitfulness of riches choke the word, and it proves unfruitful' (verse 22). Other things have displaced the kingdom from the supreme place it ought to have had.

FRUITFUL HEARING

It is the word received in good soil that bears fruit. Those in this group receive the Word and understand it. The disciples are a good example of this kind of soil. Yet when they first heard the parable of the sower, they did not understand it. So they came asking Jesus what it meant (see *Mark* 4:10, 'And when he was alone, those around him with the twelve asked him about the parables.' See also *Matt.* 13:36, 15:15). It was important to them to understand, so they came asking. We must do the same. A sermon heard is not a sermon received. A sermon preached is like a meal prepared and served, but not yet eaten. If there is to be any benefit from the meal for those at the table, they must eat and digest it. So careful listening and meditation must be given to the Word of God when we read it and when we hear it preached. What we do not understand, we must labour to understand. We must pray for understanding to be given us, and we must seek out explanations from those whom God has gifted for teaching and nurturing his church. Then we must work to apply the Word in our lives. We must remove any 'stones' that would prevent the word from taking deep root within us. We must also clear out the 'weeds' that threaten to choke out the Word as it grows. We must, in short, be doers as well as hearers of the Word. It is in such soil that the kingdom of heaven grows.

People often assume that the reason Jesus taught in parables was to make it easy for people to understand. His own explanation is rather different. When asked why he taught the crowds in parables, Jesus answered that it was because it was not given to them to understand the things of the kingdom of heaven, but only to the disciples (verse 11). Those outside the kingdom hear about it through parables, so although they hear, they do not understand, and though they see, they do not perceive (verse 14). The reason for this is that their hearts have become dull, with their ears they can barely hear, and their eyes they have closed (verse 15). But as for disciples, those who are eager not only to hear but to understand and do what Jesus teaches, to them it is given to understand the things of the kingdom of heaven. When they seek, they find; for them it is given.

SUMMARY

The teaching of Jesus in parables, like difficulties encountered in other parts of the Bible, proves to be a stumbling block to many. They do not put forth the effort necessary to understand it clearly, and they do not diligently seek to practise it faithfully. The Word is lost upon them. Let it not be so with us. Like the disciples, when we are alone with him, let us ask him to make known to us the meaning of his words (*Mark* 4:10). Let us not despair in our response to God's Word: understanding will come if we seek it with perseverance; and with understanding let there be faithful application. We will not be disappointed. We will bear good fruit, 'in one case a hundredfold, in another sixty, and in another thirty' (verse 23).

31

The Growth of the Kingdom

*H*e put another parable before them, saying, 'The kingdom of heaven may be compared to a man who sowed good seed in his field, *25* but while his men were sleeping, his enemy came and sowed weeds among the wheat and went away. *26* So when the plants came up and bore grain, then the weeds appeared also. *27* And the servants of the master of the house came and said to him, "Master, did you not sow good seed in your field? How then does it have weeds?" *28* He said to them, "An enemy has done this." So the servants said to him, "Then do you want us to go and gather them?" *29* But he said, "No, lest in gathering the weeds you root up the wheat along with them. *30* Let both grow together until the harvest, and at harvest time I will tell the reapers, Gather the weeds first and bind them in bundles to be burned, but gather the wheat into my barn."' *31* He put another parable before them, saying, 'The kingdom of heaven is like a grain of mustard seed that a man took and sowed in his field. *32* It is the smallest of all seeds, but when it has grown it is larger than all the garden plants and becomes a tree, so that the birds of the air come and make nests in its branches.' *33* He told them another parable. 'The kingdom of heaven is like leaven that a woman took and hid in three measures of flour, till it was all leavened.' *34* All these things Jesus said to the crowds in parables; indeed, he said nothing to them without a parable. *35* This was to fulfil what was spoken by the prophet: 'I will open my mouth in parables; I will utter what has been hidden since the foundation of the world.' *36* Then he left the crowds and went into the house. And his disciples came to him, saying, 'Explain to us the parable of the weeds of the field.' *37* He answered, 'The one who sows the good seed is the Son of Man. *38* The field is the world, and the good seed is the children of the kingdom. The weeds are the sons of the evil one, *39* and the enemy who sowed them is the devil. The harvest is the close of the age, and the reapers are angels. *40* Just as the weeds are gathered and burned with fire, so will it be at the close of the age. *41* The Son of Man will send his angels, and they will gather out of his *kingdom all causes of sin and all law-breakers, [42] and throw them into the fiery furnace. In that place there will be weeping and gnashing of teeth. [43] Then the righteous will shine like the sun in the kingdom of their Father. He who has ears, let him hear* (Matt. 13:24-43).

In this section there are three more parables. All three concern the growth of the kingdom of heaven in the world. In the case of one of them, the disciples come to Jesus seeking an explanation, and he provides it. There is also a further comment about the use of parables, showing us that by teaching in parables Jesus was fulfilling what was spoken by the prophet (verse 35, see *Psa.* 78:2).

THE ENEMY ALSO SOWS

The first parable in Matthew 13 presented Jesus as a sower of seed, preaching the gospel of the kingdom. In this parable too Jesus is a sower (verse 37), but this time the seed which he sows is not the Word of God, but the children of the kingdom (verse 38). The kingdom of heaven is compared to a man who sowed good seed in his field. But while his men were sleeping, his enemy came and sowed weeds among the wheat and went away. Scholars are convinced that in the parable the seed sown by the enemy is darnel. During the period of early growth, it is nearly indistinguishable from wheat. Thus the concern of the master that the workers wait until the harvest before they attempt to separate the true wheat from the weeds; otherwise they might root out the wheat along with the weeds (verses 29–30). At the harvest time, however, the reapers will separate the wheat from the weeds. The weeds shall then be gathered together and thrown into a fiery furnace where, Jesus says, there will be weeping and gnashing of teeth.

It has sometimes been thought that this is a parable about the institutional church, what theologians call the visible church, the body of all those who profess the faith. According to this view, the parable is telling us that wheat and tares, believers and unbelievers, will grow together in the church. From this it is concluded that no effort should be made to remove the unbelievers before Jesus comes again. Then his angels will do the separation. However, Jesus' own interpretation moves in another direction. He tells us that the field is the world, not the church (verse 38). Thus the wheat and the tares, the saved and the unsaved, grow together in the world. The purpose of the parable, then, is not to tell us about the presence of unbelievers in the church, but to explain God's toleration of the wicked in the world. They are not now pulled out and burned because of the damage which might be done to the wheat. For the sake of the wheat, then, the wicked are tolerated until the harvest.

Following the narrative of responses given in chapters 11 and 12, this parable and others in this series shed light upon the fact that the kingdom of God seems so insignificant in the world. Where John the Baptist and others expected immediate transformation of society by the advent of the kingdom, with a reign of righteousness abolishing all evil, the kingdom of heaven arrives inconspicuously, like seed sown in a field. Its presence does not seem to change the world very much at first. Its progress is slow, even unremarkable. Its presence is also opposed, and masked, by weeds which also grow in the field, sown by the evil one. One wonders if a kingdom of this sort has any real hope of succeeding.

FROM THE LEAST TO THE GREATEST

The next two short parables address the question of whether the kingdom's inconspicuous beginning will end in a glorious triumph. The parable of the mustard seed emphasizes that this small seed eventually produces a large plant, the largest of the garden plants, comparable to a tree in which the birds of the air can find shelter. This parable builds on Old Testament images where great kingdoms are compared to large trees, in which birds can build nests and under which beasts may find shelter (see *Ezek.* 17, 31, and *Dan.* 4). The kingdom of heaven will be just like that, despite its very small, seemingly insignificant beginning. The people of many nations will find a home in this tree.

The parable of the leaven reinforces the message of astounding growth despite a small beginning. Indeed, the idea stressed here is complete permeation. 'The kingdom of heaven is like leaven that a woman took and hid in three measures of flour, till it was all leavened' (verse 33). The kingdom of heaven is like that. No part of the world's peoples will be left untouched by its redeeming work. As leaven is 'hidden' in the flour and then permeates all the bread, so will the kingdom permeate the whole world. The teaching here is much the same as in Revelation 7:9–17. There we see a great multitude gathered before the throne of God, people 'from every nation, from all tribes and peoples and languages' (verse 9). The whole world will be touched by the saving power of the kingdom, despite its small and insignificant beginning among the children of Israel.

SUMMARY

There is great mystery in the providence of God, great mystery in the way in which he works to accomplish his purposes in the world. Like John the Baptist, we can find ourselves confused by God's ways, expecting the consummation before its time. Careful meditation upon these parables can keep us from such misunderstandings, and work patience in us while we wait for the fulfilment of his promises. Though frustrated by the slowness of the kingdom's advance, we must remember that it is this way for the sake of the wheat. Because God is still at work to save sinners, the day of judgment is delayed. The door of the ark is still open. The reaping angels are still held back. As we are grateful for the fact that the day of judgment was put off until we were called, let us also be patient while the rest of our brothers and sisters are called.

32

Teaching the Disciples

'*The kingdom of heaven is like treasure hidden in a field, which a man found and covered up. Then in his joy he goes and sells all that he has and buys that field. *[45]* Again, the kingdom of heaven is like a merchant in search of fine pearls, *[46]* who, on finding one pearl of great value, went and sold all that he had and bought it. *[47]* Again, the kingdom of heaven is like a net that was thrown into the sea and gathered fish of every kind. *[48]* When it was full, men drew it ashore and sat down and sorted the good into containers but threw away the bad. *[49]* So it will be at the close of the age. The angels will come out and separate the evil from the righteous *[50]* and throw them into the fiery furnace. In that place there will be weeping and gnashing of teeth. *[51]* Have you understood all these things?' They said to him, 'Yes.' *[52]* And he said to them, 'Therefore every scribe who has been trained for the kingdom of heaven is like a master of a house, who brings out of his treasure what is new and what is old.'* (Matt. 13:44–52).

Four more parables are now given. An important change of setting occurred in the previous section. The parable of the sower, the first in chapter 13, was told to 'the great crowds' who gathered about Jesus beside the sea (verses 1–9). Then the disciples came to Jesus privately and questioned him about his use of parables in teaching the people. Jesus explained his purpose to them (verses 10–17) and then explained the parable (verses 18–23). Next three more parables were told to the crowds (verses 24–33). After that Jesus left the crowds and the disciples again came to him privately asking him to interpret one of the parables (verses 34–36). The explanation of that parable, and the next four parables, are all told to the disciples privately, not to the crowds (verses 37–52). In verse 53 Matthew provides his standard concluding formula for the long discourse and begins a new section of narrative.

SELL ALL THAT YOU HAVE

The next two parables (verses 44–46) have the same theme: the kingdom of heaven is of such supreme value that a wise man would sell all that he has to possess it. Jesus first compares the kingdom to a treasure hidden in a field. A man finds the treasure and covers it up. Then he goes and sells all that he has and buys the field. The next parable concerns a merchant in search of fine pearls. When he finds one of great value, he sells all that he has and buys it. That both the man who found the treasure and the man who found the pearl of great value sold all that they had in order to buy what they found makes clear the main point of the two parables: the kingdom of heaven is worth more than all we have.

Readers sometimes worry about the actions of the man who found the treasure in the field, but to do so is to misunderstand the parable. The man is not being set before us as an example of what we are to do if we find a treasure in a field. Not every detail in a parable is intended as a point of application. The main point here, as in the parable of the merchant who found the pearl, is that the man considered the treasure to be of such value that he joyfully sold all that he had in order to possess it. So it should be with us. The kingdom of heaven is worth all that we have, and we should gladly part with all we have in order to possess it. This one thing, the kingdom, is worth more than everything else combined.

THE PARABLE OF THE NET

This parable also has a twin among the series given to us by Matthew, the parable of the weeds. Both stress the separation of the righteous and the wicked (see verses 30, 41–43, 48–50). Both assign this separation to the work of angels (see verses 41 and 49) at the close of the age (see verses 40 and 49). Both describe the fate of the wicked as being thrown into a 'fiery furnace', where there is 'weeping and gnashing of teeth' (see verses 42 and 50). Their point is clearly the same. But whereas the parable of the weeds stresses the need for patience on the part of the righteous, waiting until the close of the age, this parable barely hints at the need for waiting in the words, 'When it (the net) was full . . .' The main thrust in this parable is the separation itself, and the great misery that awaits the evil ones, beginning with that day.

The images used for describing the punishment of the wicked are found in Jewish literature, but it is with Jesus that this language comes into the New Testament. It is almost as if the world awaited the arrival of Jesus before it learned of the doctrine of hell. The Old Testament normally treats both judgment and salvation within the bounds of this life, judgment being equivalent to the loss of life and salvation the enjoyment of a long and blessed life. Even Isaiah's picture of the new heavens and new earth portray salvation as a very long life (see *Isa.* 65:20). From time to time the light of eternity does shine through in the Old Testament, but for the most part it is a very 'down to earth' book. The New Testament, however, opens wide the door of the future and lets us see that this world is but a prelude to another of everlasting duration, in which those who are saved will enjoy everlasting bliss while the lost will suffer everlasting torment. Jesus is the chief teacher of this doctrine, which surely underscores both the truth and the certainty of it. People who have only a general impression of what the Bible teaches sometimes suppose that the Old Testament presents a God of wrath and judgment while the New Testament presents a God of love and salvation. When the doctrine of hell is considered, we must appreciate that it is the New Testament which principally teaches this doctrine, and it is Jesus who is first among its teachers. He who has ears to hear, let him hear!

DO YOU UNDERSTAND?

The disciples came to Jesus seeking explanation, so Jesus asks them if they have understood all these things. 'Yes', they reply. Then Jesus tells them one more parable: 'Every scribe who has been trained for the kingdom of heaven is a like a master of a house, who brings out of his treasure what is new and what is old.' The parable points toward the service to the kingdom which the disciples will render. Having been trained for the kingdom of heaven, they have a treasure from which they must share. New things and old things are in that treasure, and both are to be shared. There was much that was new in the teaching brought by Jesus, at least so far as understanding is concerned, but it was all continuous with the old revelation previously given in what we call the Old Testament. Both are to be found in the teaching of the well-trained scribe who has become a disciple of the kingdom of heaven. Peter, to take just one example, had learned the lesson well:

> . . . *you should remember the predictions of the holy prophets and the commandment of the Lord and Saviour through your apostles* (2 Pet. 3:2).

SUMMARY

The kingdom of our Lord and Saviour Jesus Christ is a kingdom of surpassing value. It is worth all that we have to possess, and worth our time to understand. The disciples are our best examples of both. They left all that they had to follow Jesus (*Matt.* 19:27 and *Luke* 5:11), and they diligently sought to understand the teaching of Jesus (verse 36, also *Matt.* 15:15). Whether our time or our treasures, the kingdom of heaven is worth all that we have.

33

Rejection

And when Jesus had finished these parables, he went away from there, ⁵⁴ and coming to his home town he taught them in their synagogue, so that they were astonished, and said, 'Where did this man get this wisdom and these mighty works? ⁵⁵ Is not this the carpenter's son? Is not his mother called Mary? And are not his brothers James and Joseph and Simon and Judas? ⁵⁶ And are not all his sisters with us? Where then did this man get all these things?' ⁵⁷ And they took offence at him. But Jesus said to them, 'A prophet is not without honour except in his home town and in his own household.' ⁵⁸ And he did not do many mighty works there, because of their unbelief. ^{14:1} At that time Herod the tetrarch heard about the fame of Jesus, ² and he said to his servants, 'This is John the Baptist. He has been raised from the dead; that is why these miraculous powers are at work in him.' ³ For Herod had seized John and bound him and put him in prison for the sake of Herodias, his brother Philip's wife, ⁴ because John had been saying to him, 'It is not lawful for you to have her.' ⁵ And though he wanted to put him to death, he feared the people, because they held him to be a prophet. ⁶ But when Herod's birthday came, the daughter of Herodias danced before the company and pleased Herod, ⁷ so that he promised with an oath to give her whatever she might ask. ⁸ Prompted by her mother, she said, 'Give me the head of John the Baptist here on a platter.' ⁹ And the king was sorry, but because of his oaths and his guests he commanded it to be given. ¹⁰ He sent and had John beheaded in the prison, ¹¹ and his head was brought on a platter and given to the girl, and she brought it to her mother. ¹² And his disciples came and took the body and buried it, and they went and told Jesus (Matt. 13:53—14:12).

At the conclusion of the long section on parables, Matthew uses his standard formula to signal the end of the teaching discourse and the return to narrative, 'And when Jesus had finished these parables . . .' (verse 53). The previous narrative section

(Chapters 11–12) focused on the varied responses made to Jesus. The teaching section on parables (Chapter 13) explained those varied responses. This narrative section (Chapters 14–17) continues to present varied responses to Jesus, but the tone of the responses is increasingly hostile. Dark clouds are gathering over Jesus' head.

WITHOUT HONOUR AT HOME

Jesus goes to his home town of Nazareth and teaches in the synagogue. Matthew does not tell us what he taught them, but only their reaction. That is the main thing to notice. Matthew tells us that 'they took offence at him' (verse 57), and that, because of their unbelief, Jesus did not do many mighty works there (verse 58). It was not that he *could* not. Our faith or lack thereof does not determine the extent of Jesus' power. He is not dependent on us at all. But he may choose to apportion his works in accordance with our faith. The Roman centurion had faith to believe that Jesus could heal his servant without even coming near to his house (*Matt.* 8:5–13). He believed that Jesus need only speak the word and his servant would be healed (8:8). Jesus gave that word, in accordance with the man's faith (8:13). Now Jesus deals with Nazareth in accordance with its faith, or rather its lack of faith. The unbelief of Nazareth grieved Jesus, so he did not do many might works there. Similarly, sin in our lives, whether unbelief or otherwise, grieves the Holy Spirit (*Eph.* 4:30). Our unbelief may become a self-fulfilling prediction, leaving us distant from the transforming power of our Lord.

This incident marks the last recorded time in Matthew when Jesus speaks in a synagogue (see 4:23, 9:35, 12:9). Increasingly his dealings with official Judaism are marked by controversy and hostility. This small town becomes a harbinger of the larger rejection awaiting him in Jerusalem. He came to his own, and his own people did not receive him (*John* 1:11).

UNWELCOME FAME

Chapter 14 opens with the announcement that Herod the tetrarch 'heard about the fame of Jesus' (verse 1). Herod had been told about the 'miraculous powers' of Jesus and came to the unusual conclusion that Jesus must be John the Baptist raised from the dead (verse 2). Matthew gives us a flashback at this point and tells the story of how Herod had put John to death. He had executed John at the request of his step-daughter, who did so at the prompting of her mother. She had been angry at John for his protest against her marriage to Herod, since she had been the wife of his brother. It would appear that Herod's conscience had been troubled by the execution of John, and his confused beliefs have led him to the conclusion that John has been raised from the dead.

Why does Matthew insert the story of John's death at just this point in his narrative, since it clearly had happened some time before? It is because it serves to show how the threats against Jesus are now increasing. The next passage that we will study begins by saying, 'Now when Jesus heard this, he withdrew from there . . .' (verse 13). What Jesus heard was what Matthew reported in 14:1–2, that Herod had heard about the miraculous powers at work in Jesus and had concluded that he must be John the Baptist *redivivus*. Herod will likely seek to kill 'John' (Jesus) again, so Jesus' life is now under renewed threat. Thus, as when John was first taken into custody (4:12), and as when the Pharisees conspired to destroy him (12:15), Jesus withdrew from there (verse 13). Neither of the earlier retreats was merely defensive. Both were explained as the fulfilment of prophecy concerning the work of the Messiah, the Servant of the Lord (see 4:13–16 and 12:15–21). Though Matthew does not explicitly cite prophecy here, yet this movement is to be seen in the same light.

The fact that it is Herod who now seeks to kill Jesus is enough to tell us how threatening the situation is. His family was, of course, notorious for its murders of suspected rivals. This Herod's father (Herod the Great) had attempted to kill Jesus when he was born (2:1–18). Matthew's telling of that story thematically linked Herod the Great's massacre of the children in Bethlehem with the Egyptian Pharaoh's massacre of the children of Israel. Just as Moses was miraculously spared from Pharaoh, so Jesus was spared from Herod the Great. Within the Biblical framework, the stories of Pharaoh, Herod the Great, and now Herod the tetrarch are but particular occasions in which the perennial warfare between the seed of the woman and the seed of the serpent (*Gen.* 3:15) is played out on the pages of history (see *Rev.* 12:1–6 for this interpretation). The report of John's death is placed here both to indicate just what Herod the tetrarch was capable of doing, and to remind us of the persistent threat hanging over the head of Jesus as he goes about his ministry. Consequently, just as John served as the forerunner to Jesus in his ministry, so now he serves as the forerunner to Jesus in his death. The rejection of Jesus at Nazareth and the hostility of Herod indicate to us that the shadow of the cross is falling darkly across the path of Jesus. Jesus himself explains this generalized hatred as the fulfilment of prophecy, 'They hated me without a cause' (*John* 15:25, see *Psa.* 35:19 and 69:4).

SUMMARY

Nazareth took offence at Jesus because he did not do for them what they wished. Later the people of Israel as a whole did the same thing. Let us not follow their example. The coming of the kingdom does involve confusing aspects (such as a delay in the kingdom's consummation) that can cause us to question, as did John the Baptist when he was in prison. We must not allow these things to offend us, or cause us to turn away from Jesus. Rather, let us be content with Jesus' administration of his kingdom, recognizing that we are not worthy of the least of his mercies. Sometimes his blessings are poured out in abundance. Sometimes they are scarce. If we come in humility and faith, we shall find him ready to receive and bless us.

34

'It Is I'

*N*ow when Jesus heard this, he withdrew from there in a boat to a desolate place by himself. But when the crowds heard it, they followed him on foot from the towns. *14* When he went ashore he saw a great crowd, and he had compassion on them and healed their sick. *15* Now when it was evening, the disciples came to him and said, 'This is a desolate place, and the day is now over; send the crowds away to go into the villages and buy food for themselves.' *16* But Jesus said, 'They need not go away; you give them something to eat.' *17* They said to him, 'We have only five loaves here and two fish.' *18* And he said, 'Bring them here to me.' *19* Then he ordered the crowds to sit down on the grass, and taking the five loaves and the two fish, he looked up to heaven and said a blessing. Then he broke the loaves and gave them to the disciples, and the disciples gave them to the crowds. *20* And they all ate and were satisfied. And they took up twelve baskets full of the broken pieces left over. *21* And those who ate were about five thousand men, besides women and children. *22* Immediately he made the disciples get into the boat and go before him to the other side, while he dismissed the crowds. *23* And after he had dismissed the crowds, he went up on the mountain by himself to pray. When evening came, he was there alone, *24* but the boat by this time was a long way from the land, beaten by the waves, for the wind was against them. *25* And in the fourth watch of the night he came to them, walking on the sea. *26* But when the disciples saw him walking on the sea, they were terrified, and said, 'It is a ghost!' and they cried out in fear. *27* But immediately Jesus spoke to them, saying, 'Take heart; it is I. Do not be afraid.' *28* And Peter answered him, 'Lord, if it is you, command me to come to you on the water.' *29* He said, 'Come.' So Peter got out of the boat and walked on the water and came to Jesus. *30* But when he saw the wind, he was afraid, and beginning to sink he cried out, 'Lord, save me.' *31* Jesus immediately reached out his hand and took hold of him, saying to him, 'O you of little faith, why did you doubt?' *32* And when they got into the boat, the wind ceased. *33* And those in the boat *worshipped him, saying, 'Truly you are the Son of God.'* [34] *And when they had crossed over, they came to land at Gennesaret.* [35] *And when the men of that place recognized him, they sent around to all that region and brought to him all who were sick* [36] *and implored him that they might only touch the fringe of his garment. And as many as touched it were made well* (Matt. 14:13–36).

In Matthew 4:12, news of the arrest of John the Baptist prompted Jesus to withdraw into Galilee. Here also, news that Herod has heard about 'the fame of Jesus' prompts Jesus to withdraw into the wilderness (verse 13). As before, the movement is not purely defensive, and the location proves to be significant (see 4:13–17). Jesus moves across the pages of the New Testament silhouetted against the Old Testament acts of God. As that silhouette is brought under the light of the New Testament, we see the light of the knowledge of the glory of God shining in the face of Jesus Christ.

BREAD IN THE WILDERNESS

The feeding of the five thousand is the one miracle of Jesus, apart from the resurrection, which is found in all four of the Gospels. When Jesus withdraws 'to a desolate place' (verse 13), the multitudes follow him. There Jesus looked upon them and felt compassion for them and healed their sick (verse 14). As the day draws to a close, the disciples approach Jesus and urge him to send the multitudes away to find food in the villages. They remark that the place is 'desolate' (v. 15). The use of this term twice in such close proximity indicates to us that Matthew wants to emphasize it. In fact, this time the Greek word order puts it first in the sentence, 'Desolate is this place.' The word translated as 'desolate' in these two verses is the word for a desert or a wilderness. The location here is not, of course, a desert in the sense that there is no vegetation at all (see verse 19), but it is a wilderness, unpopulated, unfruitful, and threatening. Where have we seen this picture before, people following their Lord into the wilderness, needing to find bread? It's (Biblical) *déjà vu* all over again.

There are other details here intended to remind us of Israel's sojourn in the wilderness, where the Lord miraculously provided bread. When the people have at last been fed with the five loaves and two fish multiplied by Jesus, Matthew tells us that twelve baskets of surplus are gathered after the meal. The number twelve reminds us of the twelve tribes of Israel, which Yahweh fed in the wilderness. In addition, 'those who ate were five thousand men, besides women and children' (verse 21). Why count the multitude in this way? It is because this was how the people of Israel were counted when they came out of Egypt and marched toward the wilderness (*Exod.* 12:37). They were numbered that way to determine the number of fighting men who could do battle for Israel (see *Num.* 1).

Matthew wants us to see this multitude as representing a new Israel, one that follows the Lord into the wilderness and finds him sufficient for all their needs.

HIS WAY WAS IN THE SEA

Following the great feeding, Jesus goes up on a mountain to pray, and sends his disciples ahead of him across the sea in a boat. The journey was rough and the boat was being 'beaten by the waves, for the wind was against them' (verse 24). Where have we seen this picture before, the people of God out in the wilderness threatened by the sea? In the fourth watch of the night Jesus comes to them walking on the water. When the disciples see him, they are frightened, thinking it is a ghost. But Jesus speaks to them, 'Take heart; it is I. Do not be afraid' (verse 27).

The whole scene is replete with echoes of the Old Testament intended to create in our minds an association, indeed an identification, between Yahweh in the Old Testament and Jesus in the New. The danger from the sea in the wilderness takes us back to the crossing of the Red Sea. The details are different, of course, but the basic elements are the same. That event was foundational for Israel's faith in Yahweh, as evidenced elsewhere in the Old Testament. In *Psa.* 77:19, Israel's deliverance at the sea was recalled in these words:

> *Your way was through the sea, your path through the great waters;*
> *yet your footprints were unseen.*

Similarly, building faith for the future on this deliverance, *Isa.* 43:2a promises:

When you pass through the waters, I will be with you, and through the rivers, they shall not overwhelm you.

Significantly, the words of comfort that Jesus speaks to the disciples (verse 27) are taken from the Greek translation of *Isa*. 43, the standard version for Matthew and his readers. Jesus' exhortation, 'Do not be afraid', is found twice in that chapter (verses 1 and 5, translated in the ESV, 'Fear not'). Also, there is a phrase of self-identification for Yahweh that recurs in *Isa*. 43 and the surrounding chapters, 'I am he' (see *Isa*. 41:4; 43:10, 25; 48:12). This phrase comes from the first part of the mysterious divine name revealed at the burning bush (*Exod*. 3:14), 'I am who I am' (in Greek, 'I am he who is'). Jesus now uses this phrase in his words to the disciples, translated here as 'It is I.' Given that the disciples are now 'passing through the waters', the echoes of *Isa*. 43 in Jesus' words are surely intended to comfort them by identifying Jesus as the Saviour God revealed in that chapter, as the one who will be with them. He is indeed that God, and his way was through the sea, his path through the great waters, though his footprints were unseen.

The lesson was not lost on the disciples. Peter said, 'Lord, if it is you, command me to come to you on the water' (verse 28). Jesus did, and Peter came. But 'when he saw the wind, he was afraid', and he began to sink. 'Lord, save me', he cried (verse 30). And Jesus did. Jesus then gently rebuked him, 'O you of little faith, why did you doubt?' When they got into the boat, the wind ceased. Then the disciples worshipped him and said, 'Truly you are the Son of God.' When they arrived on the other side of the sea, the people there brought to him all who were sick, and implored him that they might touch only the fringe of his garment. 'And as many as touched it were made well' (verse 36).

SUMMARY

Against the backdrop of increasing rejection, Jesus moves forward in revealing himself to his disciples. By words and deeds reminiscent of the saving acts of Yahweh in the Old Testament, Jesus identifies himself as the true Son of God, mighty to save. Though fearful of the wind, and sinking in the sea, Peter had enough faith to cry out, 'Lord, save me.' It was enough. The Lord did save him.

The Lord is near to all who call on him, to all who call on him in truth. He fulfils the desire of those who fear him; he also hears their cry and saves them (Psa. 145:18–19).

Thanks be to God.

35

The Things Which Defile

*T*hen *Pharisees and scribes came to Jesus from Jerusalem and
said, ² 'Why do your disciples break the tradition of the elders?
For they do not wash their hands when they eat.' ³ He answered them,
'And why do you break the commandment of God for the sake of
your tradition? ⁴ For God commanded, "Honour your father and
your mother," and, "Whoever reviles father or mother must surely
die." ⁵ But you say, "If anyone tells his father or his mother, 'What
you would have gained from me is given to God,' ⁶ he need not honour his father." So for the sake of your tradition you have made
void the word of God. ⁷ You hypocrites! Well did Isaiah prophesy
of you, when he said: ⁸ "This people honours me with their lips, but
their heart is far from me; ⁹ in vain do they worship me, teaching as
doctrines the commandments of men."' ¹⁰ And he called the people to
him and said to them, 'Hear and understand: ¹¹ it is not what goes
into the mouth that defiles a person, but what comes out of the mouth;
this defiles a person.' ¹² Then the disciples came and said to him, 'Do
you know that the Pharisees were offended when they heard this saying?' ¹³ He answered, 'Every plant that my heavenly Father has not
planted will be rooted up. ¹⁴ Let them alone; they are blind guides.
And if the blind lead the blind, both will fall into a pit.' ¹⁵ But Peter
said to him, 'Explain the parable to us.' ¹⁶ And he said, 'Are you also
still without understanding? ¹⁷ Do you not see that whatever goes into
the mouth passes into the stomach and is expelled? ¹⁸ But what comes
out of the mouth proceeds from the heart, and this defiles a person.
¹⁹ For out of the heart come evil thoughts, murder, adultery, sexual
immorality, theft, false witness, slander. ²⁰ These are what defile
a person. But to eat with unwashed hands does not defile anyone.'
²¹ And Jesus went away from there and withdrew to the district of
Tyre and Sidon. ²² And behold, a Canaanite woman from that
region came out and was crying, 'Have mercy on me, O Lord, Son
of David; my daughter is severely oppressed by a demon.' ²³ But
he did not answer her a word. And his disciples came and begged
him, saying, 'Send her away, for she is crying out after us.' ²⁴ He*

answered, 'I was sent only to the lost sheep of the house of Israel.' [25] *But she came and knelt before him, saying, 'Lord, help me.'* [26] *And he answered, 'It is not right to take the children's bread and throw it to the dogs.'* [27] *She said, 'Yes, Lord, yet even the dogs eat the crumbs that fall from their masters' table.'* [28] *Then Jesus answered her, 'O woman, great is your faith! Be it done for you as you desire.'And her daughter was healed instantly* (Matt. 15:1–28).

M ore conflict with the Pharisees and scribes awaits us in this section. The controversy is sparked by the observation that Jesus' disciples do not observe the Jewish traditions concerning ritual purity before meals. Jesus seizes upon the occasion to teach us about the things which truly defile us. This is followed by the amazing story of how Jesus dealt with the Canaanite woman whose daughter was oppressed by a demon. As we shall see, it is a parallel within the Gospel context to the teaching of *Acts* 10.

PIOUS HYPOCRISY

Pharisees and scribes from Jerusalem approach Jesus with a question. They wonder why his disciples do not wash their hands according to the Jewish traditions when they eat. In their eyes this is a major fault, both in the disciples' practice and in the teaching Jesus has given them. The Pharisees and scribes are consistently portrayed in the New Testament as being very zealous for matters of ritual purity (see *Mark* 7:3–5), and yet blind to matters of great moral consequence in their own lives (*Matt.* 23:23–25 and 27:3–10). Jesus answers them with another question, 'And why do you break the commandment of God for the sake of your tradition?' (verse 3).

One of their traditions concerns the practice of devoting one's wealth to God, while yet retaining personal possession and use of it (see *Mark* 7:9–13). When dedicated in this way, such money is not available for other uses, even for helping one's father or mother. Their tradition has thus become a way of avoiding responsibility under the fifth commandment to honour their parents. Jesus says, that 'for the sake of your tradition [they] have made void the word of God' (verse 6). To drive the point home further, Jesus quotes the words of the prophet Isaiah (verses 8–9, *Isa.* 29:13)), which tell

[145]

of people who honour God with their lips while their hearts are far from him. Outwardly they look very pious, but in reality it is pious hypocrisy. Such religion finds no acceptance with God – but see next what does.

BEHOLD, A CANAANITE!

Following his encounter with the Pharisees and scribes over the issue of ritual washings, Jesus withdrew from there. It is another strategic move. How easy it would be to miss the strong connection between the controversy over what defiles a person and the incident which now follows. Jesus moves into the territory of Tyre and Sidon, places already mentioned in Matthew as legendary for the judgment of God which fell upon them (*Matt.* 11:22). A 'Canaanite' woman from that region came out and cried to Jesus to deliver her daughter, who was severely oppressed by a demon (verse 22). Matthew's characteristic 'behold' in this verse draws our attention to the woman. He calls her a Canaanite. The term is a loaded one. Mark tells us that she was 'a Gentile [literally, a *Greek*], a Syrophoenician by birth' (*Mark* 7:26). That would have been the normal way of describing her. Matthew's term is anachronistic, though quite deliberate. He intends it to remind his Jewish readers (and us) of the ancient inhabitants of this land, the people of great sin whom the Lord gave over to complete destruction (*Deut.* 7:1–5). Matthew wants us to see that just as Rahab found mercy from the Lord through Joshua (see *Josh.* 6:15–25), who was a type of Christ, so this woman finds mercy from Jesus.

But she does not find mercy easily. Three times she approaches Jesus, only to be rebuffed and answered in harsh words we never expected to hear from him.

• verse 22, she cries out to Jesus, 'Have mercy on me, O Lord, Son of David; my daughter is severely oppressed by a demon.'

• verse 23, his response: 'But he did not answer her a word.'

• verse 23, then she attempts to get to Jesus through his disciples, and they beg him to send her away (presumably, by giving her what she wanted).

• verse 24, but he refuses, saying, 'I was sent only to the lost sheep of house of Israel.'

- verse 25, again 'she came and knelt before him, saying, "Lord, help me."'
- verse 26, and again he refuses, saying, 'It is not right to take the children's bread and throw it to the dogs.'

By this time our hearts are breaking for this woman, and we are shocked to see Jesus seemingly so unfeeling in his treatment of her and so harsh in his words. His heart goes out to those who are 'harassed and helpless, like sheep without a shepherd' (*Matt.* 9:36); how can he be so untouched by this woman's pain? She is a mother desperate to find help for a daughter 'severely oppressed by a demon'. Could there be any deeper anguish a parent could feel? Why is Jesus turning away from her, and refusing her pleas, even when she kneels before him and begs?

He does it for our sake, to draw out the depth of her faith, and to show the great contrast between her and the Jews who reject and turn away from him. The people of Nazareth take great offence at Jesus. So do the Pharisees and scribes when the disciples do not wash their hands as their tradition requires. But here is a Canaanite woman, who acknowledges that she is a dog, undeserving of any of his mercies; yet she knows that he is the promised Son of David (verse 22), in whose name the Gentiles may hope (*Matt.* 12:21). Under the attack of his harsh but just refusals, she persists in calling him 'Lord' (verses 22, 25, 27). With the faith of a Jacob she wrestles with Jesus in her pleas (prayers) and refuses to let him go until he blesses her (see *Gen.* 32:26). She believes without wavering that he who abounds in steadfast love and mercy will certainly give crumbs from the children's bread to the dogs who beg under the table. Such persevering faith and sustained humility are not to be found in Israel, but here they are in full bloom among the Canaanites.

SUMMARY

As in Acts 10, where Peter's vision of the unclean animals is followed by the gift of the Holy Spirit to the unclean Gentiles, so here matters concerning religious purity are followed by a practical demonstration of how even the most defiled of Gentiles (the Canaanites) can find true acceptance with God (see *Acts* 10:35).

Together these passages teach us that the things which truly defile us are not resolved by washing our hands and watching what we eat. If we would be saved, we must come to Christ in sincerity of heart, deep humility, and persevering faith.

> *Nothing in my hand I bring, simply to thy cross I cling;*
> *Naked, come to Thee for dress, helpless, look to Thee for grace;*
> *Foul, I to the fountain fly; wash me, Saviour, or I die.*

Augustus M. Toplady,
Rock of Ages, Cleft for Me

36

Saviour of the Gentiles

Jesus went on from there and walked beside the Sea of Galilee. And he went up on the mountain and sat down there. [30] And great crowds came to him, bringing with them the lame, the blind, the crippled, the mute, and many others, and they put them at his feet, and he healed them, [31] so that the crowd wondered, when they saw the mute speaking, the crippled healthy, the lame walking, and the blind seeing. And they glorified the God of Israel. [32] Then Jesus called his disciples to him and said, 'I have compassion on the crowd because they have been with me now three days and have nothing to eat. And I am unwilling to send them away hungry, lest they faint on the way.' [33] And the disciples said to him, 'Where are we to get enough bread in such a desolate place to feed so great a crowd?' [34] And Jesus said to them, 'How many loaves do you have?' They said 'Seven, and a few small fish.' [35] And directing the crowd to sit down on the ground, [36] he took the seven loaves and the fish, and having given thanks he broke them and gave them to the disciples, and the disciples gave them to the crowds. [37] And they all ate and were satisfied. And they took up seven baskets full of the broken pieces left over. [38] Those who ate were four thousand men, besides women and children. [39] And after sending away the crowds, he got into the boat and went to the region of Magadan (Matt. 15:29–39).

From the district of Tyre and Sidon our Saviour makes his way to the Sea of Galilee. Location will prove to be a major key to understanding this section. We have a summary report of Jesus' healing ministry (verses 29–31), and then a second feeding of a multitude in a desolate place (verses 32–39). It will not be hard to discern Matthew's main point. All the distinctive clues are now well known to us.

HEALING FOR THE GENTILES

From the earliest part of his Gospel, Matthew announced the theme of salvation for the Gentiles. The genealogy of Jesus included Gentile women (*Matt.* 1:2–6), who need not have been mentioned. Gentile *magi* followed his star to the place where Jesus was born (*Matt.* 2:1–12), and these are the only visitors to Jesus mentioned by Matthew. After the arrest of John the Baptist, Jesus began his ministry in Galilee of the Gentiles, to fulfil the word of the prophet Isaiah (*Matt.* 4:12–17).

Recently in our study, Jesus has been to the region of Tyre and Sidon where a notable example of faith and salvation has been presented in the Canaanite woman. Her faith stands as a condemnation of the faithlessness that Jesus is increasingly finding among his own people. Now he returns to the region of Galilee, where his public ministry began. The location speaks of the calling of the Gentiles to partake of the salvation of God.

Jesus goes up on a mountain and sits down, just as he did when he gave the Sermon on the Mount (*Matt.* 5:1). Great crowds now come to him, bringing to him 'the lame, the blind, the crippled, the mute, and many others . . .' (verse 30). Matthew tells us that Jesus healed them, and adds that the people were amazed and wondered when they saw 'the mute speaking, the crippled healthy, the lame walking, and the blind seeing' (verse 31).

The repetition of the afflictions in the list of those who came and those who were healed throws great emphasis upon the healings performed by Jesus. It stresses the great variety of afflictions that he healed and thus indicates that there is no problem or affliction too great for Jesus.

Matthew also tells us that the crowd 'glorified the God of Israel' (verse 31). This way of referring to God, like the Galilean location, indicates that the crowd is predominantly Gentile. Had they been Israelites, we would have expected the simpler reference, 'and they glorified God' (see *Matt.* 9:8, also *Mark* 2:12, *Luke* 2:20, 5:25, 5:26, 7:16, 13:13, 17:15, 18:43, 23:47). But this crowd is glorifying the God of another nation, the God of Israel. The great healing works promised by the prophets are now being showered on the Gentiles (see *Isa.* 35).

BREAD FOR THE GENTILES

After three days of this ministry to the crowd (verse 32), Jesus tells his disciples that he is concerned for the people since they have had nothing to eat. The disciples wonder where they are to get enough bread for them in 'such a desolate place'. Again we have the term 'desolate place' as the location for feeding the multitude, so they are in the wilderness.

It is striking that the disciples approach this situation as if nothing like it had ever happened before. Are they too unbelieving? Have they forgotten the feeding of the 'five thousand men, besides women and children'? They are indeed forgetful, and they will forget this one too (see *Matt.* 16:5–12).

Jesus asks the disciples how much food they have, and they tell him that they have seven loaves and a few fish (verse 34). From this small amount, Jesus again feeds the whole multitude, and there is much surplus to pick up. This time there are seven baskets full of broken pieces (verse 37). The number of those fed is reported as 'four thousand men, besides women and children'.

Both the similarities and the differences between this story and the feeding of the five thousand are significant. Both stories take place in the wilderness and both involve Jesus giving bread in the wilderness. Both count the people as Moses counted the people of Israel in the wilderness. Both report that they all ate and were satisfied. Thus both stories are intended to present the ministry of Jesus in terms of the Exodus salvation, and to identify Jesus with Yahweh who led Israel out of the land of Egypt and gave them bread in the wilderness.

The differences in the stories, however, stress that this second crowd is mostly Gentile. There are seven baskets left over from this feeding, not twelve as in the previous one. Thus in the second feeding we are lacking the distinctive number twelve, symbolic for the people of Israel. Instead we are given the number seven, which is more generic and emphasizes completeness, those gathered from 'all' the nations. Again, the prophet Isaiah has foretold it:

> *I will make you as a light for the nations, that my salvation may reach to the end of the earth* (Isa. 49:6b).

SUMMARY

By showering miracles of healing upon the Gentiles and giving
them bread in the wilderness, Jesus is showing us that the great
salvation worked for Israel in the wilderness was a type of the
salvation to be accomplished in much greater degree for all the
nations on the face of the earth. The Yahweh of the Exodus is
indeed the one in whom the Gentiles may hope. Against the background of these saving works, the growing unbelief of Israel proves
worthy of judgment.

> *Therefore when the* LORD *heard, he was full of wrath; a fire was kin-
> dled against Jacob; his anger rose against Israel, because they did not
> believe in God and did not trust his saving power. Yet he commanded
> the skies above, and opened the doors of heaven, and he rained down
> on them manna to eat and gave them the grain of heaven. Man ate
> the bread of the angels; he sent them food in abundance* (Psa. 78:
> 21–25).

May unbelief not be found in us.

37

Pharisees and Sadducees

*A*nd the Pharisees and Sadducees came, and to test him they asked
him to show them a sign from heaven. *²* He answered them,
'When it is evening, you say, "It will be fair weather, for the sky is
red." 3 And in the morning, "It will be stormy today, for the sky is
red and threatening." You know how to interpret the appearance of
the sky, but you cannot interpret the signs of the times. *⁴ An evil and
adulterous generation seeks for a sign, but no sign will be given to it
except the sign of Jonah.' So he left them and departed. *⁵* When the
disciples reached the other side, they had forgotten to bring any bread.
*⁶ Jesus said to them, 'Watch and beware of the leaven of the Phari-
sees and Sadducees.' ⁷ And they began discussing it among themselves,
saying, 'We brought no bread.' ⁸ But Jesus, aware of this, said, 'O
you of little faith, why are you discussing among yourselves the fact
that you have no bread? ⁹ Do you not yet perceive? Do you not remember the five loaves for the five thousand, and how many baskets
you gathered? ¹⁰ Or the seven loaves for the four thousand, and how
many baskets you gathered? ¹¹ How is it that you fail to understand
that I did not speak about bread? Beware of the leaven of the Pharisees and Sadducees.' ¹² Then they understood that he did not tell them
to beware of the leaven of bread, but of the teaching of the Pharisees
and Sadducees* (Matt.16:1–12).

In this section the Pharisees and the Sadducees join together in
order to test Jesus. This is the first mention of the Sadducees
since *Matt.* 3:7 when they were part of the crowd, also including Pharisees, that came to John for baptism. It is also the first
mention of them interacting with Jesus. It is most unusual for the
Pharisees and Sadducees to join together for a common purpose,
since the theological differences between them were considerable.
Luke gives us a brief summary of their differences in the account

of Paul's hearing before the Sanhedrin after his arrest in Jerusalem (see *Acts* 23:8). Paul exploited these differences to his great advantage on that occasion and turned the groups against one another when they had come together against him.

AN UNHOLY ALLIANCE

The alliance of Pharisees and Sadducees with one another to test Jesus is an ominous development. They were such bitter opponents otherwise, but have now found common cause in their opposition to Jesus. Eventually it will lead to the cross. They demand of Jesus a sign, but he refuses (verses 1–4). In one sense, there is a certain legitimacy to their request. Jesus himself said, 'If I am not doing the works of my Father, then do not believe me; but if I do them, even though you do not believe me, believe the works, that you may know and understand that the Father is in me and I am in the Father' (*John* 10:38). The people of his day were not to accept Jesus' claims about himself merely on the basis of his claims. We are not to believe every spirit, but to test them to see whether they are from God or not, for many false prophets have gone out into the world (*1 John* 4:1).

But Jesus had already done many signs, and the reports of them had spread far and wide. Most recently he had fed a multitude of 'four thousand men, besides women and children' with seven loaves and a few fish. So this unholy alliance's demand for a sign is not a legitimate request. They have already had the evidence they need and they have hardened their hearts against it. More evidence will only aggravate their guilt. They are not seeking evidence that will convince them of the truth; they are seeking a reason for denying the truth. For such people Jesus offers only this sign: 'An evil and adulterous generation seeks for a sign, but no sign will be given to it except the sign of Jonah' (verse 4).

A fuller explanation of this 'sign of Jonah' is not given again here, but earlier in Matthew we learned that it is the resurrection of Jesus. 'For just as Jonah was three days and three nights in the belly of the great fish, so will the Son of Man be three days and three nights in the heart of the earth' (*Matt.* 12:40). On the day of Pentecost, Peter pointed to the resurrection as the decisive proof

concerning the identity of Jesus: 'Let all the house of Israel therefore know for certain that God has made him both Lord and Christ
. . .' (*Acts* 2:36). Paul likewise points the inquiring Athenians to the
resurrection of Christ as the basis for assurance that a day of judgment is approaching for all the earth:

> *The times of ignorance God overlooked, but now he commands all*
> *people everywhere to repent, because he has fixed a day on which*
> *he will judge the world in righteousness by a man whom he has*
> *appointed; and of this he has given assurance to all by raising him*
> *from the dead* (Acts 17:30–31).

UNHOLY LEAVEN

In verses 5–12 Jesus twice warned his disciples against 'the leaven
of the Pharisees and Sadducees', once at the beginning and again
near the end (verse 11). This shows that there is a single idea that
is the main point of our passage. The way in which the phrase is
formed (a singular article in the Greek text, '*the* leaven', is used
to cover both groups) suggests that, whatever and however many
sharp differences might exist between the Pharisees and Sadducees, there is a 'leaven' or teaching (verse 12) that is common to
them. What is this 'leaven' about which the disciples are so force-
fully warned to 'watch and beware'?

In the present context what the Pharisees and Sadducees have
in common is their demand for a sign from Jesus, a demand that
is clearly disingenuous, inasmuch as abundant signs have already
been given, and still they have refused to believe. Jesus warns them
against this unbelief. They can discern the signs of the weather,
but they cannot interpret the signs of the times (verses 2–4). All
around them are signs indicating that the kingdom of heaven has
arrived in the person of Jesus, yet they will not believe. The disciples must guard against this deception in their own lives, for if
they do not pay attention to what is happening, they too can miss
the advent of the kingdom of heaven. The conversation they have
with Jesus in this passage illustrates the danger before them. When
Jesus warns them against 'the leaven of the Pharisees and Sadducees', they begin to worry that they have not brought enough bread
with them. The two miraculous feedings of the multitude have

apparently been wasted on them, since they seem to forget that being without bread is really no hindrance to Jesus and, so long as they are with him, they too will not be in need. Unbelief is indeed a corrupting influence, and if we are not careful it can eat away at our lives too.

SUMMARY

Unbelievers today sometimes exhibit the same hypocrisy as the Pharisees and Sadducees of Jesus' day. They present themselves as open-minded on the issue of Jesus, and claim they only need to see the evidence. But for many this is mere pretence, for they are not really open to the truth. Their minds are made up, and they do not wish to be confused by the facts. But believers can also be corrupted by unbelief, by forgetting what the Lord has done and thus can do. We must 'watch and beware' of this leaven of the Pharisees and Sadducees in our own lives, lest we too fail to perceive. Because this danger is ever present, Paul prays for us and for all the church:

> . . . that the God of our Lord Jesus Christ, the Father of glory, may give you a spirit of wisdom and of revelation in the knowledge of him, having the eyes of your hearts enlightened, that you may know what is the hope to which he has called you, what are the riches of his glorious inheritance in the saints, and what is the immeasurable greatness of his power toward us who believe, according to the working of his great might that he worked in Christ when he raised him from the dead and seated him at his right hand in the heavenly places . . . (Eph. 1:17–20).

38

The Christ, the Church, and the Cross

*N**ow when Jesus came into the district of Caesarea Philippi, he
asked his disciples, 'Who do people say that the Son of Man is?'
[14] And they said, 'Some say John the Baptist, others say Elijah, and
others Jeremiah or one of the prophets.' [15] He said to them, 'But who
do you say that I am?' [16] Simon Peter replied, 'You are the Christ,
the Son of the living God.' [17] And Jesus answered him, 'Blessed are
you, Simon Bar-Jonah! For flesh and blood has not revealed this
to you, but my Father who is in heaven. [18] And I tell you, you are
Peter, and on this rock I will build my church, and the gates of hell
shall not prevail against it. [19] I will give you the keys of the kingdom
of heaven, and whatever you bind on earth shall be bound in heaven,
and whatever you loose on earth shall be loosed in heaven.' [20] Then
he strictly charged the disciples to tell no one that he was the Christ.
[21] From that time Jesus began to show his disciples that he must go
to Jerusalem and suffer many things from the elders and chief priests
and scribes, and be killed, and on the third day be raised. [22] And Peter
took him aside and began to rebuke him, saying, 'Far be it from you,
Lord! This shall never happen to you.' [23] But he turned and said to
Peter 'Get behind me, Satan! You are a hindrance to me. For you
are not setting your mind on the things of God, but on the things of
man.' [24] Then Jesus told his disciples, 'If anyone would come after
me, let him deny himself and take up his cross and follow me. [25] For
whoever would save his life will lose it, but whoever loses his life for
my sake will find it. [26] For what will it profit a man if he gains the
whole world and forfeits his soul? Or what shall a man give in return
for his soul? [27] For the Son of Man is going to come with his angels in
the glory of his Father, and then he will repay each person according
to what he has done. [28] Truly, I say to you, there are some standing
here who will not taste death until they see the Son of Man coming in
his kingdom'* (Matt. 16:13–28).

Jesus and his disciples now make their way to Caesarea Philippi. The place name might be familiar to Bible readers, but

probably few could confidently say that it is located in the far north of the Promised Land, about twenty-five miles north of the sea of Galilee, near the head-waters of the Jordan river. In Jesus' day it was pagan territory. Probably he had gone there to escape, as a retreat from the pressure of crowds and opponents in his own land. Jesus chooses this setting to begin preparing his disciples for a new level of understanding of who he is, what awaits him, and indeed what awaits them as his followers.

THE CHRIST AND THE CROSS

Now that he is alone with his disciples Jesus puts an important question to them, 'Who do people say that the Son of Man is?' The varied answers are intriguing, but Jesus' main concern is with what his disciples think. Peter spoke for them all and said, 'You are the Christ, the Son of the living God.'

Peter is quite correct, but it soon appears that he does not fully understand what he has said. Being the Christ means that Jesus must 'go to Jerusalem and suffer many things from the elders and chief priests and scribes, and be killed, and on the third day be raised' (verse 21). It is in this way that he will save his people from their sins. But for Peter such a fate is unthinkable: 'Far be it from you, Lord! This shall never happen to you' (verse 22). Peter envisioned a kingdom of triumph, where enemies would be defeated and the chosen people would live in peace and prosperity. Ultimately, there will be a kingdom like that, but far greater than Peter could possibly imagine. But before that would come, there would be much suffering, for the King himself as well as for his people.

That is the next surprise for Peter, for not only does the cross await Jesus, it awaits Peter and the other disciples too. The advent of the kingdom will not mean that all suffering will cease. No, that will come at the consummation. For now, Jesus must go the cross, and all who follow Jesus must take up their cross (verses 24–28).

THE ROCK AND THE CHURCH

In response to Peter's great confession Jesus pronounces on him a great benediction, 'Blessed are you, Simon Bar-Jonah! For flesh and blood did not reveal this to you, but my Father who is in heaven.'

Simon's insight was no human achievement. It was the product of divine revelation, just as it is for all who come to a true confession of Jesus as the Christ (see *1 Cor.* 12:3).

Jesus then speaks of the special role Peter will play in the church Christ will build: 'And I tell you, you are Peter, and on this rock I will build my church, and the gates of hell will not prevail against it' (verse 18). This is one of only two places where the word *church* is used in the Gospels (see also *Matt.* 18:17). This passage was an important point of debate at the time of the Reformation. Roman Catholic claims for the office and primacy of the Pope rest heavily on this verse. Protestants, eager to deny such claims, have been quick to provide alternative interpretations. They have argued that Peter is not the rock upon which Christ will build his church, but the confession he has made. Some even suggest that it is Christ himself that is the rock. But such alternatives do not do justice to Jesus' own words, which point quite directly to Peter. Are we then to suppose that Peter was the first Pope, and that the church was founded on him?

As in all such cases, each passage is to be interpreted in harmony with the rest of Scripture. Paul tells us that the church is 'built upon the foundation of the apostles and prophets, Christ Jesus himself being the cornerstone . . .' (*Eph.* 2:20). In this verse, as in the rest of the New Testament, Peter is not unique among the apostles and prophets in the role he plays in the church's foundation, not even a first among equals. It is Christ who is pre-eminent among them as the cornerstone of the foundation. Historically speaking, Peter was the first to proclaim the good news to the Gentiles (*Acts* 10; 15:7). Yet even at the council of Jerusalem, he is but one voice among several (*Acts* 15). How then is Peter the rock upon which Christ will build his church?

I would suggest that the difficulty we have in understanding this verse is that we are unconsciously reading it as if the word 'alone' had been placed in it: 'And I tell you, you are Peter, and on this rock *alone* I will build my church . . .' But that is not what Jesus said, and it is not what the New Testament reveals about Peter. Peter is indeed a rock, and upon this rock Jesus builds his church; but he is not the only rock in that foundation. Alongside him are the other apostles and the prophets. We can see this clearly in

[159]

connection with 'the keys of the kingdom', which Jesus says will be given to Peter (verse 19). The power of these keys, to bind and to loose (that is, to forgive or retain sins) are not Peter's exclusive powers, but belong to the other apostles (*John* 20:22–23), and indeed to the church generally (*Matt.* 18:18–19). This passage does not establish a papacy, but a visible church authorized to act in Christ's name. It does so as all human institutions do, fallibly, as Peter abundantly proves in this passage; but when it does act according to the principles of the Word of God the true nature of the kingdom is made visible. By the power of the keys, church officers admit to membership those who by faith truly have an inheritance in the kingdom, and they can remove from membership or deny membership to those who have no inheritance. When it acts faithfully, the church does make visible the true kingdom of heaven.

SUMMARY

Alone with his disciples at Caesarea Philippi, Jesus begins to show them the full mystery of the Christ and his kingdom. It is a lesson they will find very hard to grasp, and never fully understand until after the resurrection. The Scriptures clearly revealed it, but the disciples were 'slow of heart to believe all the prophets [had] spoken' (*Luke* 24:25). May it not be so with us. Our Lord Jesus is indeed 'the Christ, the Son of the living God', but for him there was a cross, and there is a cross for all who follow him.

> *Must Jesus bear the cross alone, and all the world go free?*
> *No, there's a cross for everyone, and there's a cross for me.*

Thomas Shepherd,
Must Jesus Bear the Cross Alone?

39

A Voice from the Cloud

*A*nd *after six days Jesus took with him Peter and James, and John his brother, and led them up a high mountain by themselves.* ² *And he was transfigured before them, and his face shone like the sun, and his clothes became white as light.* ³ *And behold, there appeared to them Moses and Elijah, talking with him.* ⁴ *And Peter said to Jesus, 'Lord, it is good that we are here. If you wish, I will make three tents here, one for you and one for Moses and one for Elijah.'* ⁵ *He was still speaking when, behold, a bright cloud overshadowed them, and a voice from the cloud said, 'This is my beloved Son with whom I am well pleased; listen to him.'* ⁶ *When the disciples heard this they fell on their faces and were terrified.* ⁷ *But Jesus came and touched them, saying, 'Rise, and have no fear.'* ⁸ *And when they lifted up their eyes, they saw no one but Jesus only.* ⁹ *And as they were coming down the mountain, Jesus commanded them, 'Tell no one the vision, until the Son of Man is raised from the dead.'* ¹⁰ *And the disciples asked him, 'Then why do the scribes say that first Elijah must come?'* ¹¹ *He answered, 'Elijah does come, and he will restore all things.* ¹² *But I tell you that Elijah has already come, and they did not recognize him, but did to him whatever they pleased. So also the Son of Man will certainly suffer at their hands.'* ¹³ *Then the disciples understood that he was speaking to them of John the Baptist* (Matt. 17:1–13).

This section will show the importance of reading the New Testament in the light of the Old. Jesus ascends a high mountain, taking with him Peter, James, and John. While there he is 'transfigured' or transformed before them: his face shines like the sun, and his clothes become white as light. There is a bright cloud that overshadows them, and from the cloud a voice speaks. Just the mention of the mountain and the cloud are enough to remind us of Sinai, but a voice speaking to them from the cloud, and Jesus' face shining like the sun, make it all too clear that we are to think of Moses on the mountain with God (*Exod.* 34:29–35). Possibly even the time notice of 'after six days' (verse 1) may be intended to remind us of Moses' meeting with God on the mountain, for it was on the seventh day when God spoke to Moses (*Exod.* 24:16). Yet, truly, one greater than Moses is now before us.

GOD'S BELOVED SON

The three disciples who are with Jesus are clearly being given a remarkable vision. Not only do they see the Lord in his glory, but appearing with him and talking with him are Moses and Elijah. Matthew does not tell us the nature of their conversation, but Luke tells us it concerned 'the *exodus*' (this is the Greek word Luke uses) that Jesus was to accomplish at Jerusalem (*Luke* 9:31).

Peter impulsively suggests that three booths should be built, one for each of the glorious figures now before him. Behind this is an assumption of the equality of the figures who now appear in glory, each deserving his own booth. But while he is still speaking, a cloud of glory overshadows them on the mountain and a voice speaks to them from out of the cloud: 'This is my beloved Son, with whom I am well pleased; listen to him.' This declaration echoes the words of 'the voice from heaven' spoken of Jesus at his baptism (*Matt.* 3:17).

In our study of that passage we saw that the declaration combined words from *Psa.* 2:7, 'You are my son', and *Isa.* 42:1, '. . . in whom my soul delights'. Here there is an addition to the baptismal declaration, '. . . listen to him.' These words echo the words of Moses in *Deut.* 18:15, 'The LORD your God will raise up for you a prophet like me from among you, from your brothers—it is to him you shall listen.' Our passage thus shows us that Jesus stands apart from, because he stands above, all the other prophets who came before him. Moses and Elijah would surely be among the greatest who came before him, but Jesus is the one to whom we are to listen.

This does not mean of course that we are now to disregard the words of Moses and Elijah. Far from it, for Jesus himself teaches us to give heed to the law and the prophets (Matt. 5:17–20). But it does mean that Jesus is supreme above all the prophets, inasmuch as he is God's Son.

[162]

The progress of Matthew's Gospel has been a steady unfolding of the identity of Jesus Christ. Various witnesses have been summoned to tell us who he is—an angel from heaven (1:21), wise men from the east (2:2), the prophets of old (2:15, 2:23, 12:17–21), John the Baptist (3:11–15), a Roman centurion (8:5–9), demons (8:29), blind men who can see more than the Jewish leaders (9:27–31), a Canaanite woman (15:22), the disciples (14:33), and Peter (16:16). But the greatest witness comes from heaven, when God himself speaks and marks out Jesus as his beloved Son. So Jesus is not just another prophet sent from God. He is the Lord of the prophets. He is the one prophesied by Moses (*Deut.* 18:15–22), whom God would raise up from among his brothers, to whom we must listen.

> *Long ago, at many times and in many ways, God spoke to our fathers by the prophets, but in these last days, he has spoken to us by his Son, whom he appointed heir of all things, through whom also he created the world. He is the radiance of the glory of God and the exact imprint of his nature, and he upholds all things by the word of his power* (Heb. 1:1–3a).

ELIJAH HAS COME

At the sounding of the voice from the cloud the disciples 'fell on their faces and were terrified' (verse 6). Jesus touched them and reassured them as he did when he walked on the sea and met them in the stormy night (verse 7; the Greek for 'have no fear' is the same as in *Matt.* 14:27, 'Do not be afraid'). When at last they lifted up their eyes, they saw only Jesus, which dramatically reinforced the lesson they had just been taught.

As they came down from the mountain, Jesus commanded them not to tell the vision to anyone until after he was raised from the dead. Several times previously Jesus has ordered silence after notable events have occurred (8:4, 9:30, 12:16). The reason for this is that there is so much misunderstanding about the work of the Messiah that wide publicity about Jesus' works will only serve to stir up distorted views of his mission and thus make it that much harder to accomplish. Even the disciples themselves do not really understand. Still having difficulty in comprehending all that has happened and all that it means, the disciples ask Jesus why the scribes said that Elijah must come first, before the Messiah. Jesus said that Elijah does come first (just as the prophet predicted, *Mal.* 4:5), and that he had indeed already come, but 'they did not recognize him'. The disciples realized that he was speaking of John the Baptist, who went before Jesus 'in the spirit and power of Elijah' (*Luke* 1:17). John had not been rightly understood, and people did to him whatever they pleased. So, as John was persecuted and killed, so it must be for Jesus also. Again Jesus speaks of the suffering that awaits him, as he had spoken of the resurrection which is to follow (verse 9), but the disciples do not comprehend.

SUMMARY

As we observe the disciples struggling to understand Jesus, we can see how easy it is to get off track with knowing and serving Jesus. Peter can mistakenly view Jesus as on a par with Moses and Elijah, and suggest that booths be made for each of them. A simple faith can save us from many mistakes, for Jesus is God's own beloved Son, in whom he is well pleased. Let us listen to him, and trust him, in all that he says and does.

> *He is the image of the invisible God, the firstborn of all creation. For by him all things were created, in heaven and on earth, visible and invisible, whether thrones or dominions or rulers or authorities—all things were created through him and for him. And he is before all things, and in him all things hold together. And he is the head of the body, the church. He is the beginning, the firstborn from the dead, that in everything he might be pre-eminent. For in him all the fullness of God was pleased to dwell, and through him to reconcile to himself all things, whether on earth or in heaven, making peace by the blood of his cross* (Col. 1:15–20).

40

Down from the Mountain

*A*nd when they came to the crowd, a man came up to him and, kneeling before him, *15* said, 'Lord, have mercy on my son, for he is an epileptic and he suffers terribly. For often he falls into the fire, and often into the water. *16* And I brought him to your disciples, and they could not heal him.' *17* And Jesus answered, 'O faithless and twisted generation, how long am I to be with you? How long am I to bear with you? Bring him here to me.' *18* And Jesus rebuked the demon, and it came out of him, and the boy was healed instantly. *19* Then the disciples came to Jesus privately and said, 'Why could we not cast it out?' *20* He said to them 'Because of your little faith. For truly, I say to you, if you have faith like a grain of mustard seed, you will say to this mountain, "Move from here to there," and it will move, and nothing will be impossible for you.' *22* As they were gathering in Galilee, Jesus said to them, 'The Son of Man is about to be delivered into the hands of men, *23* and they will kill him, and he will be raised on the third day.' And they were greatly distressed. *24* When they came to Capernaum, the collectors of the two-drachma tax went up to Peter and said, 'Does your teacher not pay the tax?' *25* He said, 'Yes.' And when he came into the house, Jesus spoke to him first, saying, 'What do you think, Simon? From whom do kings of the earth take toll or tax? From their sons or from others?' *26* And when he said, 'From others,' Jesus said to him, 'Then the sons are free. *27* However, not to give offence to them, go to the sea and cast a hook and take the first fish that comes up, and when you open its mouth you will find a shekel. Take that and give it to them for me and for yourself'* (Matt. 17:14–27).

Descending from the mountain where the transfiguration had occurred, Jesus and his disciples come upon a great crowd in turmoil and unbelief. At the centre of it all is a father seeking healing for a son who suffers grievously, and the nine remaining disciples who have failed to heal the boy. Mark and Luke also provide the same sequence of events, so we can be sure that the juxtaposition of the two events has significance in itself, apart from the meaning of the stories taken individually. When Moses came down from the mountain of Sinai, where he too saw a theophany, he found Israel in a great uproar and in deep sin (*Exod.* 32). The parallel between these two events is not merely superficial.

LITTLE FAITH, WEAK DISCIPLES

The main point of this story is easy to discern. Of the seven verses in this passage, four of them deal with the relationship between the failure to heal and the lack of faith. After the father makes his request to Jesus, he reports on the failure of the disciples to heal the boy (verse 16). Jesus responds with a word of rebuke and frustration to the 'unbelieving and perverse generation' among which he now lives (verse 17). Then Jesus heals the boy (verse 18). After that the disciples ask why they had been unable to cast out the demon (verse 19), and Jesus explains that it is because of their 'little faith' (verse 20).

'Little faith' is a recurrent term in Matthew. It first appears in the Sermon on the Mount, where Jesus warns his disciples against anxiety over their earthly needs since they have a caring heavenly Father who provides for them (*Matt.* 6:30). Next it appears when Jesus rebukes his disciples for their fear of the storm when they are in the boat with Jesus (*Matt.* 8:26). Jesus uses it to rebuke Peter, for his failure of faith as he began to sink after walking on the water (*Matt.* 14:31). It was also used to rebuke the disciples for their foolish worry about bread when Jesus warned them to beware of the leaven of the scribes and the Pharisees (*Matt.* 16:8).

Notice that it is a term dealing with Jesus' own disciples, not a general term for unbelief among the crowds, who are unbelieving (see verse 17). It points to a failure or weakness of faith. It arises from allowing other things to take our faith and focus off the power of Christ. The disciples had already been given power to heal and to cast out demons (*Matt.* 10:8), but they have now allowed their faith to become impoverished and weakened. To the one who has faith, Jesus says, even mountains can be moved (clearly a metaphorical statement—since neither Jesus nor any other biblical figure, prophet or apostle, ever performed such a feat—but it is not for that reason an empty promise).

COMING TRIALS

Now Jesus tells his disciples again of the passion which awaits him in Jerusalem (verses 22–23). They are deeply grieved by this, yet they do not press him for further understanding or explanation. It is precisely their failure to understand this properly, to see it as within and essential to the plan of God to save his people, that will lead to their further failures at the time of Jesus' arrest and crucifixion. We have seen repeated examples of their failure to understand along the way. Despite all the miracles they had seen, they are perplexed when Jesus tells them to give food to the 'five thousand' in the wilderness (*Matt.* 14:16–17). When the disciples saw Jesus walking on the water, they thought they were seeing a ghost (*Matt.* 14:26). When he explained that it was not what went into a man which defiled but what was in his heart, they did not understand his meaning (*Matt.* 15:16–19). When Jesus told them to feed the 'four thousand' in the wilderness, they were again perplexed over where to find food for so many (*Matt.* 15:33). When Jesus warns them to beware of the leaven of the Pharisees and Sadducees, they worry that they have not brought enough bread (*Matt.* 16:5–7). Peter even rebukes Jesus for his predictions of the cross, showing that his mind is not on the things of God but of men (*Matt.* 16:22–23).

Faith in us must be nurtured by prayer and meditation. Our trying circumstances must be placed within the context of God's power and love and purpose for us. Focusing too much on the things of the world, whether its problems or its comforts, can impoverish our faith and leave us weak in the face of great trials. The cross of Jesus will be just such a time for the disciples. Their present failures to pursue after a full understanding of how everything in life fits into the plan of God, and to set all their circumstances in the light of God's revelation to us, will contribute to the greater failure of their faith when Jesus is arrested.

HELP FOR WEAK FAITH

This next passage closes the narrative section (Chapter 14–17) which precedes the next long discourse (Chapter 18). It is a curious little story. The collectors have come to Peter asking whether Jesus pays the temple tax. Peter quickly answers 'Yes', though why he is so quick to answer and so confident is not clear. When he returns to the house Jesus initiates a discussion with him about whether kings tax their sons or only others. Peter says they tax only others. Jesus then draws the evident conclusion that the sons are exempt. This lesson Jesus quickly applies to the issue of the temple tax, which no doubt was a surprise to Peter, since he had not had the opportunity to discuss the matter with Jesus, if he even intended to do it. Jesus then dispatches Peter to go and pay the tax with a coin Jesus says he will find in the mouth of a fish. We could all wish for such a provision when tax time comes around, but the lesson has a much more general application. It is here to teach us faith, that whatever the need might be, our Lord can meet that need and will.

SUMMARY

While Jesus had been on the mountain in his glory, life for the disciples left behind was full of challenge and controversy. The devil's power seemed to be greater than they could overcome (verses 14–21). There were circumstances approaching they did not understand or welcome (verses 22–23). This story of the coin in the mouth of the fish and the healing by Jesus are here to show us that Jesus can take care of whatever comes our way. We must therefore have faith, and whether we must face taxes, or mountains, or unyielding powers of evil, Jesus can take care of it all. Thanks be to God.

41

The Greatness of Humility

*A*t that time the disciples came to Jesus, saying, 'Who is the great-est in the kingdom of heaven?' ² And calling to him a child, he put him in the midst of them ³ and said, 'Truly, I say to you, unless you turn and become like children, you will never enter the kingdom of heaven. ⁴ Whoever humbles himself like this child is the greatest in the kingdom of heaven. ⁵ Whoever receives one such child in my name receives me, ⁶ but whoever causes one of these little ones who believe in me to sin, it would be better for him to have a great millstone fastened around his neck and to be drowned in the depth of the sea. ⁷ Woe to the world for temptations to sin! For it is necessary that temptations come, but woe to the one by whom the temptation comes! ⁸ And if your hand or your foot causes you to sin, cut it off and throw it away. It is better for you to enter life crippled or lame than with two hands or two feet to be thrown into the eternal fire. ⁹ And if your eye causes you to sin, tear it out and throw it away. It is better for you to enter life with one eye than with two eyes to be thrown into the hell of fire (Matt. 18:1–9).

Matthew 18 contains what many have called the discourse on the church, or the ecclesiastical discourse. One reason for that is that this chapter contains one of the two uses of the word 'church' (Greek, *ekklesia*) found in Matthew. He is, as we have noted, the only Gospel writer to use the word, though the concept is certainly present in each of the others. The main focus of this discourse is on how the members of the church relate to and care for one another. It is not at all a form of government or book of dis-cipline for a church; rather, it is something of a commentary on the principle of neighbour love, or better, family love, where 'family' refers to the church community as a whole, the household of God.

SEEING OURSELVES CORRECTLY

This discourse is provoked by a question from the disciples, 'Who is the greatest in the kingdom of heaven?' Jesus calls to him a little child and puts him in the midst of the disciples. Then he tells them that unless they become like children, they will never enter the kingdom of heaven. He follows this by answering their question directly, 'Whoever humbles himself like this child is the greatest in the kingdom' (verse 4).

This answer is no doubt most unexpected by the disciples. In the next chapter in Matthew we will be told the familiar story of children being brought to Jesus, in order that he might lay hands on them and pray. The disciples rebuked the people for this, no doubt believing it was not important for Jesus to spend his time with children (*Matt.* 19:13–15). So for Jesus to use a child as the standard for kingdom entrance would have been shocking to the disciples. For Jesus to go on from there and say that the one who humbles himself to be like a child is the greatest in the kingdom would have been very far indeed from what they had expected.

Just what is it about children that Jesus is commending? The answers to this question have been many. In this context it is humility that is commended to us. Jesus says we must humble ourselves and become like children (verse 4). Some then go on to argue that children are for the most part very humble, and naturally put their trust in their parents and follow them faithfully. Such virtues are clearly among those prized in the kingdom of God but, frankly, they are not quite so universal among children as the theory proposes. Children can be selfish and arrogant, unconcerned about other children, and disrespectful to those in authority. *Prov.* 22:15 says, 'Folly is bound up in the heart of a child, but the rod of discipline drives it far from him.' Also, *Prov.* 29:15 says, 'The rod and reproof give wisdom, but a child left to himself brings shame to his mother.' The Scriptural view of children does not idolize them as innocent, naturally trusting, and humble. Such virtues must be cultivated in them; left to themselves they will bring shame upon their parents.

Why then does Jesus use children as his exemplar for kingdom greatness? The point that he is making is not that disciples in the kingdom are to become again what they were as children, or that they should become like children in their natural state, or even that they should become like the best children that they know. Rather, the point is that disciples must see themselves in the way that they see children. The disciples are self-centred men, ambitious for high places and rewards in the kingdom. They aspire after greatness, so they ask Jesus who is the greatest, so that they might become like him. Jesus does not rebuke them for ambition, and he does not despise their seeking after greatness. But he does take issue with their view of greatness, and he does despise selfish ambition.

He would redirect them in their thinking: 'Truly, I say to you, unless you turn and become like children, you will never enter the kingdom of heaven' (verse 3). His point is that they must view themselves in the way they view children. What we have here is the same as we found in Jesus' first statements about those in his kingdom, 'Blessed are the poor in spirit, for theirs is the kingdom of heaven' (*Matt.* 5:3); 'Blessed are the meek, for they shall inherit the earth' (*Matt.* 5:5).

CARING FOR OTHERS

It is when we see ourselves correctly that we can treat others correctly. After exhorting the disciples to become like children, he instructs them to receive other disciples as they would Jesus: 'Whoever receives one such child in my name receives me . . .' (verse 5). The focus here is on how we treat other disciples, not just anyone in general. True, we also have biblical commands concerning how we are to treat other people in general, regardless of whether or not they are Christians. But this passage focuses particularly upon how we are to treat 'one such child', the one who has humbled himself like a child to enter the kingdom of heaven. Such people are to be received and welcomed in Jesus' name (verse 5) because they bear his name. They are baptized into his name (*Matt.* 28:19), and called by his name (*Acts* 11:26).

Thus they are his, and how we treat those who are his is taken by him as the way we treat him. Consequently, we must be careful not to put a stumbling block in any disciple's way, that might tempt him to sin. Grave warning is given against such a thing, for Jesus says it would be better for us if we were to be drowned in the sea than to bear his wrath for causing his 'little ones' to sin (verse 6).

Furthermore, just as Jesus exhorted us to pluck out our eye or cut off our hand if either were to cause us to sin (*Matt.* 5:29–30), so now he urges us to do the same if what we do causes others to sin (verses 7–9). Twice he pronounces 'woe' upon those by whom temptation comes (verse 7). The words that follow do speak about our hand, or foot, or eye causing us to sin, but as they follow quickly upon the double warning in verse 7 we must see that in this context it is not merely our own sins that we are to guard against, but that we are also to guard against bringing temptations to sin into the lives of others.

SUMMARY

So long as we allow distorted views of greatness to predominate in our thinking, we will be slaves to selfish ambition and covetousness. But if we turn and humble ourselves, seeing ourselves like children (that is, seeing ourselves the way the disciples saw children), we will become fit instruments for service in the kingdom of Christ.

> *Have this mind among yourselves, which is yours in Christ Jesus, who, though he was in the form of God, did not regard equality with God a thing to be grasped, but made himself nothing, taking the form of a servant, being born in the likeness of men* (Phil. 2:5–7).

42

The Seeker of Lost Sheep

'See that you do not despise one of these little ones. For I tell you that in heaven their angels always see the face of my Father who is in heaven. ¹² What do you think? If a man has a hundred sheep, and one of them has gone astray, does he not leave the ninety-nine on the mountains and go in search of the one that went astray? ¹³ And if he finds it, truly, I say to you, he rejoices over it more than over the ninety-nine that never went astray. ¹⁴ So it is not the will of my Father who is in heaven that one of these little ones should perish. ¹⁵ If your brother sins against you, go and tell him his fault, between you and him alone. If he listens to you, you have gained your brother. ¹⁶ But if he does not listen, take one or two others along with you, that every charge may be established by the evidence of two or three witnesses. ¹⁷ If he refuses to listen to them, tell it to the church. And if he refuses to listen even to the church, let him be to you as a Gentile and a tax collector. ¹⁸ Truly, I say to you, whatever you bind on earth shall be bound in heaven, and whatever you loose on earth shall be loosed in heaven. ¹⁹ Again I say to you, if two of you agree on earth about anything they ask, it will be done for them by my Father in heaven. ²⁰ For where two or three are gathered in my name, there am I among them' (Matt. 18:10–20).

This section continues the theme of caring for one another within the family of God. Jesus' 'little ones' are dear to him, and each must be dear to us as well, if we too would belong to that family. The previous section ended by warning us against causing one of Christ's 'little ones' to fall into temptation. This section warns us against neglecting them if they do.

LOVING EACH ONE

It would be hard to imagine a passage of Scripture which emphasized more the concern that Christ has for each one of his sheep than this one. The passage opens with stiff warning against despising one of Christ's disciples. The reason behind this warning is rather puzzling: 'See that you do not despise one of these little ones. For I tell you that in heaven their angels always see the face of my Father who is in heaven' (verse 10). At first reading it looks like an endorsement of the widespread belief in 'guardian angels' for each of Christ's disciples. There are, however, some difficulties with this view, since Scripture nowhere clearly teaches it. Other interpretations have been offered. One is the idea that by 'angel' is meant the soul of a person who has died. *Acts* 12:15 might indicate this view. Whether this or some other interpretation proves to be best, the main point seems to be that each believer is somehow or at sometime to be represented or present before the face of God, and if so, that person must be of great value to God. Hence, to despise one who is so favoured by God is surely a great sin. We must see to it that we do not despise one who has or will have access to the very presence of God.

Further support for the high value placed on each person belonging to Christ is provided by the parable of the lost sheep that follows. If a shepherd who has one hundred sheep loses just one, he will leave the ninety-nine and go in search of the one that went astray. When he finds it, he rejoices over it more than over the ninety-nine that never went astray. 'So,' Jesus tells us, 'it is not the will of my Father who is in heaven that one of these little ones should perish' (verse 14). Each one of his sheep is so valuable that the shepherd will always go and seek for the one which has gone astray, regardless of how many others he might have.

SEEKING FOR LOST SHEEP

The next passage (verses 15-20) is generally regarded as the foundation passage for church discipline, establishing in the church power for dealing with persistent sin in the life of a believer, even to the point of excommunication. The passage clearly establishes that power in the church. It is imperative, however, that this power be rightly understood, and paying attention to what comes before it and after it will provide us with that right understanding.

Immediately before this passage we are told in verse 14 that it is not the will of the Father that even one of his little ones should perish. Then in verse 15 we are told what we should do if one of the little ones takes a path that might cause him to perish: we are to go in search of this lost sheep. First we go privately and tell him his fault. If we do not succeed in turning him back from his sin, we are to take one or two others with us, so that the fact of his sin and the need for his repentance might be confirmed by two or three witnesses. If that does not succeed we are to tell the church. This would mean informing the elders of the church, who are responsible for watching over the flock (*Ezek.* 34:1–6, *Acts* 20:28, *Heb.* 13:17). If the wayward sheep will not even listen to the church, then he must become to us like a Gentile and a tax collector.

Notice the transition that has taken place: the sheep that goes astray is a 'brother' at the beginning of the process (verse 15), one whom we regard as a fellow Christian; but when the presumed 'brother' persists in his sin against all patient and persistent appeals from other Christians and finally from the whole church, then he can no longer be regarded as a brother but as an outsider to the family of God, as Gentiles and tax collectors were regarded as outsiders to the Jewish people. This does not mean that we treat such people rudely or with contempt, but that we no longer regard them as fellow Christians. They now become the focus of the church's evangelistic efforts, whereas previously they were the focus of the church's pastoral care. All those previous efforts were aimed at reclaiming the person from a way of sin, including the final step of excommunication. Excommunication, then, is not intended to punish the sinner. It too is aimed at reclaiming the sinner. Thus, Paul calls for the excommunication of one wayward soul in hopes that his soul may be saved (*1 Cor.* 5:4–5).

The exercise of church discipline is always controversial in the life of a church. Many do not understand it and perceive it as harsh and judgmental, as foreign to the spirit of Jesus. Yet it is Jesus himself who commands it, and the reason is not hard to understand when it is understood in its context. Church discipline is the Christ-appointed means for seeking after lost sheep. A church that fails to practise church discipline is a church that does not seek after lost sheep. It is content to stay with the ninety-nine that remain, and to forget about the one who has gone astray. Not so the Good Shepherd, for it is not the will of his Father that even one of his little ones should perish.

Church discipline is even more than that. It is not only the Christ-appointed means through which we are to seek after lost sheep; it is also one means by which Christ himself seeks after lost sheep: 'For where two or three are gathered in my name, there am I among them' (verse 20). In our faithful shepherding of one another, and in faithful shepherding by elders in the church, the Great Shepherd of the sheep himself is present to act. By the shepherds whom he has called to watch over his flock, and by the Word and Spirit he has given to us, Christ himself acts 'to bind' and 'to loose', to forgive or retain sins. Such faithfulness on our part makes visible the work of Christ among his people, and what we do on earth then faithfully reflects what is done in heaven.

SUMMARY

Each one of those who comes to Christ is important to him, and each must be important to us. We must not despise Christ's 'little ones' by ignoring that one who goes astray. We ought to seek for him, in just the loving and persistent manner that Christ has appointed.

> *My brothers, if anyone among you wanders from the truth and someone brings him back, let him know that whoever brings back a sinner from his wandering will save his soul from death and will cover a multitude of sins* (James 5:19–20).

43

Forgiving Your Brother

*T*hen Peter came up and said to him, 'Lord, how often will my
brother sin against me, and I forgive him? As many as seven
times?' [22] Jesus said to him, 'I do not say to you seven times, but seventy
times seven. [23] Therefore the kingdom of heaven may be compared to a
king who wished to settle accounts with his servants. [24] When he began
to settle, one was brought to him who owed him ten thousand talents.
[25] And since he could not pay, his master ordered him to be sold, with
his wife and children and all that he had, and payment to be made.
[26] So the servant fell on his knees, imploring him, "Have patience
with me, and I will pay you everything." [27] And out of pity for him,
the master of that servant released him and forgave him the debt. [28]
But when that same servant went out, he found one of his fellow servants who owed him a hundred denarii, and seizing him, he began to
choke him, saying, "Pay what you owe." [29] So his fellow servant fell
down and pleaded with him, "Have patience with me, and I will pay
you." [30] He refused and went and put him in prison until he should
pay the debt. [31] When his fellow servants saw what had taken place,
they were greatly distressed, and they went and reported to their master all that had taken place. [32] Then his master summoned him and
said to him, "You wicked servant! I forgave you all that debt because
you pleaded with me. [33] And should not you have had mercy on your
fellow servant, as I had mercy on you?" [34] And in anger his master
delivered him to the jailers, until he should pay all his debt. [35] So also
my heavenly Father will do to every one of you, if you do not forgive
your brother from your heart'* (Matt. 18:21–35).

I n the last chapter the point was made that the section on church
discipline (verses 15–20) must be understood in the light of
both what comes before and what comes after. The parable of the
lost sheep enabled us to see that church discipline is the means
appointed and employed by Christ himself to seek after lost sheep.

In this chapter, we shall see that it is also the means by which the grace of Christ is revealed to his people.

THE BROTHER RETURNS

The previous section in Matthew ended on the sad though still hopeful note of a brother who went away into sin and did not turn back when he was reproached by the church. But what shall we do if the brother does repent? We rejoice, of course (verse 13). But what if this happens time and time again? What if our brother sins often against us? Peter wonders just how often an erring brother is to be forgiven – as many as seven times? Peter's question is not putting a limit on the number of times a brother is to be forgiven. In Jewish thinking, seven is the number of completion, so what Peter is really asking is whether we are obligated to forgive a brother *every* time he repents. Jesus' answer indicates that we are, and he intensifies the seven with 'seventy times seven' (verse 22): thus, not only should we forgive our brother every time he repents, but *every, every, every* time!

THE UNFORGIVING SERVANT

To support this teaching Jesus tells the parable of the unforgiving servant. A king wished to settle accounts with his servants. One servant owed him ten thousand talents. A 'talent' is both a measure of weight and a unit of coinage. How much did he owe? It is hard for us to put an exact amount upon this, as scholarly estimates in commentaries and dictionaries vary widely. We can perhaps gain some perspective by considering that Solomon's annual revenue was 666 talents of gold (*1 Kings* 10:14) and that David gave of his own wealth for the construction of the temple 3,000 talents of gold and 7,000 talents of silver (*1 Chron.* 29:4). So in Jesus' parable we are to picture a king's servant in debt to that king an amount roughly equivalent to David's personal contribution for the temple or fifteen years of Solomon's annual revenues. Clearly, this is an amount very far beyond anything that would be normal.

The servant is of course unable to pay the debt, so the king orders the man to be sold into slavery, along with his wife, his children, and all that he has. The man begs the king to be patient with him, and promises that he will repay him everything. The request is laughable, given the size of the debt. More time will be of no use to him, for the debt is impossibly large. Yet, amazingly, the king forgives the whole debt. He does not merely delay the time when the servant must pay, as had been requested. The king forgives all the debt that he owed.

Shortly thereafter, however, this same servant meets a fellow servant, who owes him a hundred denarii. A *denarius* was a day's wage for a common labourer, so the debt in view is about four month's pay. By comparison with the debt of ten thousand talents, this debt is a small pittance. The servant whose debt was forgiven by the king began to choke his fellow servant and demanded that he pay what he owed. The fellow servant begged the other to be patient and promised that he would repay all that he owed. But the servant who was owed the money would not be patient, and put his fellow servant into prison until he paid his debt. When the king heard of this, he summoned the unforgiving servant and rebuked him as wicked, saying that since he had been forgiven his debt he should likewise have forgiven his fellow. Then the king delivered that servant to the jailers, just as he had his fellow. Jesus then gives this solemn warning, 'So also my heavenly Father will do to every one of you, if you do not forgive your brother from your heart' (verse 35).

THE UNFORGIVING KING

Clearly this parable teaches us the necessity of forgiving our brothers if we ourselves have been forgiven. The king said, 'You wicked servant! I forgave you all that debt because you pleaded with me. And should not you have had mercy on your fellow servant, as I had mercy on you?' (verses 32–33). The point here is the same as we found in the Sermon on the Mount, 'For if you forgive others their trespasses, your heavenly Father will also forgive you, but if you do not forgive others their trespasses, neither will your Father in heaven forgive your trespasses' (*Matt.* 6:14–15).

In the parable, our sin before God is represented by the debt of ten thousand talents, an impossibly large amount that we could never repay. Now we see the purpose of introducing this wildly exaggerated figure for a servant's debt: it serves as an understatement of our own debt to God. But is the parable also teaching that those who have been forgiven their sins can forfeit that forgiveness if they fail to forgive others? To deduce that conclusion would be to push the parable too far. Not every detail in a parable is there to make a point. To suppose that God would grant forgiveness to a person, only to cancel that forgiveness later, would be to suppose that the work of Christ was not sufficient to cover all our sins. It would imply that one who came into salvation could fall from that salvation. Both of these ideas are foreign to the New Testament teaching. Jesus says that the one who comes to him he will never cast out (*John* 6:37). Likewise his apostle John tells us that if we confess our sins, he will forgive us our sins and cleanse us from all unrighteousness (*1 John* 1:9). What the parable is saying is that those who are forgiven will forgive, and thus that those who do not forgive are those who have not been forgiven. Saving and forgiving grace is transforming grace, and those who receive it from God must and can also give it to others. Those who do show it are those who know it, who have experienced that work of forgiveness in their own hearts. Thus those who are unforgiving can expect to meet an unforgiving king at the last day.

SUMMARY

Matthew 18 is addressed to the disciples about how to live within the family of God. We must humble ourselves to be like children, that we may care for one another as we should: receiving one another, guarding one another from temptation, caring for one another in pursuing after righteousness, and forgiving one another when we fail.

> *Beloved, let us love one another, for love is from God, and whoever loves has been born of God and knows God. Anyone who does not love does not know God, because God is love* (1 John 4:7–8).

44

Family Matters

*N*ow *when Jesus had finished these sayings, he went away from Galilee and entered the region of Judea beyond the Jordan. ² And large crowds followed him, and he healed them there. ³ And Pharisees came up to him and tested him by asking, 'Is it lawful to divorce one's wife for any cause?' ⁴ He answered, 'Have you not read that he who created them from the beginning made them male and female, ⁵ and said, "Therefore a man shall leave his father and his mother and hold fast to his wife, and the two shall become one flesh"? ⁶ So they are no longer two but one flesh. What therefore God has joined together, let not man separate.' ⁷ They said to him, 'Why then did Moses command one to give a certificate of divorce and to send her away?' ⁸ He said to them, 'Because of your hardness of heart Moses allowed you to divorce your wives, but from the beginning it was not so. ⁹ And I say to you: whoever divorces his wife, except for sexual immorality, and marries another, commits adultery.' ¹⁰ The disciples said to him, 'If such is the case of a man with his wife, it is better not to marry.' ¹¹ But he said to them, 'Not everyone can receive this saying, but only those to whom it is given. ¹² For there are eunuchs who have been so from birth, and there are eunuchs who have been made eunuchs by men, and there are eunuchs who have made themselves eunuchs for the sake of the kingdom of heaven. Let the one who is able to receive this receive it.' ¹³ Then children were brought to him that he might lay his hands on them and pray. The disciples rebuked the people, ¹⁴ but Jesus said, 'Let the little children come to me and do not hinder them, for to such belongs the kingdom of heaven.' ¹⁵ And he laid his hands on them and went away* (Matt. 19:1–15).

The first two verses of this chapter are the conclusion to the long discourse of Matthew 18, using the common formula to signal the end of the discourse and the transition to a new section ('Now when Jesus had finished these sayings . . .'). This transition also marks the end of the Galilean ministry in Matthew. Jesus now enters the region of Judea beyond the Jordan. His movements now are toward Jerusalem, where the cross awaits him. But there is still much ministry to accomplish before that time.

Large crowds still follow him, and he heals them (verse 2). Jesus is still concerned to make known, and to make clear, the nature of his kingdom. The two stories contained in this section provide a kingdom perspective on marriage and on children.

HARD-HEARTED PHARISEES

The Pharisees come to Jesus in order to test him (verse 3). Their question is about divorce, yet the aim is not to discover God's will for marriage and divorce; rather, they aim to entrap Jesus and impale him on the horns of a dilemma. As we shall see, the problem the Pharisees are having over divorce is the same problem they are having with Jesus – in their hardness of heart they are not seeking after God's purposes in life.

There were two schools of thought among the Jews at that time on the question of divorce:

According to one school, a man could divorce his wife 'for any cause' at all. Rabbinic examples include displeasing the man in any way, even burning his meal.

According to the other school, however, only a serious offence like adultery could justify a divorce. The Pharisees want to know which position Jesus takes. Either way, he will make some enemies.

Jesus' answer is not what either side expected. He begins by objecting to their starting point. They look at marriage and ask how much freedom a man has to break the marriage bond. One side says he has unbounded freedom, 'for any cause', while the other says his freedom is limited to serious offences. But Jesus says their starting point should be God's original purpose for marriage, that two people should become one flesh, and that what God has joined together no one should separate (*Gen.* 2:24). The concern must be with how marriages can be sustained, not on how much freedom we have to dissolve them. So the Pharisees have started at the wrong place. This can be seen by looking at the primary text being debated among them, *Deut.* 24:1–4.

This passage does not deal directly with the question of whether it is permissible to divorce; rather, the passage is aimed at prohibiting a certain type of remarriage if there has been a divorce. Divorce has been assumed to occur, but not necessarily endorsed. Jesus indicates this in pointing out that Moses gave this law due to the hardness of hearts in people.

The law was given because people were not adhering to God's purpose in marriage, and it sought to discourage divorce by erecting a 'no-return' provision for many of those who went forward in rebellion against the purposes of God. In effect, this law was saying, 'Think very carefully before you send away your wife for something "indecent" you have found in her, for it is very likely that you will never be able to undo the mistake you have made. For if after you divorce her, she marries another, you will never be able to have her as your wife again, even if her second husband dies or divorces her.'

Jesus does permit divorce where sexual immorality has occurred. This can be seen in the exception clause he attaches to his general statement about divorce: '. . . whoever divorces his wife, except for sexual immorality, and marries another, commits adultery' (verse 9). Entering a second marriage after divorce is an act of adultery, says Jesus, unless the divorce was for sexual immorality. In that case the second marriage would not be adulterous and would thus be permitted.

Notice, however, that divorce is only permitted by this provision; it is not required. Where possible, even a marriage wounded by sexual immorality need not be dissolved, as Hosea's marriage and God's marriage to Israel make plain (*Hos.* 1–3). Such marriages can reveal the healing power of forgiveness.

If that is so, then why does Jesus permit divorce at all? It is because of the hardness of our hearts. For if in hardness of heart one persists in rejection of God's purposes in marriage and pursues after sin, then he or she may indeed be cut off from the benefits of marriage, just as persistent sinners are cut off from the salvation of God. Divorce in such cases mirrors the judgment of God against the unrepentant just as faithful marriage indicates the union between Christ and his church (*Eph.* 5:22–33; see also *Additional Note* on pp. 299–300).

[183]

HARD-HEARTED DISCIPLES

It is not only Pharisees whose hearts need to be changed when it comes to marriage and serving the purposes of God. The disciples too show that their hearts are hardened. When they consider how stringent are the demands of God upon those who marry, they wonder if it is better never to marry at all.

Jesus does not dismiss the prospect of celibacy, for there are 'eunuchs' of various sorts—those who for one reason or another cannot or do not enter into marriage (verses 10–12). But not everyone can accept the demands of a celibate life. For those who can, they may devote themselves wholly to the service of the kingdom (as Jesus himself did, and Paul; see *1 Cor.* 7:1–7). For those who cannot live without the benefits of marriage, they should serve the kingdom through their full and faithful lifelong commitment to that marriage. The disciples seem to shrink from such demands, for their hearts also are much too much on their own desires and interests.

The need for change in the disciples' hearts is also seen in their treatment of children in the next verses (verses 13–15). Children had been brought to Jesus for prayer and blessing, but the disciples rebuked the people. They seem to have regarded children as an intrusion upon Jesus and his kingdom. Jesus rebuked the disciples, and commanded that the children be permitted to come to him, 'for to such belongs the kingdom of heaven' (verse 14).

Jesus finds children and marriage right at the centre of kingdom concerns. The good disciple will also view them in this way. Lifelong commitment to marriage, and welcoming children into the family, are prime kingdom services. Such commitments may seem to rob us of our freedom to do as we please, and to intrude themselves upon our own interests, but kingdom joys and blessings are found in the path of self-denial where kingdom concerns are uppermost.

SUMMARY

When we allow our hearts to be fixed upon selfish concerns and freedoms, we go against the calling and blessings of the kingdom of heaven. Jesus shows us that central to our kingdom calling is the support of lifelong marriage, and a view of children that sees them as dearly loved by our Saviour, the proper subjects of our prayers and his blessing. The one who finds a wife finds a good thing (*Prov.* 18:22), and children are a gift from the LORD (*Psa.* 127:3). The commitment required in caring for both is indeed great, but those who keep that commitment find great blessing. The one who loses his life for Jesus' sake will find it.

45

Kingdom Surprises

A nd behold, a man came up to him, saying, 'Teacher, what good deed must I do to have eternal life?' *17* And he said to him, 'Why do you ask me about what is good? There is only one who is good. If you would enter life, keep the commandments.' *18* He said to him, 'Which ones?' And Jesus said, 'You shall not murder, You shall not commit adultery, You shall not steal, You shall not bear false witness, *19* Honour your father and mother, and, You shall love your neighbour as yourself.' *20* The young man said to him, 'All these I have kept. What do I still lack?' *21* Jesus said to him, 'If you would be perfect, go, sell what you possess and give to the poor, and you will have treasure in heaven; and come, follow me.' *22* When the young man heard this he went away sorrowful, for he had great possessions. *23* And Jesus said to his disciples, 'Truly, I say to you, only with difficulty will a rich person enter the kingdom of heaven. *24* Again I tell you, it is easier for a camel to go through the eye of a needle than for a rich person to enter the kingdom of God.' *25* When the disciples heard this, they were greatly astonished, saying, 'Who then can be saved?' *26* But Jesus looked at them and said, 'With man this is impossible, but with God all things are possible.' *27* Then Peter said in reply, 'See, we have left everything and followed you. What then will we have?' *28* Jesus said to them, 'Truly, I say to you, in the new world, when the Son of Man will sit on his glorious throne, you who have followed me will also sit on twelve thrones, judging the twelve tribes of Israel. *29* And everyone who has left houses or brothers or sisters or father or mother or children or lands, for my name's sake, will receive a hundredfold and will inherit eternal life. *30* But many who are first will be last, and the last first' (Matt. 19:16–30).

T he next story is among the best known in Jesus' life. Following on the previous teachings about marriage and children, it continues the theme of the kingdom's great demands on those who would enter the kingdom. As in the previous examples too, it shows us that what stands in the way of whole-hearted service is the hardened condition of our hearts, so wedded are we to our own interests and the things of this world.

A SURPRISED RICH MAN

A man now comes to Jesus asking, 'Teacher, what good deed must I do to have eternal life?' (verse 16). Later we learn that he was a devoted keeper of the law and a young man who had great possessions (verses 20, 22). Luke also tells us that he was a ruler (*Luke* 18:18), a rather remarkable achievement for a young man in Jewish society, for their rulers were not called 'elders' for nothing.

The answer which Jesus gives to this young man might surprise readers of the New Testament. A similar question was asked by the Philippian jailer, and the answer given to him is now legendary: 'Believe in the Lord Jesus and you will be saved, you and your household' (*Acts* 16:31). Jesus does not answer in this way. Rather than the good news of the gospel, Jesus answers with the full demands of the law: 'If you would enter life, keep the commandments' (verse 17). Why the difference in the answers?

The man before Jesus is a very devout Jew (as evidenced by the fact that he became a ruler among his people), who devoted himself to keeping the commandments (verse 20). Commandment keeping is both a necessary and a noble thing, but it is also possible for such people to fall under a fatal deception: the supposition that salvation is to be earned through the doing of good things. The man in question suffered from this deception as Jesus perceived. To rid him of it, Jesus pressed upon him the full demands of the law: 'If you would be perfect, go, sell what you possess and give to the poor, and you will have treasure in heaven; and come, follow me' (verse 21). When the young man heard this he went away sorrowful, for he had great possessions (verse 22).

The purpose behind Jesus' manner of dealing with the man was to expose the true condition of his heart. Here was a man who considered himself to be a faithful keeper of the law (verse 20), but in fact he had not yet begun to keep the first and the tenth commandments (*Exod.* 20:3, 17). It is interesting to see that after

[187]

Jesus told him to keep the commandments, and he asked which ones, Jesus gave examples from what we call 'the second table of the law', the ones which deal with our relations with other people and are summarized in the commandment to love our neighbour as ourselves. But he did not mention the tenth, which deals with matters of the heart. Here the man failed miserably, for what was in his heart was a love for his great possessions, greater than his love for God. Indeed, so enslaving was this condition of his heart, that he went away from Jesus sorrowful rather than obey the commandment of the one who could give him eternal life.

ASTONISHED DISCIPLES

The rejection of the rich young man as too worldly-minded for entering the kingdom of God is not the surprise to us that it was to the disciples. For us, it is almost expected, for we tend to associate wealth with wickedness. In our literature, rich men are often the bad guys. But for the disciples, wealth was associated with the blessing of God, and those who had it were presumed to be righteous and in God's favour. When Jesus commented despairingly on the man's prospects for salvation, and those like him, the disciples were 'greatly astonished' and asked, 'Who then can be saved?' (verse 25). Jesus responded in a way which brings us full circle, back to the man's original question, 'With man this is impossible, but with God all things are possible' (verse 26).

The rich man had asked what good thing he could do to have eternal life. Jesus' answer to the disciples tells us there is nothing we can do. For if it is a matter for man to do something, then it is impossible. Our hearts are already enslaved to sin (*Gen.* 6:5, *Matt.* 15:19), and we are no more capable of changing our hearts than a leopard can his spots (*Jer.* 13:23).

But it is not impossible for God (verse 26). He can change and renew our hearts so that we may indeed repent of our sins against all the commandments, including the first and the tenth, and follow Jesus. We can indeed forsake all to follow him when he renews our hearts. Such grace had been given to the disciples, and this was evidenced by the fact that they had left everything and followed Jesus.

[188]

BIGGER SURPRISES TO COME

Judged by the standards of the day, the rich young man had risen to the top of the pile. By contrast, the disciples would not have amounted to much in the eyes of the world. But according to the standards of the kingdom, the rich young ruler fell to the bottom of the pile and the disciples rose to the top. Surprises of this sort will abound at the last day, according to Jesus, for 'many who are first will be last, and the last first' (verse 30). Such is the way of the kingdom of God, and we must learn from Jesus to see our world as he sees it, to value what he values, and to trust in him for all that will come. If in this world he calls us to great sacrifices, it will not always be so. For Jesus said to the twelve, and to all of his followers, 'Truly I say to you, in the new world, when the Son of Man will sit on his glorious throne, you who have followed me will also sit on twelve thrones, judging the twelve tribes of Israel. And everyone who has left houses or brothers or sisters or father or mother or children or lands, for my name's sake, will receive a hundredfold and will inherit eternal life' (verses 28–29).

SUMMARY

What looks good on the outside may be quite other than it appears. What looks like obedience to God's commandments may in fact be a covering for great idolatry. The kingdom of God brings with it great reversals, and the true nature of things will be revealed at the last day.

> *He has shown strength with his arm; he has scattered the proud in the thoughts of their hearts; he has brought down the mighty from their thrones and exalted those of humble estate; he has filled the hungry with good things, and the rich he has sent empty away* (Luke 1:51–53).

May we learn from the surprises of this chapter, and not be surprised at the last day.

46

Surprising Generosity

'*For* the kingdom of heaven is like a master of a house who went out early in the morning to hire labourers for his vineyard. [2] After agreeing with the labourers for a denarius a day, he sent them into his vineyard. [3] And going out about the third hour he saw others standing idle in the marketplace, [4] and to them he said, "You go into the vineyard too, and whatever is right I will give you." [5] So they went. Going out again about the sixth hour and the ninth hour, he did the same. [6] And about the eleventh hour he went out and found others standing. And he said to them, "Why do you stand here idle all day?" [7] They said to him, "Because no one has hired us." He said to them, "You go into the vineyard too." [8] And when evening came, the owner of the vineyard said to his foreman, "Call the labourers and pay them their wages, beginning with the last, up to the first." [9] And when those hired about the eleventh hour came, each of them received a denarius. [10] Now when those hired first came, they thought they would receive more, but each of them also received a denarius. [11] And on receiving it they grumbled at the master of the house, [12] saying, "These last worked only one hour, and you have made them equal to us who have borne the burden of the day and the scorching heat." [13] But he replied to one of them, "Friend, I am doing you no wrong. Did you not agree with me for a denarius? [14] Take what belongs to you and go. I choose to give to this last worker as I give to you. [15] Am I not allowed to do what I choose with what belongs to me? Or do you begrudge my generosity?" [16] So the last will be first, and the first last' (Matt. 20:1–16).

There is a very close link between this passage and the one we have just studied. We can see this by comparing the last verse in this passage with the last verse of the previous one (*Matt.* 19:30). The point made by the departure of the rich man and the promise of blessing to the disciples is that there are many who (now) are first that will be last, and many who (now) are last who will be first. The parable contained here is intended to illustrate the point further. As it does, we are surprised again.

GENEROUS TO A FAULT

Jesus tells us that the kingdom of heaven can be compared to a master of a house who hired workers for his vineyard. He went out early in the morning and hired labourers for the day, agreeing to pay them the standard wage, a *denarius*. Several times during the day he returned to the marketplace, each time hiring more labourers and promising to pay them 'whatever is right'. When the day was ended, he called his labourers together and began to pay them, beginning with the last hired and finishing with those who had been hired first. Those who were hired last were paid a full day's wage, one *denarius*. Consequently, those hired first began to expect much higher pay since they had laboured the whole day, in contrast to those who had laboured only an hour. But to their surprise and dismay, they too were paid a *denarius*, just as they had been promised at the beginning of the day. So they grumbled against the master of the house.

Those who laboured all the day considered that if the last hired were paid a *denarius*, having worked only one hour, they surely deserved far more, since they had borne 'the burden of the day and the scorching heat' (verse 12). They resented the fact that they had been made 'equal' to those who had worked only one hour. But they had considered a *denarius* a fair wage at the beginning of the day when they were hired, so why did they now grumble? Having agreed to a *denarius*, they were paid a *denarius*. Were they treated unfairly, just because others who did less than they did were paid an amount equal to their own?

To get at the meaning of this parable, we must remember that it is a parable. It is not given to us as an example to be followed in running a business and establishing a pay scale. It makes a point about the kingdom of heaven, and to do so it might depart from everyday practices, or even depart from just practices. To see this more clearly, consider the parable of the unjust steward in *Luke* 16:1–13. When faced with dismissal for bad management, the steward further mismanaged the master's wealth in order to ingratiate himself with his master's debtors, in hopes that they would be merciful to him when the master dismissed him. Jesus says the master commended the servant for his shrewdness (*Luke* 16:8). Jesus does not tell this parable to teach us how to manage someone's assets, nor does he tell us this to commend the dishonest servant for being dishonest. He tells it in order to teach us to consider the present in the light of the future and to plan accordingly. We too should look to the future and plan for it, just as the unjust steward did. Unlike him, however, we should not do evil in hopes that good may come. The parable is not intended to teach us that. So too here, the parable of the labourers in the vineyard is not intended as a model for business practice. It is intended to teach us about the Father's generosity, and to warn us about how easily we can despise it.

DESPISERS OF GRACE

Who are the people in Jesus' parable that correspond to those who despised the master's generosity? In other words, against whom was the parable told? A number of suggestions have been made. Very common is the idea that the parable is intended to warn the Jews against despising the grace of God that will be shown to the Gentiles. Like the workers hired early in the day, the Jews were called early in God's redemptive history. The point does seem to apply, but there is nothing in the immediate context to suggest such an interpretation.

Another suggestion has been the Pharisees and other self-righteous Jews. The parable warns them against despising the grace of God shown to sinners. Understood in this way, this parable would be similar to the Prodigal Son in *Luke* 15. That chapter opens by telling us that the tax collectors and sinners were drawing near to Jesus, and the Pharisees and scribes grumbled that Jesus received sinners and ate with them (*Luke* 15:1). So here, those hired first were the first to repent and to serve the master. Those hired last were lately called. One can indeed see how the parable would warn those who have served Christ a long time not to despise the grace he shows to those who have served only a short while. But again, nothing in the context indicates that specific interpretation either. Pharisees and the self-righteous are not in the nearby context.

Still another suggestion has been the disciples themselves. As we have seen, this parable is closely linked to the story of the rich young ruler in *Matt.* 19:16–30. In that story Peter asks, 'See, we have left everything and followed you. What then will we have?' (verse 27). Reward is clearly in his mind, and Jesus is quick to promise rewards to those who follow him. Perhaps the present parable is told to warn the disciples, indeed, to warn all who follow Jesus, against a mercenary approach to discipleship, expecting a just distribution of rewards on the basis of what one has earned by faithful service.

Contextually, this last interpretation would have more merit than the two others which have been suggested, but perhaps it also is too specific. That is, the parable might not have in mind any particular group of people who are represented by those who are first hired. The parable is told simply to emphasize that God's 'rewards', or better, his blessings, are distributed by a principle of grace, not merit. Our labours for the kingdom, great as they may be, involving great sacrifices such as leaving family or lands, do not earn us anything. While God will indeed return to us a hundred-fold and more, what he returns to each will be of grace; and he does not obligate himself to return more to those who sacrifice more than he does to those who sacrifice less. His grace is surprisingly generous, and sometimes seems to us generous to a fault. But that is only because of our works–righteousness mentality.

SUMMARY

Against whom is the parable told? Perhaps it is not told against anyone in particular, but to everyone in general, revealing to us all the surprising grace of God, and warning us not to despise that grace when we see it given to others, lest we be tempted to think they are less deserving of it than ourselves. For many who are first will be last, and the last first. 'It is the LORD. Let him do what seems good to him' (*1 Sam.* 3:18).

47

On Becoming Great

*A*nd as Jesus was going up to Jerusalem, he took the twelve disciples aside, and on the way he said to them, *¹⁸* 'See, we are going
up to Jerusalem. And the Son of Man will be delivered over to the
chief priests and scribes, and they will condemn him to death *¹⁹* and
deliver him over to the Gentiles to be mocked and flogged and crucified, and he will be raised on the third day.' *²⁰* Then the mother of the
sons of Zebedee came up to him with her sons, and kneeling before
him she asked him for something. *²¹* And he said to her, 'What do you
want?' She said to him, 'Say that these two sons of mine are to sit,
one at your right hand and one at your left, in your kingdom.' *²²* Jesus
answered, 'You do not know what you are asking. Are you able to
drink the cup that I am to drink?' They said to him, 'We are able.' *²³*
He said to them, 'You will drink my cup, but to sit at my right hand
and at my left is not mine to grant, but it is for those for whom it
has been prepared by my Father.' *²⁴* And when the ten heard it, they
were indignant at the two brothers. *²⁵* But Jesus called them to him
and said, 'You know that the rulers of the Gentiles lord it over them,
and their great ones exercise authority over them. *²⁶* It shall not be
so among you. But whoever would be great among you must be your
servant, *²⁷* and whoever would be first among you must be your slave,
²⁸ even as the Son of Man came not to be served but to serve, and to
give his life as a ransom for many'* (Matt. 20:17–28).

This section reminds us that Jesus is on his way to Jerusalem,
where he must suffer and die. The contrast between his own
mindset here and the one in his disciples, particularly James and
John, could not be greater. It challenges us to search our own hearts
and minds. Yet to find such insight into our own hearts is beyond
our abilities, for it is high, we cannot attain it (see *Psa.* 139:1–6).
Then let us ask the Lord to search us, and try us by this word, and
see if there be any such wicked ways in us.

THE CROSS BEFORE HIM

Matthew tells us that Jesus is on his way to Jerusalem and again he takes his disciples aside to tell them what awaits him there. He will be 'delivered over to the chief priests and the scribes, and they will condemn him to death and deliver him over to the Gentiles to be mocked and flogged and crucified, and be raised on the third day' (verses 18–19). Once again Jesus tells his disciples of his impending death in Jerusalem (see also *Matt.* 16:21; 17:12, 22–23), this time indicating specifically that he will be crucified. This reveals that the Romans will have a hand in his death, for only they had power to crucify.

This march of our Saviour to death by crucifixion must not be passed over lightly. The manner of death itself is torture, sometimes lasting days with intense pain and anguish. That in itself is enough to fear, but for Jesus his death will be more, much more indeed. For in his case, the wrath of God due to sin will be added to the mental and physical sufferings inflicted by men. He will not simply die as other men die, or even die as other crucified men die; he will die a judicial death, being 'smitten by God, and afflicted' (*Isa.* 53:4). To that cross he marches, humbling himself under the mighty hand of God (*1 Pet.* 5:6), becoming obedient to the point of death, even death on a cross (*Phil.* 2:8), entrusting himself to him who judges justly (*1 Pet.* 2:23). It was for the joy set before him that he would endure the cross, despising the shame, till he would sit down at the right hand of the throne of God. Following his example, we too must run the race that is set before us, looking to Jesus, the founder and perfecter of our faith (*Heb.* 12:1–2).

THE THRONE BEFORE THEM

No sooner has Jesus again told his disciples of the death which awaits him in Jerusalem than the mother of James and John comes to Jesus to ask him that her sons be granted the highest positions in his kingdom (verse 20). Their mother may be making the request, but it is not her ambition alone that is involved here. When Jesus answers, he speaks to them not to her (verse 22). Clearly, the fact of Jesus' death has yet to register with the disciples. Like Peter at the first revelation of his death, their minds are not on the things of

God, but on the things of men (*Matt.* 16:23). They seem to ignore the matter altogether and picture Jesus as coming into his kingdom. All they can think about are what places of privilege and power they will occupy, and they seek the highest for themselves. When Jesus asks them if they are able to drink the cup that he will drink, they reply that they are, though they have little comprehension of what they are saying. They have thrones in their minds, thrones of their own, at the right hand and left hand of Jesus' throne.

TRUE GREATNESS

It would be all too easy to look down on these disciples. It certainly was easy for the other disciples. When the other ten learned of this, they became indignant at James and John. But why? Probably not because it was so very insensitive a request coming right after Jesus had spoken of his impending death. They are indignant because they too aspire to these high places, and they are resentful of the fact that the brothers have been able to approach Jesus for this honour first, and that they have shamelessly enlisted their own mother to make the request on their behalf. They resent what has happened, but probably wished they had thought of the idea first.

It is at places like this that we can see ourselves in the disciples, as in a mirror dimly. We too want the seats of honour and the places of respect. We too want honours for ourselves and to be exalted over others. How easily are we offended when we do not receive the honour and respect we think we deserve. How different is the mindset of Jesus, and he calls us to the same mindset as he has. In his kingdom there is to be a very different mindset in those who are in high places. The rulers of the Gentiles lord it over those under them, but it is not to be so among the disciples. 'But whoever would be great among you must be your servant, and whoever would be first among you must be your slave, even as the Son of Man came not to be served but to serve, and to give his life as a ransom for many' (verses 26–28). Paul later saw this lesson clearly, and gave it to the Philippians to keep them from thinking of themselves more highly than they ought to think:

> *Do nothing from rivalry or conceit, but in humility count others more significant than yourselves. Let each of you look not only to his own interests, but also to the interests of others. Have this mind among*

yourselves, which is yours in Christ Jesus, who, though he was in the form of God, did not count equality with God a thing to be grasped, but made himself nothing, taking the form of a servant, being born in the likeness of men. And being found in human form, he humbled himself by becoming obedient to the point of death, even death on a cross. Therefore God has highly exalted him and bestowed on him the name that is above every name, so that at the name of Jesus every knee should bow, in heaven and on earth and under the earth, and every tongue confess that Jesus Christ is Lord, to the glory of God the Father (Phil. 2:3–11).

SUMMARY

Our Lord lived with the cross before him, coming not to be served but to serve, and to give his life as a ransom for many. In doing so, he gave us an example to follow in his footsteps (*1 Pet.* 2:21). Thinking more highly of ourselves than we should will lead to division among the people of God. It is love and humility that bind us together. May God purify our hearts and remove all pride from us. Let this be our prayer:

Search me, O God, and know my heart! Try me and know my thoughts! And see if there be any grievous way in me, and lead me in the way everlasting (Psa. 139:23–24).

48

Hosanna to the Son of David

*A*nd as they went out of Jericho, a great crowd followed him.
*30*And behold, there were two blind men sitting by the roadside,
and when they heard that Jesus was passing by, they cried out, 'Lord,
have mercy on us, Son of David!' *31* The crowd rebuked them, telling
them to be silent, but they cried out all the more, 'Lord, have mercy
on us, Son of David!' *32*And stopping, Jesus called them and said,
'What do you want me to do for you?' *33* They said to him, 'Lord, let
our eyes be opened.' *34* And Jesus in pity touched their eyes, and immediately they recovered their sight and followed him. *21:1* Now when
they drew near to Jerusalem and came to Bethphage, to the Mount
of Olives, then Jesus sent two disciples, *2* saying to them, 'Go into the
village in front of you, and immediately you will find a donkey tied,
and a colt with her. Untie them and bring them to me. *3* If anyone
says anything to you, you shall say, "The Lord needs them," and he
will send them at once.' *4* This took place to fulfil what was spoken
by the prophet, saying, *5* 'Say to the daughter of Zion, "Behold, your
king is coming to you, humble, and mounted on a donkey, and on a
colt, the foal of a beast of burden."' *6* The disciples went and did as
Jesus had directed them. *7* They brought the donkey and the colt and
put on them their cloaks, and he sat on them. *8* Most of the crowd
spread their cloaks on the road, and others cut branches from the trees
and spread them on the road. *9* And the crowds that went before him
and that followed him were shouting, 'Hosanna to the Son of David!
Blessed is he who comes in the name of the Lord! Hosanna in the
highest!' *10*And when he entered Jerusalem, the whole city was stirred
up, saying, 'Who is this?' *11* And the crowds said, 'This is the prophet
Jesus, from Nazareth of Galilee.' *12* And Jesus entered the temple and
drove out all who sold and bought in the temple, and he overturned
the tables of the money-changers and the seats of those who sold
pigeons. *13* He said to them, 'It is written, "My house shall be called a
house of prayer," but you make it a den of robbers.' *14* And the blind
and the lame came to him in the temple, and he healed them. *15* But

*when the chief priests and the scribes saw the wonderful things that
he did, and the children crying out in the temple, 'Hosanna to the
Son of David!' they were indignant, [16] and they said to him, 'Do
you hear what these are saying?' And Jesus said to them, 'Yes; have
you never read, "Out of the mouth of infants and nursing babies you
have prepared praise"?' [17] And leaving them, he went out of the city
to Bethany and lodged there. [18] In the morning, as he was returning
to the city, he became hungry. [19] And seeing a fig tree by the wayside,
he went to it and found nothing on it but only leaves. And he said to
it, 'May no fruit ever come from you again!' And the fig tree withered at once. [20] When the disciples saw it, they marvelled, saying,
'How did the fig tree wither at once?' [21] And Jesus answered them,
'Truly, I say to you, if you have faith and do not doubt, you will not
only do what has been done to the fig tree, but even if you say to this
mountain, "Be taken up and thrown into the sea," it will happen. [22]
And whatever you ask in prayer, you will receive, if you have faith'*
(Matt. 20:29–21:22).

The narrative of Jesus' procession into Jerusalem and its
aftermath (21:1–17) on what we now call Palm Sunday is well
known. Coming at the beginning of Matthew 21, we would be in-
clined to read it as the beginning of a new section, without considering it in connection with the healing of the two blind men in
20:29–34. But there is very good reason for connecting these two
passages. Both passages use the term 'Son of David' twice. Taken
together, four out of the ten times this phrase is applied to Jesus are
found in this one place. This title was among the first things to be
said of Jesus in this Gospel (*Matt.* 1:1). Clearly this section is very
important within Matthew's book.

LORD, HAVE MERCY ON US

As he left Jericho, a great crowd followed Jesus. Beside the road
were two blind men. When they heard that Jesus was passing by,
they cried out, 'Lord, have mercy on us, Son of David!' The crowd
rebuked them, and told them to be silent, but they cried out all the
more, 'Lord, have mercy on us, Son of David!' Mark and Luke also
tell this story, but they mention only one blind man. We have here
another story where Matthew gives us two witnesses, where Mark
and Luke give only one. The presence of two witnesses, telling us

twice that Jesus is the Son of David, puts great emphasis upon this point. Matthew does not want us to miss it.

The title also occurs once again in a context of healing, as in *Matt.* 9:27 with the other healing of two blind men. In fact, all the previous uses of the title are in the context of healing and exorcism (9:27, 12:23, 15:22), save the first use in the title to the Gospel. These healing miracles are important to Matthew in showing us the salvation that is brought by the Son of David. He delivers us from the dominion of Satan, and from the power and consequences of sin. The blind can *see* this plainly, and thus call out to him for mercy. When put off by the crowds, they call all the more. They know who Jesus is, and that is a boost to their faith. They will not be put off. They know that Jesus can heal them, and they believe that he will, if only they can make themselves known to him.

BEHOLD YOUR KING

Jesus' entrance into the city of Jerusalem is orchestrated in keeping with the prophecy of Zechariah, which Matthew quotes along with one of his fulfilment formulas (verses 4–5, see *Zech.* 9:9). As he mentioned two blind men in the previous narrative, so here we have two donkeys, a donkey and her colt. The animals are mentioned to make the tie to Zechariah's prophecy most direct. Jesus is thus announcing himself as King and Messiah, something only obliquely suggested before. The crowd cries out, 'Hosanna to the Son of David' (verse 9). The phrase means that salvation belongs to the Son of David, and is taken from *Psa.* 118:25–26, along with the benediction which follows. The healings given before (*Matt.* 20:29–34) and after his entrance into the city (21:14) demonstrate that salvation is found in him.

When Jesus comes to the temple, he is appalled by what he finds. The house of prayer (see Solomon's great prayer of dedication to that end, *1 Kings* 8:22–53) had become a den of robbers. Jesus drives out all who buy and sell there, and overturns the seats and tables of the money-changers and pigeon-sellers. Yet the blind and the lame come to him there and he heals them. The children cry out, 'Hosanna to the Son of David!' *Psa.* 118:26 indicated that the one who came in the name of the Lord would be blessed from the house of the Lord. The whole scene is replete with Messianic symbolism. The chief priests and the scribes become indignant over the acclamations, and call upon Jesus to silence his supporters (verse 15). But Jesus will not, and cites Scripture in support of the display (verse 16).

Matthew has built his case against the Jewish ruling authorities in dramatic fashion. Blind men and children can *see* clearly that Jesus is the Son of David, bringing salvation to his people. But the chief priests and the scribes remain *blind* to it all.

THE BARREN FIG TREE

After the busy events of Palm Sunday, Jesus left the city and lodged overnight in Bethany (verse 17). The next morning he returned to the city, and became hungry. He saw a fig tree by the roadside, but found nothing on it but leaves. He cursed the fig tree, saying, 'May no fruit ever come from you again!' (verse 19). At once the fig tree withered. The incident will seem very mysterious to modern readers. Admittedly, what Jesus found in Jerusalem was most disturbing. The temple, which ought to have been a house of prayer, had become a place of dishonest monetary exchange. The authorities stood in opposition to Jesus himself as the King of Israel. But why take out his anger on a tree?

The action is symbolic, as were the triumphal entry and the cleansing of the temple. Israel was represented in the Old Testament as a planting of the Lord, one intended to bear fruit (see *Psa.* 80:8–19, *Isa.* 5:1–7, *Ezek.* 17:1–24). The fig tree was in leaf, and thus should have begun to bear fruit. Mark says it was not the season for figs (*Mark* 11:13), meaning that the fruit would not have been fully ripe; but when the leaves appear there is a budding on the tree which is edible if not pleasant. The point is that the tree gave the appearance of having fruit, but it had none. So it was with the temple in Jerusalem. There was much activity there, people coming and going, animals bought and sacrificed, but it was fruitless ritual. The house of prayer had become a den of robbers. As the judgment of God would come upon that temple (*Matt.* 24: 1–2), so it came upon the fig tree. The withered fig tree foretold the ruined temple.

The disciples are amazed at the rapid withering of the tree, but Jesus assures them that prayer in faith can accomplish even greater

[201]

things (verses 21–22). The temple should have been such a place of transforming prayer, but a new temple, a new house of prayer, is now required. That temple will be built on the foundation of these disciples.

SUMMARY

The Son of David has now come to his temple with salvation and healing in his train. The blind can see it. The children can see it. Yet the religious authorities cannot, or will not. Oh that our eyes might be opened to see him in all his saving power!

> *Rejoice greatly, O daughter of Zion! Shout aloud, O daughter of Jerusalem! Behold, your king is coming to you; righteous and having salvation is he, humble and mounted on a donkey, on a colt, the foal of a donkey* (Zech. 9:9).

49

Confrontation with the Rulers

*A*nd when he entered the temple, the chief priests and the elders of the people came up to him as he was teaching, and said, 'By what authority are you doing these things, and who gave you this authority?' *24* Jesus answered them, 'I also will ask you one question, and if you tell me the answer, then I also will tell you by what authority I do these things. *25* The baptism of John, from where did it come? From heaven or from man?' And they discussed it among themselves, saying, 'If we say, "From heaven," he will say to us, "Why then did you not believe him?" *26* But if we say, "From man," we are afraid of the crowd, for they all hold that John was a prophet.' *27* So they answered Jesus, 'We do not know.' And he said to them, 'Neither will I tell you by what authority I do these things. *28* What do you think? A man had two sons. And he went to the first and said, "Son, go and work in the vineyard today." *29* And he answered, "I will not," but afterward he changed his mind and went. *30* And he went to the other son and said the same. And he answered, "I go, sir," but did not go. *31* Which of the two did the will of his father?' They said, 'The first.' Jesus said to them, 'Truly, I say to you, the tax collectors and the prostitutes go into the kingdom of God before you. *32* For John came to you in the way of righteousness, and you did not believe him, but the tax collectors and the prostitutes believed him. And even when you saw it, you did not afterward change your minds and believe him'* (Matt. 21:23–32).

From this point on there is a series of confrontations between Jesus and the Jewish authorities. Here it is with 'the chief priests and the elders', who make up the Sanhedrin, the Jewish ruling council. Later there will be confrontations with the Pharisees, the Sadducees, and the Herodians. The whole of Jewish leadership joins in opposition to Jesus, and they will draw into their conspiracy the Roman authorities as well. But all their efforts will be futile:

> *Why do the nations rage and the peoples plot in vain? The kings of the earth set themselves, and the rulers take counsel together, against the LORD and against his anointed . . .* (Psa. 2:1–2).

BY WHAT AUTHORITY?

The chief priests and the elders come to Jesus in the temple, demanding to know by what authority he acts. He has invaded the temple, driving out all who sold and bought in it, overturning the tables of the money-changers and the seats of those who sold pigeons (*Matt.* 21:12). In this action we can see the fulfilment of Malachi's prophecy:

> *Behold, I send my messenger and he will prepare the way before me. And the Lord whom you seek will suddenly come to his temple; and the messenger of the covenant in whom you delight, behold, he is coming, says the LORD of hosts. But who can endure the day of his coming, and who can stand when he appears?* (Mal. 3:1–2).

John the Baptist came as the messenger who prepared the way before the Lord. Now the Lord himself has come as the messenger of the covenant, the one in whom God's lawsuit against the covenant breakers reaches the stage of ultimatum. Symbolically Jesus has foreshadowed the judgment of God against his temple by his actions. But the covenant breakers remain unrepentant and now challenge Jesus about the authority he has to do what he has done.

Jesus responds with another question, asking them about the origin of John's baptism, whether it was from God or from men? This is no evasion by Jesus. It is part of his assault on the rulers. John was the herald for Jesus' ministry, the messenger sent before him to prepare his way. He was a man sent from God to bear witness to the light, that all might believe in him (*John* 1:9). All the people acknowledged him to be a prophet, yet the rulers did not accept John's testimony. John had pointed people to Jesus as the one who came after him, who is mightier than John, whose sandals John was not worthy to carry. John said of his own baptism that it was merely water, but the baptism of Jesus would be with the Holy

Spirit and fire. Something of that fire has just been seen in the temple, when Jesus drove out the money-changers.

Of course the rulers could not answer Jesus' question without either condemning themselves or incurring the opposition of the people, so they said they didn't know. Jesus then refused to answer their question, but in the parable which follows his answer is made perfectly clear.

THE TALE OF TWO SONS

Now Jesus tells them a parable about two sons. Both were commanded by their father to go and work in his vineyard. The 'vineyard' imagery is a clear reference to God's chosen people, as we have seen in the cursing of the fig tree. One son refuses to go at first, but later changes his mind and goes. The other at first says he will go, but afterwards does not go. Jesus asked the rulers which son did the father's will. The answer is obvious, and this time they do reply.

Ordinarily, Jesus takes time to explain his parables only to his disciples; to those outside his kingdom, Jesus hid his teaching in parables (*Matt.* 13:10–17). But this is an exception, and Jesus immediately provides the condemning interpretation: 'Truly I say to you, the tax collectors and the prostitutes go into the kingdom of God before you' (verse 31). They are the son who at first refused to go, but later changed his mind. At the preaching of John the Baptist they repented and believed. Their sins were forgiven and they were received as the children of God. The Jewish rulers, however, did not believe the preaching of John. They are the son who said he would serve but did not. Indeed, even when they could see the mighty work of God accomplished through John in the conversion of many sinners, still they did not repent and believe. Truly their hearts had been hardened into stone.

No wonder Jesus looks with such compassion upon the people, for they are truly sheep without a shepherd (*Matt.* 9:36). First in John, and then much more clearly in Jesus, the kingdom of God has drawn near. The mighty works of salvation appeared in Jesus:

> . . . *the blind receive their sight and the lame walk, lepers are cleansed and the deaf hear, and the dead are raised up, and the poor have good news preached to them* (Matt. 11:5).

No doubts should have remained, for the evidence was beyond reasonable doubt. Those unpersuaded were those who had hardened their hearts, who would not believe. Such are the rulers of the people: '. . . even when you saw it, you did not afterward change your minds and believe him' (verse 32). They are without excuse.

SUMMARY

The final confrontation between Jesus and his opponents has now begun. Earlier when Jesus met their opposition and knew their plots to take him, he withdrew into desolate places (*Matt.* 4:12, 12:15, 14:13, 15:21). This time there will be no withdrawal, for the time has now come for the Son of Man to be delivered up.

50

Repossessing the Kingdom

'*H*ear another parable. There was a master of a house who planted a vineyard and put a fence around it and dug a winepress
in it and built a tower and leased it to tenants, and went into another
country. *³⁴ When the season for fruit drew near, he sent his servants
to the tenants to get his fruit. *³⁵ And the tenants took his servants
and beat one, killed another, and stoned another. *³⁶ Again he sent
other servants, more than the first. And they did the same to them.
*³⁷ Finally he sent his son to them, saying, "They will respect my son."
*³⁸ But when the tenants saw the son, they said to themselves, "This
is the heir. Come, let us kill him and have his inheritance." *³⁹ And
they took him and threw him out of the vineyard and killed him.
*⁴⁰ When therefore the owner of the vineyard comes, what will he do
to those tenants?' *⁴¹ They said to him, 'He will put those wretches to
a miserable death and let out the vineyard to other tenants who will
give him the fruits in their seasons.' *⁴² Jesus said to them, 'Have you
never read in the Scriptures: "The stone that the builders rejected has
become the cornerstone; this was the Lord's doing, and it is marvellous
in our eyes"? *⁴³ Therefore I tell you, the kingdom of God will be taken
away from you and given to a people producing its fruits. *⁴⁴ And the
one who falls on this stone will be broken to pieces; and when it falls
on anyone, it will crush him.' *⁴⁵ When the chief priests and the Pharisees heard his parables, they perceived that he was speaking about
them. *⁴⁶ And although they were seeking to arrest him, they feared the
crowds, because they held him to be a prophet* (Matt.21:33-46).

In this section we have the parable of the wicked tenants, who
refused to pay tribute to their king and sought to take the kingdom for themselves. The parable is a survey of the whole history
of Israel in rejecting the prophets and killing God's Son. No interpretation is needed for this parable; even the chief priests and the
Pharisees can perceive its plain meaning (verse 45).

A VINEYARD PLANTED

The parable begins with the report of a master of a house 'who planted a vineyard and put a fence around it and dug a winepress in it and built a tower and leased it to tenants, and went into another country' (verse 33). These words are an unmistakable echo of the parable in *Isa.* 5:1–7. Israel is the vineyard planted by God, and everything necessary for its productivity has been done. In a new twist on the parable, Jesus says that it was leased out to tenants while the master went into another country. The 'tenants' are the caretakers of the vineyard, which would point to the religious authorities of Israel, the shepherds of God's flock, according to another image.

Ezekiel 34 tells a similar parable using the shepherd image. God's flock was committed to the care of shepherds. They were charged with guarding and caring for the flock, but the shepherds proved rebellious, not only neglecting the flock but exploiting it for their own gain. Because of this the flock will be removed from the care of these shepherds and new shepherds will be appointed. A similar ending will be given to the parable that Jesus now tells.

THE FRUIT WITHHELD

The purpose of the vineyard is to produce fruit. In Isaiah's parable, the fruit proves to be bad, an indictment of the whole nation. But in Jesus' adaptation of the parable, the problem is not with the vineyard's fruit. Rather, when the time comes for the tenants to pay tribute, to yield up the portion of the harvest rightfully belonging to the master, the tenants refuse to do so. This sharpens the parable so that it more directly focuses on the sins of the leaders. Indeed, not only do they refuse to pay, they shamefully mistreat the servants sent by the master to collect the tribute: one they beat, one they killed, and another they stoned. More servants were sent, so patient was the master. These servants were likewise rejected. Finally, the master sends his son. This really sharpens the parable, for it clearly aims to distinguish Jesus as God's Son, not merely another of his servants. Here Jesus provides us with the inner thoughts of the master, 'They will respect my son' (verse 37). Again, the master is shown to be very patient, perhaps even suggesting that he is willing to overlook all the previous rebellion and the mistreatment of his servants. But when the tenants saw him, their rebellion grew even worse. They plotted to kill the son so that the inheritance could be theirs.

The parable provides a quick overview of Israel's persistent rebellion through the years, and her rejection of the prophets. Jesus will later make this plain in his lament over the city.

> *O Jerusalem, Jerusalem, the city that kills the prophets and stones those who are sent to it! How often would I have gathered your children as a hen gathers her brood under her wings, and you would not!* (Matt. 23:37).

THE JUDGMENT FALLS

In the parable the tenants seize the son, throw him out of the vineyard, and kill him. The detail of throwing him out of the vineyard perhaps points to Jesus being crucified outside the city, a way of expressing total rejection (see *Heb*. 13:11–13). Jesus now asks, 'When therefore the owner of the vineyard comes, what will he do to those tenants?' (verse 40). Interestingly, they provide the answer to Jesus' question, showing clearly the guilt of those tenants: 'He will put those wretches to a miserable death and let out the vineyard to other tenants who will give him the fruits in their seasons' (verse 41). Jesus puts all of this in the context of *Psa*. 118:22–23: 'The stone that the builders rejected has become the cornerstone; this was the Lord's doing, and it is marvellous in our eyes.' Then Jesus spells out the application of the parable in unmistakable terms:

> *Therefore I tell you, the kingdom of God will be taken away from you and given to a people producing its fruits. And the one who falls on this stone will be broken to pieces; and when it falls on anyone, it will crush him* (verses 43–44).

The 'stone' which the builders have rejected will prove to be the stone that crushes them. They will not only lose their place of leadership, but will in fact come to a miserable death, just as they predicted for the wicked tenants.

SUMMARY

This parable, like Ezekiel's, is focused especially upon the religious leadership of Israel. They are unworthy shepherds and wicked tenants. The challenge of this passage is therefore addressed most directly to those in leadership among the people of God. They are called to be shepherds, husbandmen, and builders among God's people. Their master deserves a proper return, the fruit of their labours in worship and service. When God sees that his flock is being neglected and exploited, he rescues his flock from those leaders, and delivers them into the care of others, for he has compassion on his sheep:

And I will give you shepherds after my own heart, who will feed you with knowledge and understanding (Jer. 3:15).

Let us be thankful for the good shepherds that are given by the Great Shepherd of the sheep, and let us follow them faithfully, that our God might have the tribute that is due to his name.

51

The Wedding Feast

*A*nd again Jesus spoke to them in parables, saying, *²* '*The kingdom of heaven may be compared to a king who gave a wedding feast for his son, ³ and sent his servants to call those who were invited to the wedding feast, but they would not come. ⁴ Again he sent other servants, saying, "Tell those who are invited, See, I have prepared my dinner, my oxen and my fat calves have been slaughtered, and everything is ready. Come to the wedding feast." ⁵ But they paid no attention and went off, one to his farm, another to his business, ⁶ while the rest seized his servants, treated them shamefully, and killed them. ⁷ The king was angry, and he sent his troops and destroyed those murderers and burned their city. ⁸ Then he said to his servants, "The wedding feast is ready, but those invited were not worthy. ⁹ Go therefore to the main roads and invite to the wedding feast as many as you find." ¹⁰ And those servants went out into the roads and gathered all whom they found, both bad and good. So the wedding hall was filled with guests. ¹¹ But when the king came in to look at the guests, he saw there a man who had no wedding garment. ¹² And he said to him, "Friend, how did you get in here without a wedding garment?" And he was speechless. ¹³ Then the king said to the attendants, "Bind him hand and foot and cast him into the outer darkness. In that place there will be weeping and gnashing of teeth." ¹⁴ For many are called, but few are chosen'* (Matt. 22:1–14).

Here is a third parable which Jesus told about his rejection by the rulers. The rulers have perceived that Jesus is telling the parables about them (*Matt.* 21:45), yet their hearts remain hardened and grow even harder. They are seeking to arrest him, but they fear the crowds who take Jesus to be a prophet (21:46). In the next parable, Jesus again speaks of his rejection, but this time there is a new twist.

THE WEDDING FEAST

The parable concerns a king who gave a wedding feast for his son. This image is taken from the Old Testament where the covenant between God and his people is compared to a marriage (*Psa*. 45, *Ezek*. 16, *Hos*. 1–3). The New Testament likewise delights in this image. Indeed, Paul's treatment of this theme in *Eph*. 5:22-33 suggests that it is not a bare analogy, where marriage between a man and a woman is simply likened to the relationship between God and his people. Paul says that the one-flesh relationship between husband and wife is a profound mystery which refers to Christ and the church (*Eph*. 5:32).

In the New Testament a 'mystery' is not something obscure and unknown, but something previously hidden and now revealed (see *Eph*. 3:1–6). Thus, human marriage was specially created to reveal to us the nature of the union between Christ and his church. Notice then how at the beginning of the Bible we have the marriage of Adam and Eve (*Gen*. 2:18–25) and at the end of the Bible we have the marriage of Christ and his church (*Rev*. 19:6–10, 21:1–14). The first anticipates the second, and so when Christ appears the mystery in marriage which has been hidden for ages is now revealed.

The marriage image so powerfully expresses the union between Christ and his church that it is the capstone of the whole biblical revelation. Consequently, when Jesus tells a parable about the wedding of the king's son he is dealing with the very pinnacle of history, the main purpose of all creation.

So if we hear when the king sends out his servants to invite people to the wedding that the invitation is refused, we are dealing with a rejection of the whole purpose of God. The patience of God is revealed in that when the first invitation is refused he sends out a second (verses 3–6).

As in the parable of the wicked tenants, the servants who are sent out are mistreated and killed. This at last exhausts the patience of the king and arouses his anger. He sends forth his troops and destroys those murderers and burns their city (verse 7). We have here a prediction of the destruction of Jerusalem that took place in AD 70.

NEW GUESTS INVITED

Those who were first invited to the wedding feast proved un-worthy. They were either indifferent to the invitation (verse 5) or hostile (verse 6). Judgment fell upon them all. But the king was determined to go on with his wedding feast, so he commanded his servants to go out to the roads and to invite as many as they found, both good and evil (verse 7). Now the wedding hall was filled with guests.

This portion of the parable reveals the preaching of the gospel to the Gentiles after Jesus is rejected by Israel. Now 'whosoever will' may come. All are invited to the wedding feast. The com-mission which is given to the church at Jesus' ascension is that they are to be his witnesses first in Jerusalem, then in all Judea and Samaria, and to the end of the earth (*Acts* 1:8). Even as the gospel message begins to spread, the invitation still goes first to the Jews (*Acts* 13:46, 18:6), and then to the Gentiles. All this is familiar to us, and readily understood.

NO WEDDING GARMENT

Then the parable takes a new and surprising twist. With the wed-ding hall now filled with guests (verse 10), we are expecting great rejoicing and the conclusion of the parable. But the celebration has no sooner begun than the king enters the hall to look at his guests and finds there a man who has no wedding garment. The king con-fronts the man and asks how he got in without a wedding garment. The man is speechless, which indicates that he knew he was guilty. The king promptly orders his servants to bind the man hand and foot, and to cast him into the outer darkness, where there is weep-ing and gnashing of teeth. These are familiar symbols to us of the final judgment.

The action of the king is both surprising and disturbing. Can he really be offended by the clothes some wear? Is he not a God who has compassion on the lowly? We are, however, dealing with symbols here, not with judgments on clothing. The concluding point of the parable is that many are called, but few are chosen. So the man in question is one who has been called but has not been chosen. His 'clothing' reveals this. What might this represent?

In the parable the Jewish rulers are represented by those who rejected the invitation to come to the wedding feast. They and others like them are those who have publicly repudiated Jesus. The man without the wedding garment is among those who have responded to the invitation, and have not rejected it. He has come to the wedding feast. This man represents all those who outwardly respond to the gospel invitation and come into the church. But they do not come with faith in Christ. They are like those in the crowds who followed Jesus, but did so for reasons other than true faith. In John's Gospel such people are actually described as 'believing' in Jesus, but the context makes clear that theirs is not a true faith (see *John* 2:23–25, 8:30–59). These are the tares which grow among the wheat. So the point Jesus is making is that it is not only those who openly reject Jesus who will be judged for unbelief. Even among those who do respond there will be those who have come for other reasons. They do not come in faith, and thus do not come to the wedding in the 'garments of salvation' and the 'robe of righteousness' (*Isa.* 61:10). These are the ones who come with an outward profession of faith, but their real trust is not in the finished work of Christ on the cross.

SUMMARY

God the King will have a bride for his Son. His guests have been called and chosen from all the tribes on the face of the earth. The invitation has gone out, to good and bad alike. For those who come in faith, clothed in the righteousness of Christ, there is a place at the wedding feast. But for those who reject the invitation, and for those who come while trusting in something other than Christ, there will be the judgment of the outer darkness, where there is weeping and gnashing of teeth.

52

Taxes and Widows

*T*hen the Pharisees went and plotted how to entangle him in his words. *16* And they sent their disciples to him, along with the Herodians, saying, 'Teacher, we know that you are true and teach the way of God truthfully, and you do not care about anyone's opinion, for you are not swayed by appearances. *17* Tell us, then, what you think. Is it lawful to pay taxes to Caesar, or not?' *18* But Jesus, aware of their malice, said, 'Why put me to the test, you hypocrites? *19* Show me the coin for the tax.' And they brought him a denarius. *20* And Jesus said to them, 'Whose likeness and inscription is this?' *21* They said, 'Caesar's.' Then he said to them, 'Therefore render to Caesar the things that are Caesar's, and to God the things that are God's.' *22* When they heard it, they marvelled. And they left him and went away. *23* The same day Sadducees came to him, who say that there is no resurrection, and they asked him a question, *24* saying, 'Teacher, Moses said, "If a man dies having no children, his brother must marry the widow and raise up children for his brother." *25* Now there were seven brothers among us. The first married and died, and having no children left his wife to his brother. *26* So too the second and third, down to the seventh. *27* After them all, the woman died. *28* In the resurrection, therefore, of the seven, whose wife will she be? For they all had her.' *29* But Jesus answered them, 'You are wrong, because you know neither the Scriptures nor the power of God. *30* For in the resurrection they neither marry nor are given in marriage, but are like angels in heaven. *31* And as for the resurrection of the dead, have you not read what was said to you by God: *32* "I am the God of Abraham, and the God of Isaac, and the God of Jacob"? He is not God of the dead, but of the living.' *33* And when the crowd heard it, they were astonished at his teaching (Matt. 22:15–33).

This section contains two attempts to entrap Jesus. One comes from the Pharisees, who enlist the Herodians for good measure. The other comes from the Sadducees. The first concerns the

[215]

question of paying taxes to Caesar, where taking one side or the other is sure to bring Jesus into controversy. The second concerns marriage in the life to come, an attempt by the resurrection-denying Sadducees to catch Jesus in an absurdity. Both attempts fail, with Jesus' opponents left marvelling and astonished.

RENDER TO CAESAR

The confrontation between Jesus and the religious leaders continues. Here the Pharisees come to entangle him in controversy, and they bring with them the Herodians. The Herodians are only mentioned this once in Matthew. They are Roman sympathizers, so their enlistment here by the Pharisees is quite strategic, since the question asked is whether it is lawful (in God's eyes) to pay taxes to the Romans. Rome's taxes were not popular with the people, as anyone can imagine. So the attempt here is to bring Jesus into disfavour with one group or another. If he supports the tax, he will lose favour with the people. If he opposes the tax, then Rome will regard him as an enemy.

Jesus' answer is now legendary, for its wit and wisdom. He tells them to render to Caesar the things that are Caesar's and to God the things which are God's (verse 21). This leaves a lot unsaid, and does not directly answer the question at all. But it does set the right framework for the question. It acknowledges that under God there are things that rightfully belong to Caesar. It also sets a limit to what Caesar may claim, for there are also things that belong only to God. Paul and Peter develop this idea more fully in *Rom.* 13:1–7 and *1 Pet.* 2:13–17. There we are taught that governments in this world have been instituted by God. They are for the purpose of restraining evil and promoting good. They are, in fact, servants of God for our good (*Rom.* 13:4). As we derive benefit from them, so we should make return to them by paying taxes (*Rom.* 13:6–7).

But there are limits to what governments can regulate. Caesar may not claim for himself the right to be worshipped. That belongs only to God. He may not call what is evil good, or what is good evil. That is for God to decide. He may not contravene any commandment of God. Thus the Sanhedrin, the Jewish 'Caesar', could not command the disciples not to preach in Jesus' name, for we must all obey God rather than men (*Acts* 4:19–20, 5:29). Whether it is a husband in the home, parents over their children, elders in the church, or rulers in the civil government, none may command what God has forbidden and none may forbid what God has commanded. Each has his proper sphere of authority, and those who are under that authority are obligated to obey within that sphere. But each is also limited by God in that sphere. When they go beyond their allotted bounds, their subjects are no longer obliged to obey them. Jesus has clearly provided us with a most helpful perspective on taxes and on much else besides.

RESURRECTION PUZZLES

On the very same day the Sadducees came to Jesus. Matthew informs us that the Sadducees do not believe in the resurrection. Luke also tells us that they did not believe in angels or spirits (*Acts* 23:8). As for 'spirits', what is meant is that they do not believe that there is a 'soul' or 'spirit' that survives our body after death. Thus the Sadducees do not believe in any form of afterlife at all. So their question about the resurrection is hypothetical, and its aim is to show that the doctrine involves absurdities.

The question concerns a woman who was widowed seven times. They wonder whose wife she will be in the resurrection since there were seven men who had married her in this life. Jesus replies that they are in error with their question, for they know neither the Scriptures nor the power of God. In the resurrection, says Jesus, people do not marry and are not given in marriage. In that respect, the resurrected are like angels, who also do not marry. So the woman will not be the wife of any of the seven. Jesus is not saying, however, that we *become* angels in the life to come. Following death and before the resurrection of the body, we will be spirits without bodies and so in that sense too and for that time will be like the angels. But that is an unnatural state for us, which Paul compares to being 'naked' and 'unclothed' (*2 Cor.* 5:1–5). In the resurrection we shall receive new bodies, like the resurrected body of Jesus (*1 Cor.* 15:12–58, *Phil.* 3:20–21), and only then will our redemption be complete. Jesus did not come to save only our souls, but our bodies too.

As for the resurrection itself, Jesus points them to the Scriptures. He asks if they have not read in the Scriptures what has been

[217]

said by God, 'I am the God of Abraham, and the God of Isaac, and the God of Jacob.' He says that God is not the God of the dead, but of the living. It is most interesting that Jesus points them to this oft-repeated phrase in the Scriptures. They are Sadducees, and they do not accept as Scripture anything but the five books of Moses, the Pentateuch. The standard Old Testament texts for the doctrine of the resurrection (*Isa.* 26:19, *Dan.* 12:2) would not be accepted by them. So Jesus sends them right to the Pentateuch, to a phrase whose present-tense verb had an eternal, theological significance which they had overlooked.

SUMMARY

In these two events, first the Pharisees and then the Sadducees attempt to bring Jesus into condemnation through his own words. Both attempts fail. What they had hoped to achieve was to make Jesus responsible for his own death, through teaching what was either heresy to the Jews or treason to the Romans. They are not able to trick Jesus into such things. If they are going to execute him, they will have to kill him in their own wickedness. They will not be able to find a just cause for putting him to death. Yet die he will, the just for the unjust, that he might bring us to God (*1 Pet.* 3:18), for that is why he came. Thanks be to God.

53

The Pharisees Strike Back

B ut when the Pharisees heard that he had silenced the Sadducees,
they gathered together. ³⁵ *And one of them, a lawyer, asked him
a question to test him.* ³⁶*'Teacher, which is the great commandment
in the Law?'* ³⁷ *And he said to him, 'You shall love the Lord your
God with all your heart and with all your soul and with all your
mind.* ³⁸ *This is the great and first commandment.* ³⁹ *And a second
is like it: You shall love your neighbour as yourself.* ⁴⁰ *On these two
commandments depend all the Law and the Prophets.'* ⁴¹ *Now while
the Pharisees were gathered together, Jesus asked them a question,* ⁴²
*saying, 'What do you think about the Christ? Whose son is he?' They
said to him, 'The son of David.'* ⁴³ *He said to them, 'How is it then
that David, in the Spirit, calls him Lord, saying,* ⁴⁴ *"The Lord said
to my Lord, Sit at my right hand, until I put your enemies under
your feet"?* ⁴⁵ *If then David calls him Lord, how is he his son?'* ⁴⁶ *And
no one was able to answer him a word, nor from that day did anyone
dare to ask him any more questions* (Matt. 22:34–46).

A nother attempt to entrap Jesus is found in this passage. The
Pharisees have heard that the Sadducees have been silenced by
Jesus (verse 34), so they plot together again. One of their lawyers
will lead the assault (verses 35–40). Then Jesus will turn the questions on them (verses 41–45). Once he has silenced the Pharisees,
no further attempts will be made to ask him any more questions
(verse 46). The next move by the religious leaders (26:3–5) will be
to resort to unjust means.

THE GREATEST COMMANDMENT

The Pharisees are once again trying to entrap Jesus and bring him
into controversy. Because of their scrupulous concern with matters of the law, debates among them about the relative importance

of the various laws were common. The attempt to find the most comprehensive statement of the law is therefore a natural development of such debates, and one that would appropriately challenge experts in the law. One such expert comes forth to test him, a type of legal Goliath coming forth from the camp of the Philistine Pharisees.

Jesus' answer cites *Deut.* 6:5, recited by the Jews daily, 'You shall love the Lord your God with all your heart and with all your soul and with all your mind.' The answer would have been neither unexpected nor controversial. Jesus is quick to add that there is a second that is like it, *Lev.* 19:18, 'You shall love your neighbour as yourself.' This too was already a principle highly regarded by the Jews, and the two commandments were perhaps already commonly treated as correlative. *Luke* 10:25–28 shows Jesus getting this same combination in reply from a lawyer. Jesus says that on these two commandments depend all the Law and the Prophets (verse 40).

It is important to see that these two commandments, both framed in positive rather than negative form, are offered as summaries of the whole law. The Jews traditionally counted 613 laws in the Old Testament. Many of these are in negative form, telling us what we are not to do. This is true even of the ten commandments, which are also a summary statement of the law. By summarizing the whole law by two commandments in positive form, Jesus shows us that laws given in negative form also have positive requirements, just as laws given in positive form have negative requirements. We can see this in Jesus' exposition of the sixth and seventh commandments in the Sermon on the Mount (*Matt.* 5:21–30). With each of these laws Jesus first begins by showing that the law deals with matters of the heart as well as with outward actions (5:22, 28), prohibiting thoughts and desires as well as actions that are unlawful toward others. Then Jesus derives positive duties from the laws necessary for the keeping of the commandments (5:23–26, 29–30). Love is indeed the fulfilment of the law (*Rom.* 13:8, 10).

GREAT DAVID'S GREATER SON

There is no reply from the lawyer when Jesus gives his summary of the law. Jesus himself then goes on the offensive. He has a question for the Pharisees, 'What do you think about the Christ? Whose son is he?' (verse 32). They are quick to reply, 'The son of David.' Jesus then has a follow-up question concerning *Psa.* 110:1: Why does David in the Spirit call him 'Lord' if the Christ is his son?

We should not miss the fact that here Jesus is saying and teaching that David wrote *Psa.* 110 'in the Spirit'. This rules out the possibility that David could have misspoken in this verse. It is Jesus' own view, and it was the view of his apostles, that whatever Scripture says, God says. This is not to say that the whole of Scripture was produced in a mechanical fashion, with nothing of the human author entering into the text. No, Scripture is both human and divine. The individual characteristics of particular human authors can be clearly seen. But this in no way takes away from the fact that the words of Scripture are also the very words of God. In this case, the verse gives us the words of David and the words of God by the Spirit. The case is similar to what Luke says in *Acts* 4:25 about *Psa.* 2:1–2: It was God 'who through the mouth of our father David, your servant, said by the Holy Spirit . . .'.

The question Jesus poses is indeed a deep one, and the Pharisees have no answer to it (verse 46). If David calls him 'Lord', then the Christ must be superior to David. But if he is David's son, then David must be 'lord' to him. How can it be both? Only the mystery of the incarnation can solve this enigma. The Christ is the son of David by being born in the line of David (*Matt.* 1:1-17). But he is the Lord of David since he is the eternal Son of God, the second person of the Trinity, conceived by the Holy Spirit and born of the Virgin Mary (*Matt.* 1:20). He is God and he is man, fully God and fully man, as the Scriptures have taught (*John* 1:1–18; *Phil.* 2:6–7; *Col.* 1:19, 2:9), and the ancient creeds have declared (see the creeds of the councils of Nicaea and Chalcedon).

Following this exchange, Matthew tells us that from that day no one dared to ask him any more questions. His wisdom was the marvel of all, but his truth was not received by all. Receiving the truth is as much a matter of the heart as it is of the mind, and maybe more a matter of the heart. Earlier Jesus had already explained why his opponents did not receive his words: 'Whoever is of God hears the words of God. The reason why you do not hear them is that you are not of God' (*John* 8:47).

SUMMARY

Jesus' comprehensive knowledge of the law (verses 34–40) and his insight into the deep mysteries of the Scriptures (verses 41–46) make him just what Nicodemus found him to be, 'a teacher come from God' (*John* 3:2). Whatever he teaches must be true. Whatever he commands must be obeyed. Whatever he promises will surely be fulfilled. He who has ears to hear, let him hear.

54

Woes to Scribes and Pharisees

*T*hen *Jesus said to the crowds and to his disciples,* [2] *'The scribes
and the Pharisees sit on Moses' seat,* [3] *so practise and observe
whatever they tell you—but not what they do. For they preach, but
do not practise.* [4] *They tie up heavy burdens, hard to bear, and lay
them on people's shoulders, but they themselves are not willing to
move them with their finger.* [5] *They do all their deeds to be seen by
others. For they make their phylacteries broad and their fringes long,*
[6] *and they love the place of honour at feasts and the best seats in
the synagogues* [7] *and greetings in the marketplaces and being called
rabbi by others.* [8] *But you are not to be called rabbi, for you have one
teacher, and you are all brothers.* [9] *And call no man your father on
earth, for you have one Father, who is in heaven.* [10] *Neither be called
instructors, for you have one instructor, the Christ.* [11] *The greatest
among you shall be your servant.* [12] *Whoever exalts himself will be
humbled, and whoever humbles himself will be exalted.* [13] *But woe to
you, scribes and Pharisees, hypocrites! For you shut the kingdom of
heaven in people's faces. For you neither enter yourselves nor allow
those who would enter to go in.* [15] *Woe to you, scribes and Pharisees,
hypocrites! For you travel across sea and land to make a single proselyte, and when he becomes a proselyte, you make him twice as much
a child of hell as yourselves.* [16] *Woe to you, blind guides, who say, "If
anyone swears by the temple, it is nothing, but if anyone swears by
the gold of the temple, he is bound by his oath."* [17] *You blind fools!
For which is greater, the gold or the temple that has made the gold
sacred?* [18] *And you say, "If anyone swears by the altar, it is nothing,
but if anyone swears by the gift that is on the altar, he is bound by his
oath."* [19] *You blind men! For which is greater, the gift or the altar
that makes the gift sacred?* [20] *So whoever swears by the altar swears
by it and by everything on it.* [21] *And whoever swears by the temple
swears by it and by him who dwells in it.* [22] *And whoever swears by
heaven swears by the throne of God and by him who sits upon it.*
[23]*Woe to you, scribes and Pharisees, hypocrites! For you tithe mint*

and dill and cumin, and have neglected the weightier matters of the law: justice and mercy and faithfulness. These you ought to have done, without neglecting the others. [24] You blind guides, straining out a gnat and swallowing a camel! (Matt. 23:1–24).

Matthew 23 is a sustained critique of the religion of the scribes and the Pharisees, spoken by Jesus 'to the crowds and to the disciples' (verse 1). The audience also included a number of scribes and Pharisees and Jesus addresses them directly with seven pronouncements of woe in verses 13–36. The fact that this chapter forms a long discourse makes some wonder whether the final discourse in Matthew begins here, or whether this is the last part of the narrative before the final discourse of Chapters 24–25, which is spoken to the disciples alone. Understanding the passage is not affected by how it is classified, so we will not consider that question. We should note, however, that this chapter and the next two are parallel to the Sermon on the Mount (*Matt.* 5–7), spoken at the beginning of Jesus' public ministry. Both the sermon (*Matt.* 5:1–7:12) and the teaching of Chapter 23 focus on exposing the hypocrisy and errors of the scribes and Pharisees, and call the disciples to a very different life. The sermon ended with a view toward judgment against all false religion (*Matt.* 7:13–29). Chapters 24–25 magnify that presentation in great detail. Chapter 23 ends with Jesus' lament over Jerusalem for its history of rejecting the messengers of God and its refusal to turn and be healed. This marks the transition to the chapters on judgment that follow.

HUMILITY BEFORE EXALTATION

In the religion of the scribes and Pharisees, the aim is exaltation. Jesus, who can look upon the hearts of people, finds in the scribes and Pharisees the desire to be exalted among men. 'They do all their deeds to be seen by others . . . and they love the place of honour at feasts and the best seats in the synagogues and greetings in the marketplaces and being called rabbi by others' (verses 5–7). By contrast, the disciples are to be exactly opposite. They should not be concerned for titles and being acknowledged by others as teachers. When Jesus speaks against being called 'rabbi' and against calling others 'father' he is not prohibiting the use of certain words. The concern is how we view ourselves and others. We should not seek to become masters of others who follow after us as the scribes and Pharisees did their rabbis. The disciples are not to cultivate followers of themselves (verse 8). Nor should they seek another teacher to follow when Jesus is gone from them, making that one their father (verse 9). They are all brothers, and they have one father in heaven and one teacher, the Christ (verse 10). Seeking such honours takes one far from the path of true discipleship. Aiming for exaltation, they can expect to be humbled. But if they will humble themselves, they will be exalted.

BLIND GUIDES

After addressing the crowds and his disciples about the perversion of religion to be found in the scribes and Pharisees generally, Jesus turns directly to the scribes and Pharisees and pronounces seven woes upon them. The number seven is surely significant here, not as the exact number of faults to be found in the religion of the scribes and Pharisees, but as the number of completion, indicating a total failure of their religion and a complete rejection of it by Jesus. The first four woes concentrate on the danger this religion poses to others.

First, *the way of salvation is hidden by this religion.* The scribes and Pharisees themselves do not enter the kingdom by this road, and they shut the true door of salvation to all who follow after them (verse 13). Theirs is a religion of show and ritual, rather than of faith, humility, and sincerity of heart. Because it is focused on show and ritual, this form of religion concentrates on ritual acts of obedience, rather than on purity of heart. Consequently, in their religion, salvation is something that one achieves through ritual devotion and ceremonial obedience, rather than something one receives through faith. Simply put, it is a religion of works rather than grace; and mostly the emphasis is on ceremonial works, which are easier to do. Paul succinctly put the matter this way: 'What shall we say, then? That Gentiles who did not pursue righteousness have attained it, that is, a righteousness that is by faith; but that Israel who pursued a law that would lead to righteousness did not succeed in reaching that law. Why? Because they did not pursue it by faith, but as if it were based on works' (*Rom.* 9:30–32).

[225]

Second, *this form of religion gets worse as its passes from one to another.* Not only are their followers shut out of the kingdom of heaven, but they can become twice as much deserving of judgment as the scribes and Pharisees themselves (verse 14). Corrupt things done in moderation by the fathers are often carried to excess by the sons. So it is among the scribes and Pharisees. Some of their disciples will far exceed them in hypocrisy. We see this in the apostle Paul himself. A 'son of Pharisees' (*Acts* 23:6), a student of the chief rabbi of his time, Gamaliel (*Acts* 5:34, 22:3), Paul became very zealous for the law (*Acts* 26:5, *Phil.* 3:3–6). Yet without knowing it he became the very chief of sinners by his zeal (*2 Tim.* 1:15). The very law which promised life to him, proved to be death to him, for sin had deceived him through the law (*Rom.* 7:9–11). Paul the 'Pharisee of the Pharisees' was just the kind of fruit that grew from the vine of this religion.

Third, *they are blind guides whose 'casuistry' (handling of cases) betrays the most foolish mistakes.* Jesus illustrates this by their manner of handling vows (verses 16–22): they consider swearing by the temple a non-binding oath, but swearing by the gold of the temple a binding one. How foolish! Vows are made to God, not to temples or to gold, not to altars or to gifts on the altars. They focus so much on symbols and rituals that they entirely forget the reality behind the symbol, which leads to the next problem.

Fourth, *they promote a grotesque form of religion, one that is high on ceremonial devotion while harbouring in it extremes of moral corruption.* They tithe mint, dill, and cumin, but neglect the weightier matters of the law: justice and mercy and faithfulness (verse 23). They can pay out money to put an innocent man to death, but then shudder to put that 'blood money' into the temple treasury (*Matt.* 27:3–10). They are blind guides indeed, straining out gnats and swallowing camels.

SUMMARY

It is no wonder that Jesus calls his disciples to a righteousness that exceeds that of the scribes and Pharisees (*Matt.* 5:20). Theirs is a monstrous distortion of true religion, one that represents a total reversal of all that is good and noble and true. Seen for what it really is, it is no surprise at all that the one who outdistanced all others in the practice of this religion turned out to be the very chief of sinners. May God keep us from such deception in our own lives. Again we should pray:

Search me, O God, and know my heart! Try me and know my thoughts! And see if there be any grievous way in me, and lead me in the way everlasting (Psa. 139:23–24).

55

More Woes

'*W*oe to you, scribes and Pharisees, hypocrites! For you clean the outside of the cup and the plate, but inside they are full of greed and self-indulgence. *26* You blind Pharisee! First clean the inside of the cup and the plate, that the outside also may be clean. *27* Woe to you, scribes and Pharisees, hypocrites! For you are like whitewashed tombs, which outwardly appear beautiful, but within are full of dead people's bones and all uncleanness. *28* So you also outwardly appear righteous to others, but within you are full of hypocrisy and lawlessness. *29* Woe to you, scribes and Pharisees, hypocrites! For you build the tombs of the prophets and decorate the monuments of the righteous, *30* saying, "If we had lived in the days of our fathers, we would not have taken part with them in shedding the blood of the prophets." *31* Thus you witness against yourselves that you are sons of those who murdered the prophets. *32* Fill up, then, the measure of your fathers. *33* You serpents, you brood of vipers, how are you to escape being sentenced to hell? *34* Therefore I send you prophets and wise men and scribes, some of whom you will kill and crucify, and some you will flog in your synagogues and persecute from town to town, *35* so that on you may come all the righteous blood shed on earth, from the blood of innocent Abel to the blood of Zechariah the son of Barachiah, whom you murdered between the sanctuary and the altar. *36* Truly, I say to you, all these things will come upon this generation. *37* O Jerusalem, Jerusalem, the city that kills the prophets and stones those who are sent to it! How often would I have gathered your children together as a hen gathers her brood under her wings, and you would not! *38* See, your house is left to you desolate. *39* For I tell you, you will not see me again, until you say, "Blessed is he who comes in the name of the Lord"* (Matt. 23:25–39).

In this section three more woes are pronounced by Jesus, completing the set of seven and showing the complete failure of Pharisaic religion. The first two woes concentrate on the visible presentation of religion among the Pharisees and the neglect of the inner condition of the heart. The last woe ties the failure of the Pharisees to the same corruption that brought their forefathers to reject and kill the prophets who came before Jesus. This leads Jesus to pronounce judgment on the whole unbelieving generation among which he has come.

WHITE-WASHED RELIGION

The next two woes (verses 25–28) concentrate on the outward presentation of religion among the Pharisees which neglects the inner condition of their hearts. They clean the outside of the cup and plate, but inside are full of greed and self-indulgence (verse 25). Thus they are like white-washed tombs, which outwardly appear beautiful but inwardly are full of dead people's bones and all uncleanness (verse 27). The emphasis here is the same as we found in Jesus' exposition of the law in *Matt.* 5:27–30, where the law is shown to apply to the inner condition of the heart (the desires and motivations of the person) as well as to the outward acts. Thus a man who is angry with his brother without a cause breaks the sixth commandment, as does the man who murders his brother, and the man who lusts after his neighbour's wife breaks the seventh commandment as does the man who commits adultery with his neighbour's wife.

Pharisaic religion principally concentrates on the outward presentation of religion, but it is in the heart that sinful corruption resides. A religion which concentrates on outward rituals proves to be powerless in restraining the corrupt desires of the heart. 'For out of the heart come evil thoughts, murder, adultery, sexual immorality, theft, false witness, slander' (*Matt.* 15:19). Thus Paul warns the Colossians against focusing on outward ceremonies and ritual obligations: 'These have indeed an appearance of wisdom in promoting self-made religion and asceticism and severity to the body, but they are of no value in stopping the indulgence of the flesh' (*Col.* 2:23). Here is the deceptiveness of a religion focused primarily on ritual performance: it looks for all the world like real discipline and moral purity, but it is completely useless in curbing self-indulgence and corrupt desires. Indeed, it turns out that such ritual focus provides fertile ground in which evil desires may grow and flourish, as Paul found in himself. Sin took opportunity through the commandments, deceived him, and killed him (see *Rom.* 7:7–12).

SONS OF PROPHET KILLERS

The deceptiveness of a ritual-based religion is the main focus of the seventh and final woe Jesus pronounces against the scribes and Pharisees (verses 29–36). On the one hand, they make great effort to build tombs and monuments for the prophets and right-eous people revered by the Jews, and they believe that they would not have taken part in shedding the blood of these righteous ones had they lived in their days. Yet, on the other hand, they stand as bitter opponents to the religion of Jesus, even plotting to kill him; thus proving themselves to be the true 'sons of those who murdered the prophets' (verse 31). Failing to see the continuity of religion between Jesus and the prophets who preceded him, they likewise fail to see the continuity between themselves and their forefathers who killed the prophets. Indeed, not only are they true sons of their fathers, but they are even more monstrous. In them the sin-fulness that unites them with their fathers reaches its completion, and thus the judgment long delayed against such sinfulness will no longer be withheld. Jesus announces (verse 36) that on this gener-ation shall come all the judgment due for all the prophets who have been murdered, from the blood of innocent Abel (the first to be martyred in the Old Testament) to the blood of Zechariah the son of Barachiah (whose murder is narrated in *2 Chron.* 24, the last book of the Old Testament canon, according to the order adopted by the Jews). This generation not only continues the murderous strain, but perfects it, for they will murder the very one who sent all the previous messengers of God (verse 34).

THE PHARISEE IN US ALL

With this seventh woe, Jesus speaks his last word to the scribes and Pharisees. They will be mentioned one more time (*Matt.* 27:62), but Jesus has nothing further to say *to* them. The judgment against them has now been pronounced. What are we to take from this oracle of judgment? If we take nothing more from it than an attitude of condemnation toward the scribes and Pharisees, we could easily fall into the very same deception that blinds them. We would be like readers of the parable of the Pharisee and the tax collector (*Luke* 18:9-14) who, after seeing the arrogance and pretentiousness of the Pharisee, go away thanking God that they are not like that Pharisee! Do we fancy ourselves not to be like them, and imagine that if we had lived in their day we would not have crucified the Lord of glory? They thought the same about themselves as they looked back upon the sins of their forefathers. No, we must avoid this fatal deception and acknowledge that deep in our own hearts are the seeds of this same corrupt religion. The Galatians experienced a great work of grace when the gospel came to them, yet they quickly deserted the gospel and turned to a ritual-based religion (*Gal.* 1:6, 4:9–10). We might not be tempted with circumcision or Jewish festivals, but we can have our own rituals, be they high church (sacraments, holy days, etc.) or low church (no smoking, chewing, or card playing). All too easily we seek to substitute some form of outward purity for real purity of heart. We seek to soothe our guilty consciences with things that we can do, rather than humbling ourselves in honest confession of our corrupt hearts and ways, and seeking grace from him who is ready to receive sinners.

Often it is our view of others that tells most about ourselves. Do we look down our noses at sinners, and count ourselves so much better? Or do we weep at the sins in others and humbly search our own hearts for the same seeds of corruption? The answer to these questions will tell us if we are Pharisees or publicans (review again *Luke* 18:9–14).

SUMMARY

The scribes and Pharisees turned true religion upside down and reversed its values. They honoured pride and arrogance, while Jesus blessed the meek and poor in spirit. They cleaned and polished their outward life and left their inward life untouched. Jesus emphasized purifying the inward life that the outward life might also be clean. Most strikingly, they delivered the Righteous One over to death, whereas the Righteous One himself showed grace to the chief of sinners, the 'Pharisee of the Pharisees'—a blasphemer, persecutor, and violent opponent.

[231]

Indeed, it was for that very reason that he received mercy, so that in him, as the chief of sinners, Jesus Christ might demonstrate his perfect patience, as an example for all those who would believe in him for eternal life (*1 Tim.* 1:16).

> *To the King of ages, immortal, invisible, the only God, be honour and glory for ever and ever. Amen* (1 Tim. 1:17).

56

The Olivet Discourse

Jesus left the temple and was going away, when his disciples came to point out to him the buildings of the temple. ² But he answered them, 'You see all these, do you not? Truly, I say to you, there will not be left here one stone upon another that will not be thrown down.' ³ As he sat on the Mount of Olives, the disciples came to him privately, saying, 'Tell us, when will these things be, and what will be the sign of your coming and of the close of the age?' ⁴ And Jesus answered them, 'See that no one leads you astray. ⁵ For many will come in my name, saying, "I am the Christ," and they will lead many astray. ⁶ And you will hear of wars and rumours of wars. See that you are not alarmed, for this must take place, but the end is not yet. ⁷ For nation will rise against nation, and kingdom against kingdom, and there will be famines and earthquakes in various places. ⁸ All these are but the beginning of the birth pains. ⁹ Then they will deliver you up to tribulation and put you to death, and you will be hated by all nations for my name's sake. ¹⁰ And then many will fall away and betray one another and hate one another. ¹¹ And many false prophets will arise and lead many astray. ¹² And because lawlessness will be increased, the love of many will grow cold. ¹³ But the one who endures to the end will be saved. ¹⁴ And this gospel of the kingdom will be proclaimed throughout the whole world as a testimony to all nations, and then the end will come' (Matt. 24:1–14).

From teaching openly among the multitudes Jesus now turns to his disciples. The whole of Chapters 24 and 25 are given to this discourse. Three questions from the disciples and Jesus' reply make up the first part of the discourse (Chapter 24) and three parables make up the rest (Chapter 25). The disciples want to know the answer to the great question, 'When?' But the answer Jesus gives does not enable us to mark a date on our calendars. To understand Jesus in this chapter, we must put aside our eagerness to know

'When will the end come?', and concern ourselves with the question, 'What must we do until then?' We should follow the lead of Peter who, after a brief presentation of how things in this world would end, asked what kind of people we ought to be, seeing that things would be destroyed in this way (*2 Pet.* 3:11).

THE GLORY DEPARTS

Jesus and his disciples now leave the temple precincts and make their way toward Bethany. This movement away from the temple, noted by Matthew as immediately following the seven-fold condemnation of the temple religion in Chapter 23, indicates that the temple and the city are now abandoned by God. The Lord of glory now departs his temple, even as the glory of God departed from the temple in *Ezek.* 8–11, turning it over to judgment. When the disciples remark on the beauty of the temple, Jesus' reply is both sobering and shocking. He tells them that the beautiful temple and city they now behold will one day be destroyed and not one stone will be left upon another (verse 2). This raises great questions in the mind of the disciples: 'When will these things be, and what will be the sign of your coming and of the close of the age?' Three events are mentioned here. It appears that in the minds of the disciples all three would be simultaneous, parts of a whole, so that the return of Jesus and the end of the age would be at the same time as the destruction of Jerusalem. Historically, as we now know, the first is separated from the others by millennia, but as Jesus' answer is not intended to help them mark dates on their calendars, that fact is not made clear to them in the answers he gives. What he intends is that they should be obedient until he comes.

DECEIVERS WILL COME

In replying to his disciples' questions, Jesus' main concern is that the disciples should not be deceived about his return and the end of the age (verses 4–14). He warns that there will be many deceivers who will come claiming to be the Messiah. In addition, there will be many destructive events taking place which might seem to foretell the end of time (wars, earthquakes, famines). But these things in themselves did not mark the end of the age. These things would happen throughout the course of history, as indeed they have. They were but the beginnings of birth pangs for the age to come, not the arrival of that age. For the end will not come until the gospel of the kingdom has been preached in all the world (verse 14). The concern of the disciples must not be on figuring out when the end will come, but on preaching the gospel to the nations.

PERSECUTIONS WILL COME

In addition to the events which threaten all people before Jesus comes again ('wars and rumours of wars . . . famines and earthquakes'), there will be persecutions focused especially on those who profess to follow and serve the Lord. They will be delivered up to tribulations, put to death, and hated by all nations because of Jesus (verse 9). So harsh will these afflictions be that many who profess faith will fall away, betraying other believers and hating them (verse 10). Lawlessness will increase and the love of most people will grow cold (verse 11).

Despite such hardships, the disciples must endure to the end; only those who do will be saved (verse 13). This is one of many 'conditional' statements found in Jesus' teaching (see, for examples, *Matt.* 5:20, 7:21, 10:22, and 13:23). The New Testament contains similar statements elsewhere (*Rom.* 11:22, *1 Cor.* 15:2, *Heb.* 3:6, 14; *2 Pet.* 1:10). We could easily misunderstand their force. Some, comparing them with scriptural teaching on justification by faith apart from works of the law, dismiss them entirely or treat them as having no force at all. Yet these are words of the Holy Scriptures and must, like all the others, be true. Others read these conditional statements as implying that endurance is our work and responsibility, resting upon the use we make of the grace given to us. On this view, grace enables us to endure, but grace alone is not fully efficacious toward that end. Our own labours must complete what grace cannot supply. There is just enough truth in this view to make it both plausible and deadly. While it is true that we must indeed endure to the end, and that only those who do will be saved, yet we must never suppose that God's grace is merely enabling but not victorious. The good work which God begins in his people he brings to completion at the day of Christ Jesus (*Phil.* 1:6). None of those who truly come to Jesus will ever be cast out or perish

[235]

(*John* 6:37, 10:27–28). The conditional requirement is indeed what it appears to be, but it is not a condition that we fulfil in our own strength. The end result of God's saving grace is never in doubt, for God's grace is fully effective in completing what it begins. The reward of the enduring service of his people has been prepared for them from the foundation of the world (*Matt.* 25:34). What God requires of us, his grace secures in us. Then it is in our diligent perseverance that we make our calling and election sure (*2 Pet.* 1:10).

BE MY WITNESSES

In the face of deceivers, tribulations, and persecutions, the followers of Jesus are to continue their mission. The gospel of the kingdom announced by Jesus is to be proclaimed to all the nations (verse 14). Only when that is complete will the end come, for God will not cease his saving work until he gathers all the elect from every tribe and language and people and nation (*Rev.* 5:9). Matthew concludes his Gospel looking toward this very end (*Matt.* 28:18–20), but it has been in his view from the very beginning. The Gentile women of Jesus' genealogy hinted at this (*Matt.* 1:3-6). The arrival of Gentile magi at the birth of the Saviour anticipated it (2:1). The beginning of the public ministry in Galilee demonstrated it (4:12–17). The healings of the Roman centurion's servant (8:5–13) and the Canaanite woman's daughter (15:21–28), and the feeding of the four thousand (15:32–39), all confirm it. The people for whom Jesus has come, to save them from their sins, are to be found in every nation on earth. When we come to know that good news for ourselves, we must enter the missionary work of the church, that the gospel might indeed be preached to every nation. The end will not come until all the lost sheep have been gathered.

SUMMARY

The disciples wanted to know when the end would come, but the time of the end is hidden from us. Much as we might wish to know, what must concern us is our service in the meantime. We must be the servants whom the master will find working when he comes, as Jesus will soon emphasize (*Matt.* 24:46).

57

Days of Distress

'**S**o when you see the abomination of desolation spoken of by the prophet Daniel, standing in the holy place (let the reader understand), [16] then let those who are in Judea flee to the mountains. [17] Let the one who is on the housetop not go down to take what is in his house, [18] and let the one who is in the field not turn back to take his cloak. [19] And alas for women who are pregnant and for those who are nursing infants in those days! [20] Pray that your flight may not be in winter or on a Sabbath. [21] For then there will be great tribulation, such as has not been from the beginning of the world until now, no, and never will be. [22] And if those days had not been cut short, no human being would be saved. But for the sake of the elect those days will be cut short. [23] Then if anyone says to you, "Look, here is the Christ!" or "There he is!" do not believe it. [24] For false christs and false prophets will arise and perform great signs and wonders, so as to lead astray, if possible, even the elect. [25] See, I have told you beforehand. [26] So, if they say to you, "Look, he is in the wilderness," do not go out. If they say, "Look, he is in the inner rooms," do not believe it. [27] For as the lightning comes from the east and shines as far as the west, so will be the coming of the Son of Man. [28] Wherever the corpse is, there the vultures will gather'* (Matt. 24:15–28).

In the first part of Jesus' reply to his disciples he has stressed that the time preceding his second coming will be marked by distress and troubles for all his followers. Such difficulties are not to deter them from their mission to preach the gospel to all the nations. In the next section (verses 15–28) the focus is more particularly on the sufferings in Judah, at the time when, with respect to the temple, 'there will not be left here one stone upon another that will not be thrown down' (verse 2). This refers to the destruction of Jerusalem in AD 70. Notice that in verse 16 the instructions are directed toward 'those who are in Judea', with nothing said to those who are living elsewhere. There is, however, an important link between the events surrounding the destruction of Jerusalem, and the return of Jesus at the close of the age. It is because of that link that Jesus treats them all together in his reply to the disciples.

THE FORETASTE OF THINGS TO COME

The return of Christ and the close of the age will not occur until very long after the city and temple of Jerusalem are destroyed, but what occurs at that time is very similar to the coming of Christ at the close of the age. The latter will be a judgment of the whole world. The former anticipates and foreshadows that day, bringing judgment on a part of the whole, as a warning to the rest. It is a judgment against the nation of Israel for their rejection of Christ and of all God's messengers that preceded him. Jesus spoke of this as a judgment that would come upon this generation for 'all the righteous blood shed on earth, from the blood of innocent Abel to the blood of Zechariah the son of Barachiah' (*Matt.* 23:35). It will mark the end of God's patience, which has waited long for Israel to repent and return. Jesus lamented the approach of that day, for he dearly wished it would be otherwise:

> O *Jerusalem, Jerusalem, the city that kills the prophets and stones those who are sent to it! How often would I have gathered your children together as a hen gathers her brood under her wings, and you would not! See, your house is left to you desolate. For I tell you, you will not see me again, until you say, 'Blessed is he who comes in the name of the Lord'* (Matt. 23:37–39).

UNPARALLELED SUFFERING TO COME

The judgment to come on the nation of Israel will be a time of unparalleled suffering, 'such as has not been from the beginning of the world until now, no, and never will be' (verse 21). The report of the siege on Jerusalem by the Romans given by the Jewish historian Josephus certainly confirms this. Anticipating this dreadful period, Jesus warns the Christian believers of that time in order that they might not be caught unawares and then go through more suffering than necessary. First, they must flee Judea when they see 'the abomination of desolation spoken of by the prophet Daniel standing in the holy place' (verse 15). The reference is to a phrase found in *Dan.* 8:13, 9:27, 11:31, and 12:11. In at least one of these places Daniel has in view the desecration of the temple carried out by Antiochus Epiphanes. He converted the altar of burnt offering in the Jerusalem temple into an altar to the Greek god Zeus and sacrificed a pig on it. What Jesus means by the phrase here is not specified, but clearly he means something equally abominable and perhaps very similar to that done by Antiochus. When this occurs, the disciples are to flee to the mountains. One must see here that our Lord cares deeply for his people, and that he seeks to mitigate their suffering.

He also instructs them to pray that, when it is time to flee, they will not be in circumstances that will make their flight more difficult. He says they should pray that, if mothers, they will not be pregnant or nursing infants in those days, and that their flight will not be in winter or on a Sabbath. These are but illustrations of the kind of circumstances that could make their flight more difficult and arduous. Here too we see our Lord's concern to ease our sufferings, and he invites us to pray toward that end. What he says about the times of suffering would be true of other times as well. We are frequently encouraged in the Scriptures to pray for our own well-being. For instance, we should pray for our daily bread (*Matt.* 6:11), that we be delivered from temptation (*Matt.* 6:13, 26:41), and that we might live 'a peaceful and quiet life, godly and dignified in every way' (*1 Tim.* 2:2). Indeed, we are told: 'In everything by prayer and supplication with thanksgiving let your requests be made known to God' (*Phil.* 4:6). Clearly, prayer changes things. We must never doubt the truth of this. A belief in God's sovereignty and omniscience is never to be regarded as a reason to give up praying for things to change, for God ordains the means to his ends as well as the ends themselves. Indeed, prayer is among the means which God has appointed for the accomplishment of his ends.

Even before we ask, our Father works to provide for our comfort and well-being. Our Lord tells us that the sufferings to come in the time of his judgment will be so great that were they permitted to go on without limit, no human being would be saved. But, 'for the sake of the elect those days will be cut short' (verse 22). See

[239]

then how carefully the Lord watches over his own. None will be lost (*John* 6:37–39). He cuts short the days of their suffering, so that they will not be tested beyond what they can endure (see also *1 Cor.* 10:13). Thus, whatever uncertainties await us in the future, whatever difficulties may come, however long the trials may last, our Lord will keep us to the end.

> *Fear not, little flock, for it is your Father's good pleasure to give you the kingdom* (Luke 12:32).

BEWARE OF FALSE PROPHETS

In terrible times it is easy to become confused about how to respond. Such confusion of mind, coupled with great suffering, can make us vulnerable to being misled. So our Lord warns us that in difficult times 'false Christs and false prophets' will arise. They will encourage us to seek the Lord according to their words and their guidance. Jesus says we must not give in to their deceptions. When he comes at last to claim his own, there will be no mistaking where he is. How we should live until then is likewise clear.

> *My sheep hear my voice, and I know them, and they follow me. I give them eternal life, and they will never perish, and no one will snatch them out of my hand* (John 10:27–28).

SUMMARY

Like the disciples we would very much like to know, 'When will these things be, and what will be the sign of your coming and the close of the age?' But it is not for us to know 'times or seasons that the Father has fixed by his own authority' (*Acts* 1:7). How we are to live and serve him, today and tomorrow, whenever he might come – that is our concern. On this, our Lord has not left us without clear instruction.

58

The Coming of the Son of Man

'*Immediately after the tribulation of those days the sun will be darkened, and the moon will not give its light, and the stars will fall from heaven, and the powers of the heavens will be shaken.* ³⁰ *Then will appear in heaven the sign of the Son of Man, and then all the tribes of the earth will mourn, and they will see the Son of Man coming on the clouds of heaven with power and great glory.* ³¹ *And he will send out his angels with a loud trumpet call, and they will gather his elect from the four winds, from one end of heaven to the other.* ³² *From the fig tree learn its lesson: as soon as its branch becomes tender and puts out its leaves, you know that summer is near.* ³³ *So also, when you see all these things, you know that he is near, at the very gates.* ³⁴ *Truly, I say to you, this generation will not pass away until all these things take place.* ³⁵ *Heaven and earth will pass away, but my words will not pass away.* ³⁶ *But concerning that day and hour no one knows, not even the angels of heaven, nor the Son, but the Father only.* ³⁷ *For as were the days of Noah, so will be the coming of the Son of Man.* ³⁸ *For as in those days before the flood they were eating and drinking, marrying and giving in marriage, until the day when Noah entered the ark,* ³⁹ *and they were unaware until the flood came and swept them all away, so will be the coming of the Son of Man.* ⁴⁰ *Then two men will be in the field; one will be taken and one left.* ⁴¹ *Two women will be grinding at the mill; one will be taken and one left.* ⁴² *Therefore, stay awake, for you do not know on what day your Lord is coming.* ⁴³ *But know this, that if the master of the house had known in what part of the night the thief was coming, he would have stayed awake and would not have let his house be broken into.* ⁴⁴ *Therefore you also must be ready, for the Son of Man is coming at an hour you do not expect.* ⁴⁵ *Who then is the faithful and wise servant, whom his master has set over his household, to give them their food at the proper time?* ⁴⁶ *Blessed is that servant whom his master will find so doing when he comes.* ⁴⁷ *Truly, I say to you, he will set him over all his possessions.* ⁴⁸ *But if that wicked servant says to himself, "My master is delayed,"* ⁴⁹ *and begins to beat his fellow servants and eats and drinks with drunkards, [50] the master of that servant will come on a day when he does not expect him and at an hour he does not know [51] and will cut him in pieces and put him with the hypocrites. In that place there will be weeping and gnashing of teeth* (Matt. 24:29–51).

The remainder of this chapter focuses on the return of Christ and on how we are to live as we await that day. The opening words of this section, 'Immediately after the tribulation of those days . . .', are the source of much debate over the time when the things mentioned in verses 29–31 are to take place. Since the previous section (especially verses 15–28) discussed events surrounding the destruction of Jerusalem that took place in AD 70, some have concluded that this section is teaching that Jesus himself expected, or that the early church expected, that Jesus would return within the lifetime of his disciples. Such hypotheses are entirely without basis. Jesus makes very clear in this chapter that only the Father knows the time of his return (verse 36), and much of the chapter is devoted to teaching the need for patience when Jesus' return seems to be delayed. While giving a glimpse of what we can expect until he comes, his main concern is to instruct us concerning how we are to live until that day comes. He is not giving a time line upon which to plan our schedules. Consequently, we must understand him to be teaching that his return will not occur within any predictable period of time.

THE DAYS OF TRIBULATION

In the opening verses of this section, Christ's coming is said to be 'immediately after the tribulation of those days'. The word 'tribulation' is also used in verses 9 and 21 of this chapter. Its use helps us in getting some perspective on this passage. In verse 21, the word is used with an adjective, '*great* tribulation', but here and in verse 9 it is used without qualification. From this we may see that Jesus is telling us that the whole period of history between his first and second comings will be a period of tribulation for his disciples. This is clearly taught elsewhere (see *John* 16:33). In comparison with this, the time of Jerusalem's destruction will be a time of *great* tribulation, a period of suffering much more severe than that experienced in other times. So Jesus' remark that he will return 'immediately after the tribulation of those days' is not a reference to the time of 'great tribulation' at the destruction of Jerusalem, but to the whole period of tribulation that will occur between his first and second comings. Thus what he says here gives us no basis on which to speculate concerning when he will return. Given that this discourse is not intended to answer our 'When?' questions, this is what we should expect. Rather than tell us when he is coming, Jesus aims to assure us that he will return for us, despite the seeming delays; to instruct us in how to live while we wait; and to warn us against being misled about his coming by false prophets and false teachers.

The imagery which Jesus uses to describe his second coming is most important. In particular, the mention of his 'coming on the clouds of heaven with power and great glory' is taken directly from *Dan.* 7:13–14. It is a clear claim to be the Messiah. When Jesus speaks of his return in these terms before the high priest Caiaphas, he is accused of blasphemy (*Matt.* 26:64–54). It is not a weather report that Jesus gives, but a reference to the glory-cloud which led the people in the wilderness (*Exod.* 13:21), which covered the mountain of Sinai (*Exod.* 19:6), which descended upon the tabernacle (*Exod.* 40:34), which filled the temple at its dedication (*2 Chron.* 5:13–14), and which descended on the mount of transfiguration (*Matt.* 17:5). For Jesus to return 'on the clouds of heaven' is for him to return in the glory of his Father (*Matt.* 16:27). In comparison with the storm of tribulation which is to come upon the disciples until he comes, Jesus' return will be (so to speak) a tremendous change in the weather. 'Weeping may tarry for the night, but joy comes with the morning' (*Psa.* 30:5). He will gather his elect from one end of heaven to the other, and all who have believed will be safe in the protection of Christ for ever and ever. Amen.

AN IMMINENT RETURN

In the remaining verses of this chapter Jesus uses a number of comparisons to drive home important points about his return: the lessons of *the fig tree*, of *the days of Noah*, and of *the faithful and wise steward*. From the lesson of the *fig tree*, Jesus wants us to learn that his coming is imminent, not in the sense that it would happen soon after his resurrection, but that it could happen at any moment, '. . . know that he is near, right at the gates' (verse 33). He underscores this by insisting that all the things he has mentioned will take place before 'this generation' (that is, his own generation) passes away. Here is another place where some have thought that Jesus was predicting his return within the lifetime of his disciples. For the reasons already mentioned, that view should not be accepted. What Jesus is saying is that all 'these things', all the things which belong to the period of tribulation, including the period of 'great tribulation' at Jerusalem's fall, will occur within 'this generation'. But that does not mean they will all be completed within this generation and it does not therefore imply that Jesus will return within that generation. Again, the time of his return was unknown, even to him (verse 36).

From the comparison with Noah, Jesus teaches us that his coming will catch many unaware, just as the people of Noah's day were 'unaware until the flood came and swept them all away' (verse 39). Our sinful nature encourages us to delay making changes in our life, even when we clearly know that we must. We find reasons to put it off to some future day when, we tell ourselves, it will be more convenient. We must, however, be ready at any moment, for 'the Son of Man is coming at an hour you do not expect' (verse 44).

The way to be ready is to be found doing what our Master has commanded us to do until he returns. This is the lesson of the *faithful and wise steward*, whom his master finds working when he returns (verses 45–46). That servant will be highly rewarded by his master (verse 47); but a wicked servant who exploits the time of delay to indulge in disobedience will be caught unawares when the master does return, and he will be judged with the hypocrites (verses 48–51).

SUMMARY

This chapter challenges us in many ways. Our natural curiosity about what the future holds prompts us to search the chapter for clues as to what will happen and when. But as our Lord elsewhere teaches, 'It is not for [us] to know times or seasons that the Father has fixed by his own authority' (*Acts* 1:7). The main purpose of the chapter is not to satisfy that urge in us. Rather, Jesus warns us against being deceived, telling us that we will live in hard times of tribulation until he comes, and that we must not be confused or discouraged because of them. We are to rest secure in the promise of his return, and live in that expectation, however long we must wait, and however long we must endure until he comes. But while we wait, we must be about our Master's work, proclaiming the gospel of his kingdom throughout the whole world as a testimony to the nations, 'and then the end will come'. 'Amen. Come, Lord Jesus!' (*Rev.* 22:20).

59

Wise and Foolish Virgins

'*T*hen the kingdom of heaven will be like ten virgins who took
their lamps and went to meet the bridegroom. *²* Five of them
were foolish, and five were wise. *³* For when the foolish took their
lamps, they took no oil with them, *⁴* but the wise took flasks of oil with
their lamps. *⁵* As the bridegroom was delayed, they all became drowsy
and slept. *⁶* But at midnight there was a cry, "Here is the bridegroom!
Come out to meet him." *⁷* Then all those virgins rose and trimmed
their lamps. *⁸* And the foolish said to the wise, "Give us some of your
oil, for our lamps are going out." *⁹* But the wise answered, saying,
"Since there will not be enough for us and for you, go rather to the
dealers and buy for yourselves." *¹⁰* And while they were going to buy,
the bridegroom came, and those who were ready went in with him to
the marriage feast, and the door was shut. *¹¹* Afterward the other virgins came also, saying, "Lord, lord, open to us." *¹²* But he answered,
"Truly, I say to you, I do not know you." *¹³* Watch therefore, for you
know neither the day nor the hour' (Matt. 25:1–13).

This chapter contains three parables which continue the teaching of the previous chapter and support it. By these parables we are again instructed to be patient in waiting for the Lord's
return, to be ready for him to return at any moment, to be faithful
while we wait, and to rest assured that our labour for the Lord will
not be in vain, but richly rewarded at his coming.

AWAITING THE BRIDEGROOM

The parable of the ten virgins is a scene of anticipation. A wedding is approaching, and a bridegroom is expected to come and
claim his bride. This is a truth about the second coming which
must never be forgotten. The day of Christ's return is, to be sure,
a day of judgment, and this chapter will bring that truth before

us in unforgettable terms. On that day Christ will come as Judge over all the nations. But he will also come as a loving husband to rescue his bride from the tribulations just foretold in the previous chapter, to claim her as his own, and to take her to the home he has prepared for her, that where he is she may also be (*John* 14:3): 'As the bridegroom rejoices over the bride, so shall your God rejoice over you" (*Isa.* 62:5b). Believers should look forward to this day, not shrink from it in fear (*1 John* 2:28). This chapter prepares us to do that.

There are ten virgins awaiting this bridegroom, not as potential brides, but as the friends of the bride. They have been invited to the wedding feast and are expecting to join in the festivities. The bride herself is not mentioned in this parable, and that should not be a matter of concern or speculation for us. The point of the parable does not concern the bride, but those who will be admitted to the marriage feast.

Two kinds of virgins are presented to us for consideration, the *wise* and the *foolish*. The wise were prepared to wait long for the bridegroom, for they took flasks of oil with them to ensure that they had enough oil for their lamps, whenever the bridegroom might come. The foolish virgins, however, took no oil with them. When at last the call was given that the bridegroom was approaching, all the virgins began to trim their lamps; but the foolish virgins did not have sufficient oil to keep their lamps alight. They begged their wise companions to give them some of their oil, but the wise virgins protested that there was not enough for all of them. So the foolish virgins had to leave their post and seek additional oil from dealers elsewhere. While they were gone, the bridegroom came. Those who were ready were admitted to the marriage feast, and the door was shut. When later the foolish virgins returned, they were turned away by the bridegroom. The point of the parable is clear: since we do not know the hour when the bridegroom will come, we must be prepared to meet him at any time, and to wait long for him if necessary.

STICKING TO THE POINT

It would be easy to get confused over some of the details of this parable. First, some look at the 'wise virgins' and think that their

[247]

reaction was very selfish. Does not the Bible encourage us to share with others who are in need? The Bible does indeed encourage sharing with those in need, but this parable is not told to teach that truth, and not all the details of this or any parable are intended for interpretation. For example, when Jesus told the parable of the dishonest manager (*Luke* 16:1–9), and commended the man 'for his shrewdness' (*Luke* 16:8), he was not commending the man's dishonesty. The parable was told to show that, in the face of impending judgment, we must make wise preparations for that day. The dishonest steward was commended for his foresight and preparation, not for being dishonest. So here, the main point is not whether it is right to refuse to share when one has but limited resources; the point is simply that each one must be prepared to meet the Lord when he comes, whenever that might be.

Another detail in the parable is the source of much speculation. What does the oil represent? Because elsewhere in Scripture oil, particularly anointing with oil, is used as a symbol for the Holy Spirit, some have argued that the 'oil' we must have is the Holy Spirit. There can be no doubt that possession of the Holy Spirit is absolutely essential to our being admitted to the wedding feast. 'Anyone who does not have the Spirit of Christ does not belong to him' (*Rom.* 8:9). However, this parable should not be turned toward making that point.

This parable is teaching us to be prepared for the coming of the Lord, whenever that might be. To limit that preparation to possessing the Holy Spirit would ignore the emphasis in this discourse on faithfulness in all that the Lord has commanded us. In the face of tribulations, we must proclaim the gospel of the kingdom to all the nations (*Matt.* 24:14). While our master is 'away' (that is, before he returns for us) we must be busy in doing what he has entrusted to us (*Matt.* 24:45–47), and using the 'talents' he has given us (*Matt.* 25:14–30). In the third parable of this chapter, we are exhorted toward feeding the hungry, giving drink to the thirsty, welcoming the stranger, clothing the naked, and visiting the sick and imprisoned (*Matt.* 25:31–46). The 'oil' of this passage, then, is not one thing, but many. It encompasses the whole Christian life, which we are to be living faithfully while we await the coming of our Lord.

THE DOOR WHICH IS SHUT

It is only when we appreciate that the 'oil' which the foolish virgins lacked is not one thing but many that we can best understand the significance of the shut door (verse 10). A novice reading this parable might not only wonder about the selfishness of the wise virgins, but also about the harshness of the bridegroom. Does it not seem cruel that the bridegroom should exclude from the wedding feast those who simply lacked enough oil for their lamps? But, when we consider that the lack of oil symbolized that the foolish virgins were not faithful in their waiting, that they were unfaithful servants not doing what their master had told them to do while he was gone, that they were wicked servants not using the 'talents' entrusted to them, and that they did not feed the hungry, or clothe the naked, or care for the sick and imprisoned, then we see that their rejection is justly deserved, not arbitrarily imposed. Such judgment does await the unfaithful and disobedient. As in the days of Noah, there will come an end to the period of grace, and the door will be shut (*Gen.* 7:16). When that door is shut, no man can open it. He who has ears to hear, let him hear!

SUMMARY

We must be wise, not foolish, virgins. We must wait patiently for our Lord's return, which we do, not by passive looking, but by active serving. By the power of the Holy Spirit we are to give ourselves to do our Lord's bidding, serving faithfully until he comes. May the grace of God be with us, that while we wait upon the Lord we might renew our strength, and mount up with wings like eagles, run and not be weary, walk and not faint (*Isa.* 40:31). 'Come, Lord Jesus!' (*Rev.* 22:20).

60

The Parable of the Talents

'*F*or it will be like a man going on a journey, who called his servants and entrusted to them his property. *15* To one he gave five talents, to another two, to another one, to each according to his ability. Then he went away. *16* He who had received the five talents went at once and traded with them, and he made five talents more. *17* So also he who had the two talents made two talents more. *18* But he who had received the one talent went and dug in the ground and hid his master's money. *19* Now after a long time the master of those servants came and settled accounts with them. *20* And he who had received the five talents came forward, bringing five talents more, saying, "Master, you delivered to me five talents; here I have made five talents more." *21* His master said to him, "Well done, good and faithful servant. You have been faithful over a little; I will set you over much. Enter into the joy of your master." *22* And he also who had the two talents came forward, saying, "Master, you delivered to me two talents; here I have made two talents more." *23* His master said to him, "Well done, good and faithful servant. You have been faithful over a little; I will set you over much. Enter into the joy of your master." *24* He also who had received the one talent came forward, saying, "Master, I knew you to be a hard man, reaping where you did not sow, and gathering where you scattered no seed, *25* so I was afraid, and I went and hid your talent in the ground. Here you have what is yours." *26* But his master answered him, "You wicked and slothful servant! You knew that I reap where I have not sown and gather where I scattered no seed? *27* Then you ought to have invested my money with the bankers, and at my coming I should have received what was my own with interest. *28* So take the talent from him and give it to him who has the ten talents. *29* For to everyone who has will more be given, and he will have an abundance. But from the one who has not, even what he has will be taken away. *30* And cast the worthless servant into the outer darkness. In that place there will be weeping and gnashing of teeth"' (Matt. 25:14-30).

Like the previous parable in this chapter, this one also deals with the period of time between our Lord's departure from this world by his ascension and his coming again. The issue is how we are to live in the interim.

That perspective is quite apparent, for this parable concerns 'a man going on a journey' and entrusting to his servants a portion of his wealth. After a while he returns, and each servant is then called to account for what he has done with what had been entrusted to him. Taken together, this parable and the one which follows in this chapter teach us that when our Lord returns we too shall be called to account for how we have lived.

EACH ACCORDING TO HIS ABILITY

As the master prepares to go on his journey, he calls his servants and entrusts to them a certain portion of his wealth. The division is not equal. To one is given five talents (a *talent* is a measure of weight or value), to another two talents, and to a third just one. The division is made according to the ability of each (verse 15). An equal division is not made, because the servants' abilities differ. So it is among people. People have not all received the same advantages and gifts. They differ from one another and vary in their abilities and opportunities. The service expected of them likewise varies. But however varied our abilities, faithfulness and diligence are expected of all. From the one to whom more is given, more is required. From the one to whom less is given, less is required. But from each, faithfulness and diligence are required.

Notice that what is given to the servants is 'entrusted' to them (verse 14) and when the master returns the servants are called 'to settle accounts' with the master. Here we are reminded that all that we have and all that is given to us is not really ours, but belongs to our master. It is entrusted to us and we are expected to make good use of it. It is not ours to do with as we please, but ours to use for the advantage of our Master. A day is coming when we will have to settle accounts with him.

GOOD AND FAITHFUL SERVANTS

Two of the servants proved to be good and faithful servants. The one who received five talents traded with them and made five talents more (verse 16). The one who received two talents did likewise and made two talents more (verse 17). When the master returned to settle accounts with them, each one was able to return all that had been entrusted to him and double besides. Each is commended for his faithfulness and each is rewarded accordingly, being entrusted with yet greater responsibilities and standing (verses 21, 23).

This matter of reward for service is sometimes thought to be contrary to the New Testament teaching which tells us that we are saved by grace through faith, and not because of our works, so that no one may boast (*Eph.* 2:8–9). It is thought that reward for service is a legalistic notion, as if the work done merited the reward, and thus gave grounds for boasting. But it is not true that, if one receives a reward for service, he has thereby a ground for boasting.

The New Testament teaches that there *will* be rewards for service (as in this parable, and also *1 Cor.* 3:5–15, *2 John* 8), yet it also teaches that it is all by God's grace that any man accomplishes anything. Thus Paul says that he labours according to the grace of God which is given to him (*1 Cor.* 3:10), and that all that he has done is 'what Christ has accomplished' through him (*Rom.* 15:18). In effect, therefore, the rewards given to us for our labours are themselves gifts of God's grace, for they crown in us the work of Christ done through us.

There is no ground for boasting in this, for each of us must confess that the glory belongs to God alone. Rewards there will be, for all that we have done; but when all that we have done is by the grace of God given to us, we have no ground for boasting in ourselves.

A WICKED AND SLOTHFUL SERVANT

The servant who received the one talent likewise is called to account, but in his case no use was made of the talent and so there is no profit. All he can do is return the one talent he first received. The explanation he offers for his failure is revealing.

He regarded the master as 'a hard man, reaping where (he) did not sow, and gathering where [he] scattered no seed' (verse 24). In view of this, the servant said he was afraid and hid the talent in the ground.

The explanation given by the servant is hypocritical, as the master quickly exposes. For if the servant had indeed believed the master to be so hard and unscrupulous as to reap where he did not sow and to gather where he did not scatter seed, then the servant would have at least invested the money with the bankers, to guarantee against its loss and to insure at least a minimum of profit. But no, he hid the talent in the ground.

The explanation for his failure was not fear, but wickedness and sloth. The judgment he receives is frightful, but it is equal to his sin. He is cast into the outer darkness, where there is weeping and gnashing of teeth (verse 30).

A SURPRISING TWIST

There is a surprising twist to this parable. Ordinarily we expect that it is the rich, the ones most highly favoured with this world's goods and opportunities, who are the examples of wickedness (as in the parable of the rich man and the poor man named Lazarus, *Luke* 16:19–31). But here, it is not the servant with five talents who proves to be unfaithful, nor even the one with two, but the servant who has only one. As each received 'according to his ability', this servant had less ability than the others.

The point is sobering, for the 'wicked and slothful servant' had indeed received much less than the others, yet he too was expected to be faithful in the little that he had, and in all that he had. Consequently, what little he had, and all that he had, was taken from him (verse 28), and he was cast into the outer darkness. Let none of us evade our calling and responsibility on the ground that our gifts and abilities are so much less than others. Whatever we have received, however little it might be, must be put to use in the Master's service.

SUMMARY

'Who then is the faithful and wise servant, whom his master has set over his household, to give them their food at the proper time?' It is the servant 'whom his master finds so doing when he comes' (*Matt.* 24:45–46). From our God we have each received a measure of time, talent, and treasure. It is all to be used for the service of God. He is not a hard man, who reaps where he does not sow, or harvests where he has scattered no seed. He is a good and gracious

[253]

God, who takes the little that we have and, when given to him, blesses and multiplies it so that it might do great things (see *Matt.* 14:17–21). Neither five-, nor two-, nor one-talent servants should ever fear him, but always trust him and serve him; and when he comes again, he will graciously reward our faithful service.

61

The Final Judgment

'*When the Son of Man comes in his glory, and all the angels with him, then he will sit on his glorious throne. ³² Before him will be gathered all the nations, and he will separate people one from another as a shepherd separates the sheep from the goats. ³³ And he will place the sheep on his right, but the goats on the left. ³⁴ Then the King will say to those on his right, "Come, you who are blessed by my Father, inherit the kingdom prepared for you from the foundation of the world. ³⁵ For I was hungry and you gave me food, I was thirsty and you gave me drink, I was a stranger and you welcomed me, ³⁶ I was naked and you clothed me, I was sick and you visited me, I was in prison and you came to me." ³⁷ Then the righteous will answer him, saying, "Lord, when did we see you hungry and feed you, or thirsty and give you drink? ³⁸ And when did we see you a stranger and welcome you, or naked and clothe you? ³⁹ And when did we see you sick or in prison and visit you?" ⁴⁰ And the King will answer them, "Truly, I say to you, as you did it to one of the least of these my brothers, you did it to me." ⁴¹ Then he will say to those on his left, "Depart from me, you cursed, into the eternal fire prepared for the devil and his angels. ⁴² For I was hungry and you gave me no food, I was thirsty and you gave me no drink, ⁴³ I was a stranger and you did not welcome me, naked and you did not clothe me, sick and in prison and you did not visit me." ⁴⁴ Then they also will answer, saying, "Lord, when did we see you hungry or thirsty or a stranger or naked or sick or in prison, and did not minister to you?" ⁴⁵ Then he will answer them, saying, "Truly, I say to you, as you did not do it to one of the least of these, you did not do it to me." ⁴⁶ And these will go away into eternal punishment, but the righteous into eternal life*' (Matt. 25:31–46).

This final parable is one of the best known in all the New Testament. It is a judgment scene, when all the nations are called before the great king of all the earth. The people will be separated from one another, even as a shepherd separates the sheep from the goats in his flock. The one group will enter into the king's favour and receive his blessing, while the other will fall under his judgment and receive his wrath. It is the final judgment that is in view here, and the consequences of it will go on for all eternity (verse 46). May the Lord give us much grace as we study this passage, that we may each be brought to a true understanding of our own spiritual condition.

JUDGMENT BY THE SON

The great judge in this parable is none other than the Son of Man himself. He first came to us in weakness, but when he comes again it will be in power and glory, and all the angels of heaven will be with him (verse 31). As we have seen before, the title 'Son of Man' is peculiarly apt for our Lord Jesus Christ. On the one hand, it was a title that did not automatically carry with it any messianic symbolism and would not have aroused suspicions among his enemies. For Ezekiel, it meant simply his lowliness (*Ezek.* 2:1, 3:1, 4:1, etc.), his lowly human condition as one made from dust as he stood before God. But in *Dan.* 7:13–14, this title speaks of one in lowly human form to whom is given 'dominion and glory and a kingdom, that all peoples, nations, and languages should serve him'. The Daniel passage is the one most in view now as Jesus reveals the sober realities of the approaching day of judgment. He has all the authority in heaven and earth, and all judgment has been given to him (*John* 5:22)

THE SHEEP AND THE GOATS

A great separation of the human race is to occur at the time of the final judgment, presented here as a separation between 'the sheep and the goats'. The sheep are placed at the king's right hand (verse 33), the place of favour. Favour is given to them and they are praised for the works they have performed – feeding the hungry, giving drink to the thirsty, welcoming strangers, clothing the naked, and visiting the sick and the imprisoned. These works are presented as works done to the Son of Man himself. This is a surprising revelation to the sheep, for they wonder when they have ever given such kindness to the great king himself. He replies that they did it to him when they did it to the very least of his brothers (verse 40).

This passage is often cited as showing the necessity of doing good to all people. The Bible does indeed teach that lesson, both in the Old Testament and in the New. The simple but profound principle of 'love your neighbour as yourself' teaches this (*Luke* 10:25–37). Nothing said here should obscure this fundamental and important biblical teaching. But this passage in Matthew 25 does not echo that teaching. Here the focus is more narrow. Those in need are the 'brothers' of Jesus, particularly 'the least' of them. Jesus says that he receives the service of the sheep to his brothers as service to himself. We see this principle taught elsewhere (*Matt.* 10:40).

In the New Testament, Jesus does not identify himself as a brother to every person on the earth, or even to every needy person on the earth. Those who are the brothers and sisters of Jesus are those who do the will of God (*Matt.* 12:50). Those who have God as their Father are those who have come to God in Jesus Christ (*John* 1:12–13). What is in view here is particularly how people have treated those who belong to Christ's family. It is precisely this matter that marks out Christians as distinct from the world: 'By this all people will know that you are my disciples, if you have love for one another' (*John* 13:35). It is that important mark that is highlighted on the last day.

The goats are placed at the left hand of the king (verse 33), opposite the position of favour. They are condemned and rejected because they did not treat the Son of Man with kindness when he was in need. They too are surprised, for they wonder when they ever saw him in need and did not minister to him. But again, they failed to do these things, when they failed to do it for 'the least of these' (verse 45). Neglect, rejection, and mistreatment of the servants of Christ has brought upon them unimaginable punishment.

JUDGMENT BY WORKS?

Reading about this final judgment, focused as it is on the works performed by the sheep and the goats, Christian readers are likely to be as surprised as the sheep and the goats. For if judgment is to be on the basis of our works, who can hope for salvation? Have not we all sinned, and fallen short of the glory of God? Have we not been taught to look away from our own works and trust in Christ alone for salvation, to trust that his works will be received as our own and that his death be received as our own? Yes, indeed, we are taught these things. But we must also remember that while faith alone saves, the faith that saves us is never alone (*James* 2:14–26). We show our faith by our works. When we are saved by faith, we become new creatures in Christ. We are not yet made *perfect* creatures in Christ, but we do become *new* creatures in Christ. Thus, our lives show our salvation, and on the last day our works will be used to vindicate our faith; showing that it was a true and living faith by which we were saved, and by which we served. Because of that faith, we were united to Christ, and being united to Christ we received his Holy Spirit. By his Holy Spirit we are enabled more and more to live for Christ, and more and more to die to our sins. We hear our Shepherd's voice, and we follow him (*John* 10:27). As he went about doing good (*Acts* 10:38), so do we, that by doing good we might silence the ignorance of foolish people (*1 Pet.* 2:15). At the last day, our Lord himself will use those good works to silence the mouths of the wicked.

SUMMARY

The day of final judgment is one of everlasting consequence, for the verdict rendered on that day continues throughout eternity. Those who enter the kingdom will live there for ever; likewise, those who are rejected go away into eternal punishment (verse 46). The result of our response to Christ could not be more important. Let us then examine ourselves to see if we be in the faith (*2 Cor.* 13:5), for if Christ is in us, he will shine through us. We will never shine perfectly in this life, but the light in us will shine in the darkness, and the darkness will not overcome it. Our good works will indeed 'glorify God in the day of visitation' (*1 Pet.* 2:12).

62

The Saviour's Worth

*W*hen *Jesus had finished all these sayings, he said to his disciples,*
² 'You know that after two days the Passover is coming, and
the Son of Man will be delivered up to be crucified.' ³ Then the chief
priests and the elders of the people gathered in the palace of the high
priest, whose name was Caiaphas, ⁴ and plotted together in order to
arrest Jesus by stealth and kill him. ⁵ But they said, 'Not during the
feast, lest there be an uproar among the people.' ⁶ Now when Jesus
was at Bethany in the house of Simon the leper, ⁷ a woman came up
to him with an alabaster flask of very expensive ointment, and she
poured it on his head as he reclined at table. ⁸ And when the disciples
saw it, they were indignant, saying, 'Why this waste? ⁹ For this could
have been sold for a large sum and given to the poor.' ¹⁰ But Jesus,
aware of this, said to them, 'Why do you trouble the woman? For she
has done a beautiful thing to me. ¹¹ For you always have the poor
with you, but you will not always have me. ¹² In pouring this oint-
ment on my body, she has done it to prepare me for burial. ¹³ Truly,
I say to you, wherever this gospel is proclaimed in the whole world,
what she has done will also be told in memory of her.' ¹⁴ Then one of
the twelve, whose name was Judas Iscariot, went to the chief priests
¹⁵ and said, 'What will you give me if I deliver him over to you?'
And they paid him thirty pieces of silver. ¹⁶ And from that moment he
sought an opportunity to betray him (Matt. 26:1–16).

Another great discourse in Matthew's Gospel is now completed, and he notes it in his characteristic manner: 'When Jesus
had finished all these sayings . . .' This time, however, there is a
difference. Jesus has now finished *all* his sayings. This is the last
of the five major blocks of instruction. Jesus' teaching ministry has
concluded. In the remaining chapters the cross is at hand. Jesus'
final Passover will be observed in Jerusalem, and there he will be
delivered over to be crucified. This section tells us of the plot of

the chief priests and the elders to put Jesus to death (verses 3–5), and of Judas to betray him (verses 14–16). In between these plots, Matthew strategically places the anointing of Jesus for his burial (verses 6–13). This arrangement has much to teach us.

THE PLOT AGAINST HIM

In the home of the high priest Caiaphas the chief priests and elders gather to plot the death of Jesus (verses 3–5). Matthew's way of describing this scene is suggestive of *Psa*. 31:13 which, in the Greek version, reads, 'When they were gathered together against me, they took counsel to take my life.' This Psalm provides one of the words from the cross in Luke's Gospel (verse 5, see *Luke* 23:46), 'Into your hands I commit my spirit.' By this Psalm and much else in the Old Testament we are to understand the life and death of Jesus. The Psalm also declares (verse 15), 'My times are in your hand.' This will become clear, for while the Jewish leaders want to take Jesus away to death, they also fear an uproar from the people, so they say, 'Not during the feast . . .' Yet during the feast it *will* and *must* take place, for Christ our Passover lamb (*1 Cor.* 5:7) must be sacrificed at that time. Not the Jewish leaders, but God himself will determine the time. 'Many are the plans in the mind of a man, but it is the purpose of the LORD that will stand' (*Prov.* 19:21). Before the leaders even meet, Jesus again tells his disciples of his impending death (verse 2).

At about the same time, Judas is plotting to betray Jesus (verses 14–16). He goes to the chief priests asking what they will give him if he betrays Jesus to them. Thirty pieces of silver is the agreed price. It is the price of compensation paid for a dead slave in the law (*Exod.* 21:32). Matthew will show how it fulfilled prophecy in *Matt.* 27:3–9. Here, however, he is content to note that the agreement had been reached. The plot is now complete: the authorities are seeking to take him and kill him, and Judas has agreed to betray him.

ANOINTED FOR HIS BURIAL

Between the stories of the Jewish leaders who plotted against Jesus and Judas who bargained to betray him, Matthew inserts the story of Jesus' anointing at Bethany. The chief act of the Messiah ('Anointed One') will be to die for his people, so the story of his anointing is most appropriate at this place. John places this story just before the triumphal entry into Jerusalem on Palm Sunday. In Matthew the meeting of the Jewish leaders is placed after that, just two days before the Passover (verse 2). Matthew's placement of the anointing story here seems to be motivated by topical rather than chronological concerns. Its placement is intended to tell us something important.

In comparison with the way this story is told by Mark and John, Matthew's version is sparse (see *Mark* 14:1–9, *John* 12:1-8). What he tells us, and what he does not, helps us to see what he wants to emphasize. He does not tell us that it was Mary who anointed Jesus, or that Martha and Lazarus were there (see *John* 12:1). He does not tell us the estimated price of the perfume (see *Mark* 14:5), though he does mention that it was 'very expensive ointment'. Like Mark and John, he does note the protest against this 'waste' (verse 8), with the observation that the alabaster flask might have been sold for a large sum and the money given to the poor (verse 9). Like them also, Matthew tells us that Jesus rebuked this protest sternly, defending the woman's service as a 'beautiful thing', and prophesying that she will always be remembered for this wherever 'this gospel of the kingdom is proclaimed in the whole world' (verse 13). In the story of Judas which immediately follows in Mark and Matthew, both tell us that Judas went to the chief priests in order to betray Jesus, and received money for it; but only Matthew tells us that Judas *asked* for the money.

The placement of this story between the plotting of the Jewish leaders and the plan of Judas to betray Jesus provides a striking contrast in how Jesus is regarded. Judas and the Jewish leaders settle on a mere thirty pieces of silver (estimated at about 120 *denarii*, wages for about four months), while Mary lavishly pours upon his head a 'very expensive ointment'. It could have been sold for 300 *denarii*, about a year's wages, according to Judas' own estimate, *John* 12:5, and he would likely know. Matthew shows that even the disciples are uncomprehending of the woman's gift, and themselves join the protest against its 'waste'. But Jesus welcomes the gift, commends the woman, and promises that she will have enduring fame for it. Then once again Jesus points his disciples toward the cross which is now before him (verse 12). How little did they understand how precious were the moments they now shared with Jesus. If they had, they would have counted the woman's anointing as far too little tribute, not too much.

SUMMARY

The placement of the plotting against Jesus alongside his anointing with the costly perfume serves to highlight both. The plots stand out as that much more wicked in comparison with the loving devotion shown by the woman. Her lavish display of love is that much greater in the light of the plotters' perfidy. So the text both warns us and instructs us. It tells us to spare nothing in our service and devotion to Christ, and it sternly warns us against any thought or course of action that fails to recognize the supreme worth he must have in our lives. May God help us to live after this woman's example, and give to him all that we have and are.

Love so amazing, so divine, demands my soul, my life, my all.

Isaac Watts,
When I Survey the Wondrous Cross

63

With You

*N*ow *on the first day of Unleavened Bread the disciples came to Jesus, saying, 'Where will you have us prepare for you to eat the Passover?' [18] He said, 'Go into the city to a certain man and say to him, "The Teacher says, My time is at hand. I will keep the Passover at your house with my disciples."' [19] And the disciples did as Jesus had directed them, and they prepared the Passover. [20] When it was evening, he reclined at table with the twelve. [21] And as they were eating, he said, 'Truly, I say to you, one of you will betray me.' [22] And they were very sorrowful and began to say to him one after another, 'Is it I, Lord?' [23] He answered, 'He who has dipped his hand in the dish with me will betray me. [24] The Son of Man goes as it is written of him, but woe to that man by whom the Son of Man is betrayed! It would have been better for that man if he had not been born.' [25] Judas, who would betray him, answered, 'Is it I, Rabbi?' He said to him, 'You have said so.' [26] Now as they were eating, Jesus took bread, and after blessing it broke it and gave it to the disciples, and said, 'Take, eat; this is my body.' [27] And he took a cup, and when he had given thanks he gave it to them, saying, 'Drink of it, all of you, [28] for this is my blood of the covenant, which is poured out for many for the forgiveness of sins. [29] I tell you I will not drink again of this fruit of the vine until that day when I drink it new with you in my Father's kingdom'* (Matt. 26:17–29).

The feast of the Passover was instituted for Israel on the night they left Egypt, and year after year it commemorated that deliverance (*Exod.* 12). The very name of God was attached to the great salvation of the Passover night (see *Exod.* 6:2–8), so central was it for understanding the nature of God and his covenant with his people. But Passover was much more than just a memory of a great deliverance now past.

[263]

The prophets spoke of a greater exodus to come, one which would culminate in a greater deliverance and a greater inheritance (*Isa.* 40–55; see *Jer.* 16:14–15, 23:7–8). In Christ that greater exodus has been fulfilled. The Lord's Supper which Jesus instituted at the Passover meal now proclaims that greater exodus and points us to its consummation.

DIVINE PREPARATION

Jesus is in full control of the events which are now speeding toward his crucifixion. When his disciples ask where they should prepare the Passover meal, Jesus' reply indicates that the place is already determined. They are simply to go into Jerusalem where they will see a certain man and tell him what Jesus says. The disciples do as they are told.

The simple telling of these preparations, much condensed by Matthew from what we find in Mark and Luke, could cause us to miss the fact that all that now takes place is fully under the sovereign control of the Lord. For instance, Matthew omits the detail given by Mark and Luke of how the disciples are to recognize the man (see *Mark* 14:13 and *Luke* 22:10). Nothing has been left to chance. 'The Son of Man goes as it is written of him . . .' (verse 24). Some might read this story as a tragic unfolding of events in which an innocent man suffers an unjust death, betrayed by a misguided follower.

But believers know it as the story of amazing grace and redeeming love, by which our Saviour God entered into our flesh and blood and ordered all the events of history, in order that he might offer himself in our place and that we might receive the forgiveness of sins. No one takes his life from him; he lays it down of his own accord (see *John* 10:11–18).

EVIL BETRAYAL

This sovereign control of events includes the free and wicked choice of Judas to betray the Christ. Judas did this of his own accord. No compulsion was upon him. Yet at the same time his free and wicked act was under the sovereign control of the Lord of history, who ordered it for the accomplishment of the divine purpose.

As with the brothers of Joseph (see *Gen.* 50:20), what Judas meant for evil God meant for good. What happened was exactly what had been written and prophesied in the Holy Scriptures (verse 24; see also verses 54–56; *John* 13:18, 17:12; *Acts* 1:16–20). Luke puts it even more pointedly: 'For the Son of Man goes as it has been determined' (*Luke* 22:22).

How God's sovereign determination of all events governs and directs the free and responsible acts of wicked people is a great mystery to us, but we can no more deny it than explain it. The Scriptures assert both these truths without embarrassment (see *Isa.* 10:5–19 and *Acts* 4:24–28). Sometimes, as here, both are asserted within the very same verse: 'The Son of Man goes as it is written of him' (divine sovereignty), 'but woe to that man by whom the Son of Man is betrayed' (human responsibility, verse 24, see also *Luke* 22:22 and *Acts* 2:23). All things are under his control and ordered by his will. 'The LORD has made everything for its purpose, even the wicked for the day of trouble' (*Prov.* 16:4).

PERSONAL LOVE

Jesus transformed this celebration of the Passover meal into the Lord's Supper. He took the bread, blessed it, broke it, and gave it to his disciples saying, 'Take, eat; this is my body' (verse 26). Then he took a cup and when he had given thanks for it, he gave it to his disciples saying, 'Drink of it, all of you, for this is my blood of the covenant, which is poured out for many for the forgiveness of sins' (verse 28).

Henceforth the bread and wine would speak to Christians of the body and blood of Christ, given in the place of his people, that they might receive forgiveness of sins.

Matthew and Mark do not record for us the backward-looking instruction of Jesus, 'Do this in remembrance of me', as does Luke (*Luke* 22:19; see also Paul, *1 Cor.* 11:24f.), though it is surely implied. Matthew does, however, share with Mark and Luke the forward-looking word: 'I tell you I will not drink again of this fruit of the vine until that day when I drink it new with you in my Father's kingdom.'

Matthew has recorded a part of Jesus' words which Mark and Luke did not, '. . . *with you* . . .'. As a single instance, this might not seem to tell us much; but viewed within Matthew's Gospel as a whole it highlights something which is very important to him and to us. This Gospel begins and ends with emphasis upon 'God with us' (see *Matt.* 1:23 and 28:20). Here in this passage that point is also being emphasized. In verse 18 Jesus indicates that he wants to eat the Passover 'with my disciples'. In verse 20 his desire is fulfilled, for 'he reclined at table with the twelve'. Now as he shares his last supper with the disciples, he looks forward to that day when he will once again drink the cup new *'with you'* in his Father's kingdom.

We must not miss the strong note of personal love which is to be found in these words. Jesus spoke of this personal love in his high priestly prayer recorded in *John* 17. There in verses 6–19 he prays most movingly for his disciples. In verse 20 he turns to the rest of his church, those who would believe in him through the word of his disciples.

Then of his whole church he prays (verse 24), 'Father, I desire that they also, whom you have given me, may be with me where I am, to see my glory that you have given me because you loved me before the foundation of the world.' It is to that day in the Father's kingdom that Jesus now looks as he shares the fruit of the vine with his disciples, one last time in this world. Until that day of reunion comes, he will abstain from the cup, unwilling to partake of its sweetness until we can join him in it. He waits for that day when he can share it new *'with you'* – with those whom he has loved, for whom he died, and who have believed and trusted in him.

SUMMARY

As the lens of history zooms in on the Last Supper, the total sovereignty of God over all the events of history comes into view in a most marvellous way. Everything in the whole historical process of the world is governed by a plan, the outlines of which are revealed in what has been written in the Holy Scriptures. Even the most wicked deeds imaginable are under the control of the Sovereign Lord, and ordered for the divine purpose; yet they are brought to pass through the freedom of the evildoers, who therefore are fully responsible for their evil.

Furthermore, and to our amazement and comfort, the goal in view is the salvation of the people of God, that they might be with God, and God with them. Truly he is Immanuel, *God with us.* What comfort it is to know that we who believe will be with God, for ever and ever. Amen.

64

Meeting Temptation

*A*nd *when they had sung a hymn, they went out to the Mount of Olives.* [31] *Then Jesus said to them, 'You will all fall away because of me this night. For it is written, "I will strike the shepherd, and the sheep of the flock will be scattered."* [32] *But after I am raised up, I will go before you to Galilee.'* [33] *Peter answered him, 'Though they all fall away because of you, I will never fall away.'* [34] *Jesus said to him, 'Truly, I tell you, this very night, before the cock crows, you will deny me three times.'* [35] *Peter said to him, 'Even if I must die with you, I will not deny you!' And all the disciples said the same.* [36] *Then Jesus went with them to a place called Gethsemane, and he said to his disciples, 'Sit here, while I go over there and pray.'* [37] *And taking with him Peter and the two sons of Zebedee, he began to be sorrowful and troubled.* [38] *Then he said to them, 'My soul is very sorrowful, even to death; remain here, and watch with me.'* [39] *And going a little farther he fell on his face and prayed, saying, 'My Father, if it be possible, let this cup pass from me; nevertheless, not as I will, but as you will.'* [40] *And he came to the disciples and found them sleeping. And he said to Peter, 'So, could you not watch with me one hour?* [41] *Watch and pray that you may not enter into temptation. The spirit indeed is willing, but the flesh is weak.'* [42] *Again, for the second time, he went away and prayed, 'My Father, if this cannot pass unless I drink it, your will be done.'* [43] *And again he came and found them sleeping, for their eyes were heavy.* [44] *So, leaving them again, he went away and prayed for the third time, saying the same words again.* [45] *Then he came to the disciples and said to them, 'Sleep and take your rest later on. See, the hour is at hand, and the Son of Man is betrayed into the hands of sinners.* [46] *Rise, let us be going; see, my betrayer is at hand'* (Matt. 26:30–46).

*A*fter they completed the Passover meal, Jesus and his disciples went out to the Mount of Olives. There Jesus would pray as he prepared for his arrest and crucifixion. He also sought to prepare his disciples for their temptations, but they proved to be heedless of his warnings. The section is most instructive to us about how to meet temptation. What Jesus does, and what his disciples fail to do, shows us the way.

SELF-DECEPTION

Jesus told his disciples numerous times what awaited *him* in Jerusalem. Now he reveals what awaits *them*. 'You will all fall away because of me this night. For it is written,"I will strike the shepherd and the sheep will be scattered." But after I am raised up, I will go before you to Galilee' (verses 31–32). Peter, who often replied too quickly, foolishly asserted the steadfastness of his faith: 'Though they all fall away because of you, I will never fall away' (verse 33). Such was Peter's view of himself. But Jesus told him it would be otherwise, and indicated that Peter would also fall, even denying Jesus three times before the cock crowed in the morning. All the disciples then joined with Peter in denying that they would ever fall away (verses 34–35). They have still not come to have that regard for the Lord's teaching that they should have, nor for what is written in the Scriptures.

Our Lord's knowledge of us, of our weakness and our needs, is so much greater than our own. We are ignorant and deceive ourselves about our spiritual maturity and strength. How much wiser it would be to accept our Lord's assessment of what we can do and what we need. Yet Peter and the other disciples reject the Lord's predictions about their actions. As a result, they also reject his instructions about how to prepare for that night. When the hour of testing arrives, they will not be able to meet it. 'Therefore, let anyone who thinks that he stands take heed lest he fall' (*1 Cor.* 10:12). When the shepherd is struck, the sheep will indeed be scattered.

FAILING TO WATCH

Jesus went with the eleven remaining disciples to Gethsemane. Then, taking Peter and 'the two sons of Zebedee' a little beyond the rest, he told them that his soul was very sorrowful, even to death, and asked them to remain there and watch with him, while he went off a little farther to pray (verses 37–39). Jesus agonized in prayer (*Luke* 22:44), but the disciples fell asleep. Returning to them after prayer, Jesus found them sleeping (verse 40). Then he said to Peter (notice how the passage narrowly focuses on Peter— he alone is named, and to him particularly Jesus speaks), 'So, could you not watch with me for one hour? Watch and pray that you may not enter into temptation. The spirit indeed is willing, but the flesh is weak.'

Minutes before the disciples had been told by Jesus that they would fall away that night. They had all denied it vehemently (verse 35). Jesus had indicated to them that the Scriptures spoke of this very result (verse 31). One would think that this would be enough to put them on their guard, and to reach out for any help they could find that they might be better able to meet the challenge ahead. Yet the warnings did not avail. Not believing that they were capable of falling so, they did not sense the urgency to watch and pray lest they enter into temptation. How foolish they were. How deceived about themselves. Are we not like them all too much? Do we not likewise reject what the Scriptures teach us about ourselves and our needs? Oh that we might have ears to hear and eyes to see.

OUR LORD'S FAITHFULNESS

What the Scriptures and our Lord teach us about the weakness of our flesh should be enough to move us to diligence in prayer. But if not, his example of persevering prayer for the strengthening of his own spirit and flesh puts the exclamation point on the matter. Our Lord himself needed to pray as he faced the temptations of that night and the day to come. He prayed and he prayed. These repeated prayers were not empty repetitions, but the outpouring of a heart in agony over what was to come. He called out to God first in hopes that the cup might pass from him, and then for the strength to drink that cup if he must. If our Lord needed such prayers to face his temptations, do we not also?

We have here a most perfect example for our own praying. It was not wrong for Jesus to ask that the cup might pass from him. It was a bitter cup, one no one could think about drinking without the greatest apprehension. When we too are confronted with difficult trials, we have the example of our Lord to encourage us to pray that the cup might pass from us, while also praying that if that cup must be drunk, then let God's will be done, and let us have strength to do it. Then our persistent prayers become the channel for our strengthening, fortifying us to meet trials with faith and courage. What a privilege it is to be let into this secret chamber of prayer, where the incarnate Son of God pours out fervent petitions to his heavenly Father (see *Heb.* 5:7). That night even his closest disciples were kept at a distance, but here the Holy Spirit gives us all an intimate knowledge of what transpired that night, as the Son of God yielded himself to the Father's will in going to the cross. Oh that such a spirit of prayer would be given to us, for we too must pick up our cross if we would be his disciples (*Matt.* 16:24). How much we need it. How weak we are.

SUMMARY

Peter's self-confidence that night proved altogether misplaced, and so is ours if we ever believe that we are beyond the reach of great temptations to sin. Our spirit may indeed be willing, but our flesh is weak. Only by prayer and by diligent use of all the means of grace, only by putting on the whole armour of God, are we able to stand in the time of temptation (*Eph.* 6:10–20). Let anyone who thinks that he stands take heed lest he fall (*1 Cor.* 10:12).

> *Rise, my soul, to watch and pray, from thy sleep awaken;*
> *Be not by the evil day unawares o'ertaken.*
> *For the foe, well we know, oft his harvest reapeth*
> *While the Christian sleepeth.*

Johann B. Freystein,
Rise, My Soul, to Watch and Pray

65

It Must Be So

*W*hile he was still speaking, Judas came, one of the twelve, and with him a great crowd with swords and clubs, from the chief priests and the elders of the people. *48* Now the betrayer had given them a sign, saying, 'The one I will kiss is the man; seize him.' *49* And he came up to Jesus at once and said, 'Greetings, Rabbi!' And he kissed him. *50* Jesus said to him, 'Friend, do what you came to do.' Then they came up and laid hands on Jesus and seized him. *51* And behold, one of those who were with Jesus stretched out his hand and drew his sword and struck the servant of the high priest and cut off his ear. *52* Then Jesus said to him, 'Put your sword back into its place. For all who take the sword will perish by the sword. *53* Do you think that I cannot appeal to my Father, and he will at once send me more than twelve legions of angels? *54* But how then should the Scriptures be fulfilled, that it must be so?' *55* At that hour Jesus said to the crowds, 'Have you come out as against a robber, with swords and clubs to capture me? Day after day I sat in the temple teaching, and you did not seize me. *56* But all this has taken place that the Scriptures of the prophets might be fulfilled.' Then all the disciples left him and fled. *57* Then those who had seized Jesus led him to Caiaphas the high priest, where the scribes and the elders had gathered. *58* And Peter was following him at a distance, as far as the courtyard of the high priest, and going inside he sat with the guards to see the end. *59* Now the chief priests and the whole Council were seeking false testimony against Jesus that they might put him to death, *60* but they found none, though many false witnesses came forward. At last two came forward *61* and said, 'This man said, "I am able to destroy the temple of God, and to rebuild it in three days."' *62* And the high priest stood up and said, 'Have you no answer to make? What is it that these men testify against you?' *63* But Jesus remained silent. And the high priest said to him, 'I adjure you by the living God, tell us if you are the Christ, the Son of God.' *64* Jesus said to him, 'You have said so. But I tell you, from now on you will see the Son of Man seated at the right hand of Power and coming on the clouds of heaven.'

*⁶⁵ Then the high priest tore his robes and said, 'He has uttered blas-
phemy. What further witnesses do we need? You have now heard his
blasphemy. ⁶⁶ What is your judgment?' They answered, 'He deserves
death.' ⁶⁷ Then they spat in his face and struck him. And some slapped
him, ⁶⁸ saying, 'Prophesy to us, you Christ! Who is it that struck
you?'* (Matt. 26:47–68).

The prayer time in the garden ended suddenly, and the action
now moves swiftly to the cross. Judas arrives with a 'great
crowd' of people wielding swords and clubs, sent from the chief
priests and the elders of the people. There will be a brief attempt
by the disciples to resist the arrest, but Jesus will order them to
cease. He gives himself over to the arrest and is quickly taken
before Caiaphas and the Sanhedrin. The prayer time in the garden
has settled for him the issue of the cross: *It must be so*.

THE SCRIPTURES MUST BE FULFILLED

Though Judas arrives with a great crowd to arrest Jesus, it is clear
that Jesus is in control of all that unfolds. Jesus responds to the
kiss of betrayal, saying, 'Friend, do what you came to do' (verse
50). When Jesus is arrested, one of the disciples draws a sword
and cuts off the ear of the high priest's servant (John tells us it was
Peter, *John* 18:10). Jesus orders him to put away his sword, explaining that if resistance were appropriate he could easily call upon his
Father, who would immediately send forth more than twelve
legions of angels. But doing so would divert him from what he
came to do. He tells them that the Scriptures must be fulfilled, for
'it must be so' (verse 54).

There is a necessity to all that now happens, but it is not the out-
working of a blind, inexorable fate. It is rather the unfolding of the
eternal counsel of God's will, to save a people for himself through
the mediation of his Son. It must be so! Not because fate demands
it, but because omnipotent love has decreed it. From all eternity
God has chosen a people for himself and in love predestined them
for adoption through Jesus Christ, according to the purpose of his
will (*Eph.* 1:5). The prayer in the garden had been, 'My Father, if it
be possible, let this cup pass from me . . .' (*Matt.* 26:39). But it was
not possible, if the beloved and chosen people were to be saved. So

[273]

Judas and the guards come to do as they will, Peter and the disciples do as they are told, and Jesus willingly submits to arrest, for thus the Scriptures have prophesied, and 'it must be so'.

HE WAS DESERTED BY ALL

After Jesus was taken away, 'all the disciples left him and fled' (verse 56). This too was just as had been prophesied. Jesus had earlier that night predicted that they would all fall away, and he quoted to them from the prophet Zechariah, 'I will strike the shepherd, and the sheep of the flock will be scattered' (*Matt.* 26:31). Peter had denied that would happen, along with all the others (26:35). Yet it happened just as Jesus had said, just as it had been written. Nothing had been left to chance. Everything was ordered for the accomplishment of the divine purpose.

Here is a wonderful window into the mystery of God's love. For God shows his love for us in that while we were still sinners, Christ died for us (*Rom.* 5:8). On this night when Jesus faced the agony of giving himself over to the cross, not just to his accusers and the bodily pain of crucifixion, but to the wrath of God for sin, he gave himself to die for those who deserted him. Even his closest disciples could not stay and watch with him while he prayed for the strength to go forward in his mission. No wonder Paul dates the institution of the Lord's Supper to 'the night when he was betrayed' (*1 Cor.* 11:23).

> *Depth of mercy! Can there be*
> *Mercy still reserved for me?*
> *Can my God his wrath forbear?*
> *Me, the chief of sinners, spare?*
>
> *I have long withstood his grace,*
> *Long provoked him to his face;*
> *Would not hearken to his calls,*
> *Grieved him by a thousand falls.*
>
> *Still for me the Saviour stands,*
> *Shows his wounds, and spreads his hands;*
> *God is love! I know, I feel;*
> *Jesus weeps, and loves me still.*

Charles Wesley, *Depth of Mercy!*

THE SON OF MAN IN GLORY

When Jesus had been seized he was taken before Caiaphas and the Sanhedrin. They were seeking charges against him to put him to death (verse 59). After two witnesses had finally testified against him, Caiaphas demanded that he tell them whether he was the Christ or not. Jesus answered him, 'You have said so' (meaning, 'It is exactly as you say'). Then Jesus tells Caiaphas and the whole council that from this time on they 'will see the Son of Man seated at the right hand of Power and coming on the clouds of heaven' (verse 64). For the Jewish leaders, the reference is unmistakable. Jesus is identifying himself with the 'son of man' figure in *Dan.* 7:13–14, to whom is given everlasting dominion over all peoples and over all the earth. The reference to the 'clouds of heaven' is to the glory-cloud of God himself. Jesus has clearly equated himself with God. Caiaphas concludes that no further witnesses will be necessary since Jesus has committed blasphemy. Jesus is immediately condemned to death (verse 66). Then they spat upon him and mocked him.

In the eyes of the Jewish leaders, Jesus would be given the death he fully deserved, the most humiliating and shameful death that could be given. But in the cross is the very glory of Christ, dying in the place of his people, bearing the penalty for their sins. Jesus looked upon this time as 'the hour . . . for the Son of Man to be glorified' (*John* 12:23). Here too is all our glory, for nothing can surpass the glory of being one for whom Christ died (see *Gal.* 6:14).

SUMMARY

Seen from one perspective, the events of this 'night when he was betrayed' are shocking for what they reveal of human sinfulness. At the same time, however, these events reveal the divine glory in all its fullness. What amazing love it is! The Scriptures prophesied all that came to pass, and all did come to pass, just as it had been foretold. Had there been another way to save us, another cup he could drink to save us, it would have been so. But there was not. It must be so! And so it was. Thanks be to God.

66

Two Subplots

*N*ow *Peter was sitting outside in the courtyard. And a servant girl came up to him and said, 'You also were with Jesus the Galilean.'* [70] *But he denied it before them all, saying, 'I do not know what you mean.'* [71] *And when he went out to the entrance, another servant girl saw him, and she said to the bystanders, 'This man was with Jesus of Nazareth.'* [72] *And again he denied it with an oath: 'I do not know the man.'* [73] *After a little while the bystanders came up and said to Peter, 'Certainly you too are one of them, for your accent betrays you.'* [74] *Then he began to invoke a curse on himself and to swear, 'I do not know the man.' And immediately the cock crowed.* [75] *And Peter remembered the saying of Jesus, 'Before the cock crows, you will deny me three times.'' And he went out and wept bitterly.* [27:1] *When morning came, all the chief priests and the elders of the people took counsel against Jesus to put him to death.* [2] *And they bound him and led him away and delivered him over to Pilate the governor.* [3] *Then when Judas, his betrayer, saw that Jesus was condemned, he changed his mind and brought back the thirty pieces of silver to the chief priests and the elders,* [4] *saying, 'I have sinned by betraying innocent blood.' They said, 'What is that to us? See to it yourself.'* [5] *And throwing down the pieces of silver into the temple, he departed, and he went and hanged himself.* [6] *But the chief priests, taking the pieces of silver, said, 'It is not lawful to put them into the treasury, since it is blood money.'* [7] *So they took counsel and bought with them the potter's field as a burial place for strangers.* [8] *Therefore that field has been called the Field of Blood to this day.* [9] *Then was fulfilled what had been spoken by the prophet Jeremiah, saying, 'And they took the thirty pieces of silver, the price of him on whom a price had been set by some of the sons of Israel,* [10] *and they gave them for the potter's field, as the Lord directed me'* (Matt. 26:69–27:10).

This section tells us little about Jesus, only that Jesus was condemned by the Sanhedrin and taken to Pilate. The focus is on two others, Peter and Judas. As Jesus is being examined, Peter is in the courtyard outside. There he is identified as a follower of Jesus, but he denies it; just as Jesus had predicted. When Judas sees that Jesus is condemned by the Sanhedrin, he regrets what he has done, and he hangs himself. Both stories have much to teach us.

VAIN SELF-CONFIDENCE

Peter had vehemently denied that he would ever betray Jesus, when Jesus said that the disciples would all fall away. He protested that even if all the other disciples fell away, he would not (*Matt.* 26:33). Jesus then predicted that Peter would in fact deny him three times before the cock crowed the next morning. Again Peter emphatically denied it and said to Jesus, 'Even if I must die with you, I will not deny you!' All the disciples then said the same (26:35).

Peter and the other disciples could not believe about themselves what Jesus said, yet it all proved to be true. Of the other disciples we are only told that they all fled when Jesus was arrested (26:56). But for Peter we get a detailed account of each of his three denials (verses 69–75). How the proud boaster has fallen! Peter could not believe it himself. When immediately the cock crowed after his third denial, the words of Jesus came back to him and pierced his soul. He went out and wept bitterly.

VAIN REGRET

When Judas saw that Jesus had been condemned, Matthew says 'he changed his mind' and brought back the thirty pieces of silver (*Matt.* 27:3). He also confessed that he had 'sinned by betraying innocent blood' (verse 4). This might look like repentance, but it is not. How can we tell? From other places in Scripture we know that Judas was lost. Jesus said he was the son of destruction, the only one lost from among the twelve (*John* 17:12). He was the one for whom it would have been better if he had not been born (*Matt.* 26:24). The Scriptures were fulfilled in his destruction (*John* 17:12, *Acts* 1:20). If he had truly confessed his sins, he would have been forgiven (*1 John* 1:9). If he had repented, he would have been saved, for all who call upon the name of the Lord Jesus Christ will be saved (*Rom.* 10:13). So, since he is known to have perished, we must conclude that whatever he did, he did not repent.

[277]

What then did he do? He came to regret what he had done. *Regret* is not the same as *repentance*. We can regret doing something merely because of how things turned out, not because we came to despise the thing itself. In repentance, we sorrow over our sins. If we regret what we have done, we might be sorrowful only over the consequences of our sins. Outwardly it might be hard for others to tell the difference, but inwardly there is a world of difference, and the difference is known to him who looks upon the heart (*1 Sam.* 16:7, *Jer.* 17:10). Any sinner can come to regret his sins, merely for the consequences they bring. But repentance is a work of grace in the heart, making us hate our very sins, and causing us to turn from them and in faith turn to Christ that we might be saved.

AVOIDING A FALL

Our Lord Jesus Christ knows us all through and through. He knows the evil corruption that is within us, and how easily we can fall. He knows us far better than we know ourselves. Consequently it is vitally important for us to believe our Lord's word when he tells us what he sees in us. He told Peter and the other disciples to pray that they might not enter into temptation (*Matt.* 26:41). But Peter and the others did not take heed to this word. The means of grace are given to us so that we might grow spiritually and become strong, yet how neglectful we are of these means. Our Bibles can easily remain closed books to us, or our reading in the Bible can be without meditation and application. Our prayers can be superficial and sporadic. Our attendance at worship can likewise be sporadic, and even if faithful in attendance we can become mechanical in our approach. The fall of Peter should be a warning to all of us. He himself tells us that a vital, growing, spiritual life is the best means to keep us from falling (*2 Pet.* 1:5–11).

The presence of Judas among the disciples also stands as a witness to us. There must have been something that attracted him to follow Jesus, yet in the end he betrayed him. It is too easy for us simply to dismiss him as a reprobate and sinner, as if he was altogether unlike the rest of us. We must remember that he was so much like the other disciples that they never suspected what he was plotting. Even when Jesus identified him as the one who would betray him, the disciples did not understand (*John* 13:21–30). This must tell us that outwardly there was little difference between Judas and the other disciples. He seemed to be one of them. That is what must challenge us. We might suppose that people capable of great sins are nothing like us, that there is some special wickedness in them (not present in us) that leads them to do such things. But all the wickedness we need to commit such sins is already in each of us. Certainly there was in David enough to lead him into great sin. There was enough in Peter to lead him to deny Christ. 'Therefore, let anyone who thinks he stands take heed lest he fall' (*1 Cor.* 10:12).

SUMMARY

The stories of Peter's denial and Judas' betrayal are placed side by side for our instruction. Both fell into sin. One found repentance and forgiveness. The other found only regret, and everlasting destruction. The difference between Peter and Judas was in their hearts, a difference only God can make. So call upon him, and trust him; then follow him and obey him. The one sure hope of avoiding a fall is to grow in the grace and knowledge of our Lord and Saviour Jesus Christ (*2 Pet.* 3:18).

67

Suffered under Pontius Pilate

Now Jesus stood before the governor, and the governor asked him, 'Are you the King of the Jews?' Jesus said, 'You have said so.' [12] But when he was accused by the chief priests and elders, he gave no answer. [13] Then Pilate said to him, 'Do you not hear how many things they testify against you?' [14] But he gave him no answer, not even to a single charge, so that the governor was greatly amazed. [15] Now at the feast the governor was accustomed to release for the crowd any one prisoner whom they wanted. [16] And they had then a notorious prisoner called Barabbas. [17] So when they had gathered, Pilate said to them, 'Whom do you want me to release for you: Barabbas, or Jesus who is called Christ?' [18] For he knew that it was out of envy that they had delivered him up. [19] Besides, while he was sitting on the judgment seat, his wife sent word to him, 'Have nothing to do with that righteous man, for I have suffered much because of him today in a dream.' [20] Now the chief priests and the elders persuaded the crowd to ask for Barabbas and destroy Jesus. [21] The governor again said to them, 'Which of the two do you want me to release for you?' And they said, 'Barabbas.' [22] Pilate said to them, 'Then what shall I do with Jesus who is called Christ?' They all said, 'Let him be crucified!' [23] And he said, 'Why, what evil has he done?' But they shouted all the more, 'Let him be crucified!' [24] So when Pilate saw that he was gaining nothing, but rather that a riot was beginning, he took water and washed his hands before the crowd, saying, 'I am innocent of this man's blood; see to it yourselves.' [25] And all the people answered, 'His blood be on us and on our children!' [26] Then he released for them Barabbas, and having scourged Jesus, delivered him to be crucified. [27] Then the soldiers of the governor took Jesus into the governor's headquarters, and they gathered the whole battalion before him. [28] And they stripped him and put a scarlet robe on him, [29] and twisting together a crown of thorns, they put it on his head and put a reed in his right hand. And kneeling before him, they mocked him, saying, 'Hail, King of the Jews!' [30] And they spit on him and took the reed and struck him on the head. *³¹ And when they had mocked him, they stripped him of the robe and put his own clothes on him and led him away to crucify him* (Matt. 27:11–31).

B etween the stories of Peter's denial and Judas' betrayal, Matthew inserted a brief report of the outcome of Jesus' trial before the Jews and his transfer to the court of Pilate (*Matt.* 27:1, 2). The Sanhedrin voted for his condemnation and they took him to Pilate in hopes of having him executed. This section picks up the story left off there.

THE KING OF THE JEWS

Matthew tells us very little about the interrogation of Jesus before Pilate. Pilate asks if he is the King of the Jews, and Jesus answers him affirmatively. That is the last time Jesus speaks in this Gospel until his cry of dereliction from the cross, 'My God, My God, why have you forsaken me?' (27:46). Further questions from Pilate are met with silence, to Pilate's great amazement (verse 14). Matthew no doubts wants us to see the obvious connection to *Isa.* 53:7.

> *He was oppressed, and he was afflicted, yet he opened not his mouth; like a lamb that is led to the slaughter, and like a sheep that before its shearers is silent, so he opened not his mouth.*

The reference to Jesus as King will come up again in this section (verse 29). The soldiers of Pilate mock and abuse Jesus. They put a scarlet robe on him and twist together a crown of thorns; then they kneel before him and mock him, 'Hail, King of the Jews!' Then they spit on him and strike him, and lead him away to be crucified (verses 27–31). This title will be used once more in the next section (verse 37), where it is placed as a marker on Jesus' cross. Each time the title is used in derision. Jesus is also mockingly called 'the king of Israel' by the chief priests, scribes, and elders (verse 42). In the eyes of his enemies, Jesus cannot possibly be a king if he is undergoing such treatment, yet it is precisely these things that will secure his kingdom. By his death the kingdom of evil and death itself will be overthrown. Jesus will hereby secure for himself 'all authority in heaven and on earth' (*Matt.* 28:18).

[281]

And being found in human form, he humbled himself by becoming obedient to the point of death, even death on a cross. Therefore God has highly exalted him and bestowed on him the name that is above every name, so that at the name of Jesus every knee should bow, in heaven and on earth and under the earth, and every tongue confess that Jesus Christ is Lord, to the glory of God the Father (Phil. 2:8–11).

BARABBAS

So far in Matthew's narrative we have seen Jesus betrayed by Judas, denied by Peter, deserted by the rest of the twelve, and falsely accused and condemned by the Jewish leaders. Now the crowds turn against him as well. There was a custom at that time that the governor would release a prisoner during the feast of Passover. At that time Pilate was holding a notorious man by the name of Barabbas (verse 18). Mark tells us that 'he had committed murder in the insurrection', so perhaps he was a popular hero with the people for opposing Rome (*Mark* 15:7, see also *Luke* 23:19). Pilate gave the crowd a choice: Barabbas or Jesus? Persuaded by their leaders, the crowds demand to have Barabbas released and not Jesus. When Pilate asks what then should be done to Jesus, 'They all said, "Let him be crucified!"' (verse 22). Pilate asks them, 'Why, what evil has he done?' They simply shout all the more, 'Let him be crucified!' (verse 23). It is just as Isaiah predicted:

He was despised and rejected by men; a man of sorrows, and acquainted with grief; and as one from whom men hide their faces he was despised, and we esteemed him not (Isa. 53:3)

Or as David said:

But I am a worm and not a man, scorned by mankind and despised by the people (Psa. 22:6).

THAT RIGHTEOUS MAN

During the trial before Pilate, Matthew tells us something unique, something not mentioned by the other evangelists. While Pilate is seated on his judgment seat, his wife sends him word: 'Have nothing to do with that righteous man, for I have suffered much because of him today in a dream' (verse 19). Dreams have had special value in this Gospel. Four times Joseph was instructed by an angel of the Lord appearing to him in a dream (*Matt.* 1:20; 2:13, 19, 22). The magi from the east were also warned in a dream not to return to Herod (2:12). Now again a dream is used to provide divine guidance, although this time it is ignored. Yet the dream provides significant commentary on the whole proceeding. Pilate's wife says that Jesus is a righteous man, and Pilate himself gives ample testimony to Jesus' innocence. He asks the crowd what evil he has done (verse 23), and when the crowd demands that Jesus be crucified, he seeks to wash his hands of the innocent man's blood (verse 24), for he knows this is a travesty of justice. Two witnesses have thus confirmed his innocence, including Pilate himself; yet he delivers Jesus over to be crucified (verse 26). Isaiah had foretold it: 'By oppression and judgment he was taken away . . .' (*Isa.* 53:8).

SUMMARY

He died as a righteous man for the unrighteous (*1 Pet.* 3:18). Pilate could find no guilt in him, yet had him scourged and delivered him over to crucifixion. Through all the false accusations, and all the mockings, 'he opened not his mouth'. He went without protest, for this was why he came.

> *He committed no sin, neither was deceit found in his mouth. When he was reviled, he did not revile in return; when he suffered, he did not threaten, but continued entrusting himself to him who judges justly* (1 Pet. 2:22, 23).

68

Crucified, Dead, and Buried

*A*s they went out, they found a man of Cyrene, Simon by name.
They compelled this man to carry his cross. *³³ And when they
came to a place called Golgotha (which means Place of a Skull),
³⁴ they offered him wine to drink, mixed with gall, but when he tasted
it, he would not drink it. ³⁵ And when they had crucified him, they
divided his garments among them by casting lots. ³⁶ Then they sat
down and kept watch over him there. ³⁷ And over his head they put
the charge against him, which read, 'This is Jesus, the King of the
Jews.' ³⁸ Then two robbers were crucified with him, one on the right
and one on the left. ³⁹ And those who passed by derided him, wagging
their heads ⁴⁰ and saying, 'You who would destroy the temple and
rebuild it in three days, save yourself! If you are the Son of God,
come down from the cross.' ⁴¹ So also the chief priests, with the scribes
and elders, mocked him, saying, ⁴² 'He saved others; he cannot save
himself. He is the King of Israel; let him come down now from the
cross, and we will believe in him. ⁴³ He trusts in God; let God deliver
him now, if he desires him. For he said, "I am the Son of God."'
⁴⁴ And the robbers who were crucified with him also reviled him in the
same way. ⁴⁵ Now from the sixth hour there was darkness over all the
land until the ninth hour. ⁴⁶ And about the ninth hour Jesus cried out
with a loud voice, saying, 'Eli, Eli, lema sabachthani?' that is, 'My
God, my God, why have you forsaken me?' ⁴⁷ And some of the bystanders, hearing it, said, 'This man is calling Elijah.' ⁴⁸ And one of
them at once ran and took a sponge, filled it with sour wine, and put
it on a reed and gave it to him to drink. ⁴⁹ But the others said, 'Wait,
let us see whether Elijah will come to save him.' ⁵⁰ And Jesus cried
out again with a loud voice and yielded up his spirit. ⁵¹ And behold,
the curtain of the temple was torn in two, from top to bottom. And the
earth shook, and the rocks were split. ⁵² The tombs also were opened.
And many bodies of the saints who had fallen asleep were raised,
⁵³ and coming out of the tombs after his resurrection they went into
the holy city and appeared to many. ⁵⁴ When the centurion and those
who were with him, keeping watch over Jesus, saw the earthquake*

and what took place, they were filled with awe and said, 'Truly this was the Son of God!' *⁵⁵ There were also many women there, looking on from a distance, who had followed Jesus from Galilee, ministering to him,* *⁵⁶ among whom were Mary Magdalene and Mary the mother of James and Joseph and the mother of the sons of Zebedee.* *⁵⁷ When it was evening, there came a rich man from Arimathea, named Joseph, who also was a disciple of Jesus.* *⁵⁸ He went to Pilate and asked for the body of Jesus. Then Pilate ordered it to be given to him.* *⁵⁹ And Joseph took the body and wrapped it in a clean linen shroud* *⁶⁰ and laid it in his own new tomb, which he had cut in the rock. And he rolled a great stone to the entrance of the tomb and went away.* *⁶¹ Mary Magdalene and the other Mary were there, sitting opposite the tomb* (Matt. 27:32–61).

The crucifixion, death, and burial of Jesus are recounted in this section. Again, the Old Testament becomes our guide in understanding what takes place. Matthew is indeed a scribe well trained for the kingdom of heaven, who brings forth from his treasure what is new and what is old (*Matt.* 13:52).

HE DIED ACCORDING TO THE SCRIPTURES

The brief summary of the faith given to us by Paul in *1 Cor.* 15:1–10 tells us that 'Christ died for our sins according to the Scriptures' (verse 3). Matthew certainly makes this point clear. The language he uses to recount the crucifixion is replete with phrases taken from the Old Testament. The most notable of these are the following:

- verse 34: 'they offered him wine to drink, mixed with gall' – see *Psa.* 69:21a.

- verse 35: 'they divided his garments among them by casting lots' – see *Psa.* 22:18.

- verse 38: 'Then two robbers were crucified with him' – see *Isa.* 53:9a.

- verse 39: 'those who passed by derided him, wagging their heads' – see *Psa.* 22:7.

- verse 43: The chief priests, scribes, and elders unwittingly fulfil the Scriptures when they say, 'He trusts in God; let God deliver him now, if he desires him' – see *Psa.* 22:8.

- verse 48: 'one of them at once ran and took a sponge, filled it with sour wine, and put it on a reed and gave it to him to drink' – see *Psa.* 69:21b.
- verse 57: 'there came a rich man from Arimathea' – see *Isa.* 53:9b.

As Matthew himself would say, all these things took place to fulfil what had been spoken by the prophets.

HE DESCENDED INTO HELL

Some preachers and moviemakers have believed that people will be helped in understanding the work of Christ on the cross if they are given a more graphic presentation of the crucifixion than what can be found in the Gospel narratives. In comparison with such presentations, the Gospel narratives seem almost sanitized. The barest descriptions are given to us of the physical torments inflicted on Jesus. There is good reason for this moderation: detailed emphasis upon the physical sufferings of Christ will not take us deeper into an understanding of what happened at the cross or what he accomplished there. Of greater help to us is the cry of dereliction (verse 46), 'My God, my God, why have you forsaken me?' Quoted from *Psa.* 22:1, these words reveal the deep and agonizing separation from God the Father that the Son experienced in his human nature and consciousness, when the wrath of God came upon him for the sins of his people. If hell is what our sins deserve, then hell must be what Christ suffers for us.

John Calvin rightly taught that Christ descended into hell while he hung on the cross (*Institutes*, II. xvi. 8–12). Paul describes the torments of hell as being 'away from the presence of the Lord and from the glory of his might' (*2 Thess.* 1:9). Our Saviour knew that separation and cried out in agony. No impassioned rhetoric or film portrayal can possibly convey to us what it was like to suffer under the wrath of God the due penalty of sin for all who will be saved. When 'from the sixth hour there was darkness over all the land until the ninth hour' (verse 45), Christ experienced 'the outer darkness' (*Matt.* 8:12). He did not journey to hell in his spirit after he died, for he completed the payment for sin while still on the cross. This is indicated by his words, 'It is finished' (*John* 19:30). In addition, he assured the penitent thief that he would be in Paradise with him that very day (*Luke* 23:43). So the descent into hell is on the cross, where the Son of God dies under the wrath of God to save his people from their sins. The details of the physical torments of scourging and crucifixion do not begin to tell us what we most need to know.

By means of his own shed blood, Jesus has secured for us an eternal redemption (*Heb.* 9:12). Therefore we have confidence to enter into the presence of God 'by the new and living way that he opened for us through the curtain, that is, through his flesh . . .' (*Heb.* 10:19). Because Christ did descend into hell to make full payment for our sin, the curtain of the temple was torn in two, from top to bottom (*Matt.* 27:51); signifying that the separation between God and his people has now been removed, since a sacrifice has been made which has put away sin for all time (see *Heb.* 10:11–14). A great earthquake caused the curtain to tear and, just as it opened the way into the temple's most holy place, so it also opened many tombs. Many bodies of the saints who had died were raised and, coming out of their tombs after the resurrection, they went into the city and appeared to many people (verses 51–53). When the soldiers who carried out the execution saw these things, they were filled with awe and confessed, 'Truly this was the Son of God' (verse 54).

HE WAS BURIED

The details of Jesus burial are remarkable. Considering all who have turned against him, one wonders if there are any who will step forward to bury him. There were faithful women who had been looking on from a distance (verse 55–56). They had followed Jesus from Galilee, and they remained faithful to the end. But a surprising figure emerges to carry out the burial, a rich man from Arimathea named Joseph (verse 57). Matthew tells us that he was a disciple of Jesus. Mark tells us that he was a respected member of the Sanhedrin, who was looking for the kingdom of God (*Mark* 15:43). Luke says he was 'a good and righteous man, who had not consented to their decision and action . . .' (*Luke* 23:50–51). John tells us that he was a disciple of Jesus, but 'secretly for fear of the Jews' (*John* 19:38). Yet now, in the midst of Passover feast, he 'took courage' (*Mark* 15:43) and – with Nicodemus (see *John* 19:39) – dared to touch the dead body of a crucified man (*Num.* 19:11–22, *Deut.* 21:22–23). Ceremonially, his Passover ended at that moment, but it mattered little. For Christ, our Passover lamb, had been sacrificed. We can all now celebrate the festival (*1 Cor.* 5:7–8).

SUMMARY

Crucified, dead, and buried – so says the Apostles' Creed. In that brief summary is nearly the whole work of salvation. When Jesus foretold these events to his disciples, they could not believe this would ever happen to Jesus (*Matt.* 16:22). Yet the Scriptures had foretold that it was necessary for the Christ to suffer these things, and then on the third day . . .

69

The Third Day He Rose Again
from the Dead

*N*ext day, that is, after the day of Preparation, the chief priests and the Pharisees gathered before Pilate [63] and said, 'Sir, we remember how that impostor said, while he was still alive, "After three days I will rise." [64] Therefore order the tomb to be made secure until the third day, lest his disciples go and steal him away and tell the people, "He has risen from the dead," and the last fraud will be worse than the first.' [65] Pilate said to them, 'You have a guard of soldiers. Go, make it as secure as you can.' [66] So they went and made the tomb secure by sealing the stone and setting a guard. [28:1] Now after the Sabbath, toward the dawn of the first day of the week, Mary Magdalene and the other Mary went to see the tomb. [2] And behold, there was a great earthquake, for an angel of the Lord descended from heaven and came and rolled back the stone and sat on it. [3] His appearance was like lightning, and his clothing white as snow. [4] And for fear of him the guards trembled and became like dead men. [5] But the angel said to the women, 'Do not be afraid, for I know that you seek Jesus who was crucified. [6] He is not here, for he has risen, as he said. Come, see the place where he lay. [7] Then go quickly and tell his disciples that he has risen from the dead, and behold, he is going before you to Galilee; there you will see him. See, I have told you.' [8] So they departed quickly from the tomb with fear and great joy, and ran to tell his disciples. [9] And behold, Jesus met them and said, 'Greetings!' And they came up and took hold of his feet and worshipped him. [10] Then Jesus said to them, 'Do not be afraid; go and tell my brothers to go to Galilee, and there they will see me.' [11] While they were going, behold, some of the guard went into the city and told the chief priests all that had taken place. [12] And when they had assembled with the elders and taken counsel, they gave a sufficient sum of money to the soldiers [13] and said, 'Tell people, "His disciples came by night and stole him away while we were asleep." [14] And if this comes to the *governor's ears, we will satisfy him and keep you out of trouble.'* [15] *So they took the money and did as they were directed. And this story has been spread among the Jews to this day* (Matt. 27:62–28:15).

We have arrived at the final chapter in Matthew's Gospel, and in this section we have the account of the resurrection. As with the other Gospels, Matthew stresses the empty tomb and the resurrection appearances. The women are first in connection with both. Matthew uniquely preserves the report of the guards to the Jewish authorities and the ensuing strategy to discredit the report of the supernatural. Overall, however, Matthew shows little interest in what takes place in Jerusalem on that Resurrection Day. His special emphasis is on the resurrection appearance in Galilee.

NOT HERE, BUT THERE

Following the burial of Jesus, the chief priests and Pharisees go to Pilate to make sure that the tomb of Jesus is made secure. They seal it with a stone and post a guard (*Matt.* 27:62–66). The women who had been watching all these things from a distance saw where Joseph had laid the body (27:61). The next day was the Sabbath, so on the following day, the first day of the week, the women go to the tomb at the break of day. They discover that the stone has been rolled away from the tomb. The explanation is that an earthquake occurred, and an angel of the Lord descended from heaven and rolled back the stone. The women find him sitting on the stone. The guards also saw the angel, and they became as dead men. To the women the angel speaks, telling them not to be afraid, and explaining that Jesus has risen from the dead, 'as he said' (28:1–6). Prophecy has once again been fulfilled. The women are then invited to see that the tomb is indeed empty. Then the women are instructed to go quickly and tell the disciples that Jesus has risen from the dead, and that they will see him in Galilee (verse 7). When the women depart to obey these instructions, they are met by Jesus on the way (verse 9). He too instructs them to tell his disciples to go to Galilee, where he will see them.

Matthew does not tell us about the other resurrection appearances that took place in Jerusalem (see *Luke* 24:13–49, *John* 20:1–23). As we noted, his main interest lies with Galilee, for twice in this section instructions are given to tell the disciples to go there, because they will see Jesus there. Then in the final section of this chapter, verse 16–20, the disciples make their way to Galilee where Jesus had directed them (see *Matt.* 26:32). The reason for the emphasis on Galilee is not hard to understand. It was in Galilee that Jesus began his public ministry, and Matthew showed that this was in fulfilment of Isaiah's prophecy (*Matt.* 4:12-17), where it is called 'Galilee of the Gentiles'. Given Matthew's special emphasis on the inclusion of the Gentiles, he took particular interest in this part of Jesus' ministry (in contrast with John's interest in the Jerusalem ministry of Jesus). Matthew concludes his Gospel with Jesus in Galilee, sending his disciples to the nations, that is, to the Gentiles (Greek, *ethnoi*). As most readers of this commentary will be from among those Gentiles, we can be most grateful for Matthew's emphasis on this point.

JERUSALEM, JERUSALEM!

But what about the chief priests and the elders? What do they make of the empty tomb? Matthew tells us that some of the guards went to the chief priests and reported 'all that had happened'. One would very much like to know just what the guards had to say. In any event, the chief priests and elders wasted no time in devising a scheme to suppress any information that might give credence to the account of the resurrection. They bribed the guards to say that while they had slept the disciples came and stole the body by night (verses 11–13).

It was quite a tale! If the guards were sleeping, they could hardly know what had happened to the body of Jesus, let alone that the disciples had come and stolen it. Moreover, such a report would condemn the guards for gross dereliction of duty, exposing them to the death penalty. The Jewish authorities pledged to intervene on the guards' behalf if they should have any trouble with the governor (verse 14).

The picture of the Jewish authorities we are given here is the capstone on what Matthew has been showing us about their rejection of Jesus. Despite all that the guards tell them, they do not give a moment's thought to the possibility that Jesus might have been raised from the dead. Immediately, all their energies are

[291]

focused on suppressing the truth in unrighteousness, exchanging the truth of God for a lie (*Rom.* 1:25). Their hearts must have been extremely hardened to persist in their rejection in the face of the overwhelming testimony they had received from the guards.

FAITHFUL SERVANTS

So far in our meditation on these verses we have concentrated on matters which are unique to Matthew and which receive his special emphasis. But we must not leave this section without pausing to reflect upon a feature which is common to all the Gospels: the role of the women who discovered the empty tomb and became the first witnesses to the resurrection (*Matt.* 27:62–66). The women did not come to investigate whether Jesus had been raised as he had said. Though Matthew does not tell us why they came, from the other Gospels we learn that they hoped to complete the preparation of the body of Jesus for burial, and that they wondered how they would get access to the body when the tomb was sealed with a stone larger than they could move (*Mark* 16:1–3, *Luke* 23:55–24:1). However, when they saw the stone rolled away from the tomb and the angel sitting on the stone, and received the angel's report of Jesus' resurrection, they were not slow to believe what they were told. They departed quickly to tell the disciples (verse 8).

The women obeyed without question, though as yet they themselves had not seen him alive. 'Blessed are those who have not seen and yet have believed' (*John* 20:28). Their faithful service to Jesus over many years – supporting him from their own resources, ministering to him, remaining with him at the cross, and now, as a final tribute, coming to complete the preparations for his burial – is acknowledged by their receiving the first audience with the risen King, who makes them his first witnesses (verse 9). The fact that, according to the prejudices of the first century, women generally were not thought reliable witnesses makes this report that much more credible, for no one seeking to fabricate a resurrection story would put such people in the role of primary witnesses. Yet Jesus chose them for this role, and the Gospel writers faithfully report it. Oh, that such faith might be in us, to believe all that Jesus has told us, and to obey all that he commands us to do.

SUMMARY

The resurrection provides the final seal of truth on the person and work of Jesus Christ, the son of David, the son of Abraham. The empty tomb reveals his victory over the grave and, by his appearance to the women, he shows himself alive, 'as he had said'. Jesus' instructions to go to Galilee help to underscore the fact that his mission is not yet complete, for the 'gospel of the kingdom' must be proclaimed and disciples made in all the nations. Just as Galilee was chosen as the place for Jesus to begin his ministry, so Galilee will be the place where the disciples will receive their commission from the risen Christ to continue his mission. Against this background of obedience and faith, the hardness of heart seen in the Jewish leaders stands out as a great sin, well-deserving of the judgment which Jesus had declared against them.

70

The All-Embracing Gospel

N̄ow the eleven disciples went to Galilee, to the mountain to which Jesus had directed them. *[17]* *And when they saw him they worshipped him, but some doubted.* *[18]* *And Jesus came and said to them, 'All authority in heaven and on earth has been given to me.* *[19]* *Go therefore and make disciples of all nations, baptizing them in the name of the Father and of the Son and of the Holy Spirit,* *[20]* *teaching them to observe all that I have commanded you. And behold, I am with you always, to the end of the age'* (Matt. 28: 16–20).

Matthew now draws his Gospel to a conclusion. The disciples are now transformed into apostles, receiving a commission which is from the one to whom *all authority* has been given, which embraces *all the nations*, which concerns *all Jesus has commanded*, and which is sustained by Jesus' personal presence *all the days* to the end of the age.

ALL AUTHORITY

Jesus appears to his disciples in 'Galilee of the Gentiles', high up on a mountain. Mountains have been significant places in Jesus' life and ministry (*Matt.* 4:8, 5:1, 17:1). Of special note here is the scene in *Matt.* 4:8, when Satan took Jesus 'to a very high mountain and showed him all the kingdoms of the world and their glory'. Satan said that he would give all of them to Jesus if only Jesus would bow down and worship him. Satan had only a temporary and limited hold on those kingdoms, so he could not have bestowed them upon Jesus or anyone else forever. Now 'the ruler of this world' has been cast out (*John* 12:31, *Col.* 2:15). Now Jesus possesses all that Satan had offered and so much more, and he has it forever.

Now, from this highly symbolic vantage point, standing as it were between heaven and earth, he reveals himself in victory over sin and death, for himself and for his people. 'All authority in heaven and on earth has been given to me', he says (verse 18). All things have now been subjected to him, and he has been given as head over all things to the church (*Eph.* 1:22). Nothing is outside of his power and authority, and no purpose of his can be thwarted (*Job* 42:2); therefore we can be confident that he both can and will work all things according to the counsel of his own will (*Eph.* 1:11), and make them all work together for good for those who love God, who are called according to his purpose (*Rom.* 8:28).

ALL THE NATIONS

Having all authority over heaven and earth, Jesus commissions the disciples to go to all the nations. It is not enough that he should be only the Saviour of Israel; his salvation shall reach to the end of the earth (*Isa.* 49:6). This 'gospel of the kingdom will be proclaimed throughout the whole world as a testimony to all nations' (*Matt.* 24:14), and disciples will be made from among all tribes, languages, peoples, and nations (*Rev.* 5:9). Matthew was anticipating this when he gave us the genealogy of Jesus, and included the Gentile women (*Matt.* 1:3, 5). He indicated this too when he told of the Gentile magi who came seeking 'the born king of the Jews' (2:2). He emphasized it at the beginning of Jesus' public ministry in 'Galilee of the Gentiles', fulfilling the words of the prophet Isaiah that 'the people dwelling in darkness have seen a great light' (4:16). Token examples of this were given in the Roman centurion who came seeking healing for his servant (8:5), and in the Canaanite woman who sought deliverance for her daughter (15:22). The one who comes to save 'his people' from their sins (1:21), now tells us that his people will come from *every nation*.

ALL THE COMMANDMENTS

Disciples are followers, and they are to follow their Master. What their Master commands they must do. Hence the disciples must be taught all that the Master has commanded (verse 20). It was for this reason that Jesus said that we must not think that he came to abolish the Law and the Prophets, for 'until heaven and earth pass away, not an iota, not a dot, will pass from the Law until all is accomplished' (5:18). Thus these well-trained 'scribes of the kingdom of heaven' (13:52) will go forward into the world with a treasure of both new things and old, and they must teach each new disciple to obey all that Jesus has commanded.

These disciples from the nations will be baptized into the name of the Father, the Son, and the Holy Spirit (verse 19). This baptism is the sign and seal of the covenant God makes with them. In that covenant and by this sign he assures them of the truth of his promises, to forgive and save all who repent and believe. He also binds them under his name as those who belong to God and who therefore must live for God, obeying all that he commands. Those who love him will keep his commandments (*John* 14:15).

ALL THE DAYS

Such a challenging task would be enough to make even the bravest souls hesitate, but these apostles (and those who will become disciples through them) are not sent out on their own. Rather, they are promised the sustaining presence of Christ himself: 'And behold, I am with you always, to the end of the age' (verse 20). For this final point in his book, Matthew uses his great word of emphasis, 'Behold'. The assurance is not to be missed or undervalued – *always*, he says, *to the end of the age*. Indeed, a literal translation of Matthew's Greek would be '*all the days* to the end of the age'. Our assurance therefore concerns each and every day in which we live, the bad days as well as the good, the hard as well as the easy, the sorrowful as well as the joyful. How comforting it is to know that not a single day will pass in which the presence of Christ is missing from His people.

As we noted at the beginning of our study, Matthew concludes his book with the same theme that opened it, 'God with us'. Our study has now fully revealed that Jesus is God. He is the Son, and a distinct Person from the Father, but he is God as the Father is God, and as the Spirit is God. There is only one God, but there are three Persons in the Godhead. So in Jesus Christ God is truly with us, in our own flesh and blood, and in all our temptations. Having been obedient to the point of death, even death on a cross, God the Father has now highly exalted him, and bestowed on him the name that is above every name, so that at the name of Jesus every knee will bow, in heaven and on earth and under the earth, and every tongue will confess that Jesus Christ is Lord, to the glory of God the Father (*Phil.* 2:8–11).

SUMMARY

So Matthew ends where he began, speaking to us of the God who is with us, who is *Immanuel*. Having made a promise to Abraham and to David, he has fulfilled that promise. He came to save his people from their sins, and he has done so. Now he is calling those people to himself, from all the nations on the earth. Having all authority in heaven and on earth, he commands his people to go into all the world, to make disciples of all the nations, that his salvation might reach to the end of the earth.

Here then is the missing discourse in Matthew's Gospel. Up till now all his narrative sections (Chapters 1–4, 8–9, 11–12, 14–17, 19–22) have been followed by long discourses (Chapters 5–7, 10, 13, 18, 23–25). But his final narrative (Chapters 26–28) has no concluding discourse. That is because we are to provide the final discourse. We who are his disciples are to make disciples of all the nations, teaching them to observe all that he has commanded. It is a daunting task that he gives us, but – behold! – his power (all authority in heaven and on earth) and his assurance (all the days to the end of the age) are more than sufficient to guarantee our success. Thanks be to God.

Additional Note

Marriage, Divorce, and Remarriage
in Matthew's Gospel

One of the distinctive features of Matthew's Gospel in comparison with Mark and Luke is the 'exception' clause in the teaching of Jesus on divorce and remarriage. 'But I say to you that everyone who divorces his wife, except on the ground of sexual immorality, makes her commit adultery, and whoever marries a divorced woman commits adultery' (5:32). Similarly, 'And I say to you: whoever divorces his wife, except for sexual immorality, and marries another, commits adultery' (19:9).

Neither Mark 10:11–12 nor Luke 16:18 has the exception clause, and when read in isolation from Matthew they might be thought to teach that Jesus prohibited all divorced persons from marrying again (unless they remarried their former spouse, see *1 Cor.* 7:10–11). But the exception noted by Matthew is not an innovation. It was one already widely accepted in Judaism, as illustrated in the decision of Joseph to divorce Mary when she was suspected of immorality (*Matt.* 1:18–19). Matthew, then, simply makes explicit what Mark and Luke assume. So we may conclude that divorce on the grounds of sexual immorality was permitted by Jesus, and that a person who divorces a guilty spouse for that reason would be free to marry another. Paul extends this permission to those who are divorced because they have been deserted by an unbelieving spouse (see *1 Cor.* 7:12–16).

A further question arises, however, about the status of second marriages when the first marriage was not dissolved by divorce with a biblical warrant. Jesus says that those who enter such marriages are committing adultery. Would that mean that all such marriages are continuously adulterous and should be dissolved by another divorce?

[299]

The issues here are certainly complex and various opinions have been offered. Readers will have to consult the various specialized studies that have been published on this subject. The present author would agree with those who say that while such second marriages are acts of adultery in their inception (and thus now provide the grounds for divorce from the first marriage), the second marriages are to be honoured once they have occurred. Many first marriages are such that they should never have been made, but once they are they must be honoured. So with second marriages involving a person who has been divorced for reasons not permitted in Scripture: though the second marriage should not have been formed, it still must be honoured with godly devotion.

In studying the Holy Scriptures people often have their eyes opened to see that they have done or are doing things they ought not to have done. So it may be that readers here will now see that the divorce which dissolved their first marriage was not with biblical warrant, and thus that they had no biblical permission for entering a second marriage.

If that is your discovery, dear reader, know that Jesus delivers from that sin as from all other sins. Confess it to him, and ask his forgiveness; then commit yourself to walk in faithfulness hereafter. If you are in a second marriage that should not have been formed, it is nonetheless the marriage you should now honour. There are many decisions made in life that should not have been made, and in some cases we cannot undo what has been done but must simply move forward in faithfulness, under the forgiveness of Christ. A second marriage could be one of those decisions. But when that second marriage is offered to the Lord in humble repentance from previous sin, and sincere commitment is made to live in faithfulness hereafter, that marriage too can become a place of blessing and honour under the transforming grace of God.

Look back upon the genealogy of Jesus found in Matthew 1:1–17. He is not ashamed to make us his family, though our lives be marred with many sins.

Group Study Guide

Study Passage	Chapters
1. Matthew 1	1–3
2. Matthew 2	4–5
3. Matthew 3	6–7
4. Matthew 4	8–9
5. Matthew 5	10–14
6. Matthew 6	15–16
7. Matthew 7	17–18
8. Matthew 8–9	19–21
9. Matthew 10:1–11:1	22–24
10. Matthew 11:2–30	25–26
11. Matthew 12	27–29
12. Matthew 13:1–52	30–32
13. Matthew 13:53–14:36	33–34
14. Matthew 15	35–36
15. Matthew 16–17	37–40
16. Matthew 18	41–43
17. Matthew 19	44–45
18. Matthew 20:1–28	46–47
19. Matthew 20:29–21:46	48–50
20. Matthew 22	51–53
21. Matthew 23	54–55
22. Matthew 24	56–58

This Study Guide has been prepared for group Bible study, but it can also be used individually. Those who use it on their own may find it helpful to keep a note of their responses in a notebook.

The way in which group Bible studies are led can greatly enhance their value. A well-conducted study will appear as though it has been easy to lead, but that is usually because the leader has worked hard and planned well. Clear aims are essential.

AIMS

In all Bible study, individual or corporate, we have several aims:

1. To gain an understanding of the original meaning of the particular passage of Scripture;

2. To apply this to ourselves and our own situation;

3. To develop some specific ways of putting the biblical teaching into practice.

2 Timothy 3:16–17 provides a helpful structure. Paul says that Scripture is useful for:

(i)   teaching us;

(ii)   rebuking us;

(iii)   correcting, or changing us;

(iv)   training us in righteousness.

Consequently, in studying any passage of Scripture, we should always have in mind these questions:

What does this passage teach us (about God, ourselves, etc.)?

Does it rebuke us in some way?

How can its teaching transform us?

What equipment does it give us for serving Christ?

[302]

In fact, these four questions alone would provide a safe guide in any Bible study.

PRINCIPLES

In group Bible study we meet in order to learn about God's Word and ways 'with all the saints' (*Eph.* 3:18). But our own experience, as well as Scripture, tells us that the saints are not always what they are called to be in every situation – including group Bible study! Leaders ordinarily have to work hard and prepare well if the work of the group is to be spiritually profitable. The following guidelines for leaders may help to make this a reality.

Preparation:

1. Study and understand the passage yourself. The better prepared and more sure of the direction of the study you are, the more likely it is that the group will have a beneficial and enjoyable study. Ask: What are the main things this passage is saying? How can this be made clear? This is not the same question as the more common 'What does this passage "say to you"?', which expects a reaction rather than an exposition of the passage. Be clear about that distinction yourself, and work at making it clear in the group study.

2. On the basis of your own study form a clear idea *before* the group meets of (i) the main theme(s) of the passage which should be opened out for discussion, and (ii) some general conclusions the group ought to reach as a result of the study. Here the questions which arise from 2 Timothy 3:16–17 should act as our guide.

3. The guidelines and questions which follow may help to provide a general framework for each discussion; leaders should use them as starting places which can be further developed. It is usually helpful to have a specific goal or theme in mind for group discussion, and one is suggested for each study. But even more important than tracing a single theme is understanding the teaching and the implications of the passage.

[303]

Leading the Group:

1. Announce the passage and theme for the study, and begin with prayer. In group studies it may be helpful to invite a different person to lead in prayer each time you meet.

2. Introduce the passage and theme, briefly reminding people of its outline and highlighting the content of each subsidiary section.

3. Lead the group through the discussion questions. Use your own if you are comfortable in doing so; those provided may be used, developing them with your own points. As discussion proceeds, continue to encourage the group first of all to discuss the significance of the passage (teaching) and only then its application (meaning for us). It may be helpful to write important points and applications on a board by way of summary as well as visual aid.

4. At the end of each meeting, remind members of the group of their assignments for the next meeting, and encourage them to come prepared. Be sufficiently prepared as the leader to give specific assignments to individuals, or even couples or groups, to come with specific contributions.

5. Remember that you are the leader of the group! Encourage clear contributions, and do not be embarrassed to ask someone to explain what they have said more fully or to help them to do so ('Do you mean . . . ?').

Most groups include the 'over-talkative', the 'over-silent' and the 'red-herring raisers'! Leaders must control the first, encourage the second and redirect the third! Each leader will develop his or her own most natural way of doing that; but it will be helpful to think out what that is before the occasion arises! The first two groups can be helped by some judicious direction of questions to specific individuals or even groups (for example, 'Jane, you know something about this from personal experience . . .'); the third by redirecting the discussion to the passage itself ('That is an interesting point, but isn't it true that this passage really concentrates on . . . ?'). It may be helpful to break the group up into smaller groups sometimes, giving each subgroup specific points to discuss and to report back on. A wise arranging of these smaller groups may also help each member to participate.

More important than any techniques we may develop is the help of the Spirit enabling us to understand and to apply the Scriptures. Have and encourage a humble, prayerful spirit.

6. Keep faith with the schedule; it is better that some of the group wished the study could have been longer than that others are inconvenienced by it stretching beyond the time limits set.

7. Close in prayer. As time permits, spend the closing minutes in corporate prayer, encouraging the group to apply what they have learned in praise and thanks, intercession and petition.

STUDY 1: Matthew 1

AIM: To begin to discover who Jesus is and what he came to do.

1. What names and titles are given to Jesus in this chapter? See verses 1, 23.

2. What is notable about the family tree of this person? See verses 1–16.

3. What reason is given for the name which the angel commands to be given to the child? See verse 21.

4. What important truth is assured to us in the birth of Jesus? See verse 23.

5. Both sections of this chapter (verses 1–17, 18–25) aim to establish that Jesus is connected to the house of David. What is significant about this?

6. What do we find in this passage to lead us to praise, thanksgiving, confession of sin, intercession for others, and petition for ourselves?

For STUDY 2:
Read Matthew 2 and chapters 4–5 of the commentary.

[305]

STUDY 2: Matthew 2

AIM: To understand the birth and infancy of Christ in the light of Old Testament prophecy.

1.   Identify the various people and groups mentioned in this chapter. How does each react to the news of Jesus' birth?

2.   Seen in the light of Numbers 24, Psalm 72, and Isaiah 60, what does the arrival of the magi from the east represent?

3.   Hosea 11:1 refers to an event in the past from Hosea's time, so how does Jesus' coming out of Egypt *fulfil* this verse?

4.   Seen in the light of Jeremiah 31, what *hope* is given to us by the 'weeping of Rachel' mentioned in Matthew 2:16–18?

5.   How does Isaiah 53 illuminate Matthew 2:23?

6.   What *warnings* and *comforts* are given to us in Matthew 1–2 and their Old Testament background?

7.   What do we find in this passage to lead us to praise, thanksgiving, confession of sin, intercession for others, and petition for ourselves?

For STUDY 3:
Read Matthew 3 and chapters 6-7 of the commentary.

STUDY 3: Matthew 3

AIM: To understand what the advent of the kingdom of heaven means and how we should respond to it.

Group Study Guide

1. Why does the arrival of the kingdom of heaven mean that people should repent (verse 2)?

2. Why do you suppose Matthew bothered to tell us how John was dressed? See Malachi 4:5–6, 2 Kings 1:1–8; Matthew 11:7–10.

3. What can this chapter teach us about the relationship between faith and works? See verses 7–10. Compare with James 2:14-26; 1 John 3:11-24.

4. In this passage, what similarities are to be found in the baptism of John and the baptism that will come with Jesus? What are th edifferences? See verses 6–12.

5. Why was it 'fitting' for Jesus to be baptized (verse 15)?

6. What affirmation does Jesus receive at his baptism? See verse 17.

7. What do we find in this passage to lead us to praise, thanksgiving, confession of sin, intercession for others, and petition for ourselves?

For STUDY 4:

Read Matthew 4 and chapters 8–9 of the commentary.

STUDY 4: Matthew 4

AIM: To understand the consummation of Christ's kingdom as it is anticipated in its beginning.

1. What parallels can be drawn between Jesus' time in the wilderness and Israel's? See verses 1–3 and Exodus 4:22.

2. What light does Deuteronomy 8 throw on the purpose for sending both Jesus and Israel into the wilderness? See verse 4, Deuteronomy 8, and Hebrews 5:8.

3. How do the disciples exemplify the appropriate response to the advent of the kingdom? See verses 18–22 and Heb. 11:8.

4. What is significant about the fact that Jesus begins his public ministry in Galilee? See verses 12–17 and Isaiah 9:1–7.

5. How do the miracles of Jesus contribute to our understanding of the kingdom of heaven? See verses 23–25 and Isaiah 35.

6. What do we find in this passage to lead us to praise, thanksgiving, confession of sin, intercession for others, and petition for ourselves?

For STUDY 5:

Read Matthew 5 and chapters 10–14 of the commentary.

STUDY 5: Matthew 5

AIM: To know the character of Christ's disciples and to increase our longing for that character.

1. The first and the eighth beatitudes promise the same blessing. What does that suggest about the whole set? The first and eighth beatitudes promise present blessings while those in between promise future blessings. What does this teach us about our life in this world as disciples of Christ? See verses 3–10.

2. What can we learn about the church's calling from the images of salt and light used by Jesus to describe his disciples? See verses 13–16.

Group Study Guide

3. How are we to think about the teaching of Jesus in the New Testament in relation to the Old Testament? See verses 17–20.

4. What is the fundamental error in the religion of the scribes and the Pharisees? See verses 17–20 and Matthew 23:1–39.

5. How does Jesus summarize the teaching on Christian character found in this chapter? See verse 48.

6. What do we find in this passage to lead us to praise, thanksgiving, confession of sin, intercession for others, and petition for ourselves?

For STUDY 6:

Read Matthew 6 and chapters 15–16 of the commentary.

STUDY 6: Matthew 6

AIM: To know the righteousness which is pleasing in the sight of God and to seek for that righteousness in our own lives.

1. How do the scribes and Pharisees pervert the practice of righteousness? See verse 1.

2. Is it right to seek after reward from God in the performance of religious duties?

3. What comfort does Jesus give his disciples for the practice of secret piety? See verses 4, 6, and 18.

4. Why is it so important to focus on the outcome of our life in heaven, rather than earthly treasure? See verses 19–21.

5. Since we do have many earthly needs, what comfort does Jesus give his disciples concerning their life on earth? See verses 25–34.

6. What do we find in this passage to lead us to praise, thanksgiving, confession of sin, intercession for others, and petition for ourselves?

For STUDY 7:
Read Matthew 7 and chapters 17–18 of the commentary.

STUDY 7: Matthew 7

AIM: To understand the continuity between the teaching of the Old Testament and Jesus, and to make a wise response to that teaching.

1. What do we learn about the character of God from verses 7–11? Where else do we see this emphasis in the Sermon on the Mount?

2. What summary of the Law does Jesus give us in this chapter? See verse 12. How does this compare with other summaries of the Law given to us in Scripture? See Matthew 22:34–40 and Romans 13:8–10.

3. How is the Biblical theme of the two ways in life developed in the conclusion to Jesus' sermon? See verses 13–27.

4. Compare verses 21–23 with James 2:14–26. What do we learn about the importance of good works from these passages?

5. What was the response of the crowds to the teaching of Jesus found in Matthew 5–7? See verses 28–29. What is your response?

6. What do we find in this passage to lead us to praise, thanksgiving, confession of sin, intercession for others, and petition for ourselves?

For STUDY 8:
Read Matthew 8–9 and chapters 19–21 of the commentary.

STUDY 8: Matthew 8–9

AIM: To understand the miracles of Christ and what they
mean for our comfort today and for the future.

1. How do chapters 5–7 and 8–9 fit with the summary of Jesus'
ministry given in 4:23 and 9:35?

2. How do the healings in these chapters fulfill the prophecy of
Isaiah 53:4?

3. According to verse 16 there were many people brought
to Jesus and he healed them all. Since there are many
believers today who are not healed, what hope does this
passage give us? Review the commentary notes on 4:23–
25.

4. What do the miracles have to teach us about the forgiveness
of sins? See 9:1–8.

5. Matthew gives his own testimony in 9:9 and tells how others
like him came to salvation in 9:10–13. In what way does the
healing of the paralysed man link with Matthew's testimony
and that of his friends?

6. What does this chapter teach us about how Jesus felt toward
suffering people? See verse 36 especially. What comfort do
these chapters give us?

7. What do we find in this passage to lead us to praise,
thanksgiving, confession of sin, intercession for others,
and petition for ourselves?

For STUDY 9:
Read Matthew 10:1–11:1 and chapters 22–24 of
the commentary.

STUDY 9: Matthew 10:1–11:1

AIM: To understand the ministry of the church today in the light of Jesus' ministry.

1.   In 9:37–38 the disciples were urged to pray earnestly to the Lord of the harvest to send out labourers into his harvest. How does the teaching of chapter 10 link to this prayer?

2.   How does the ministry of the disciples compare with the ministry of Jesus? See verse 1.

3.   What treatment from the world should the disciples of Jesus expect? See verses 16–25. Do we see this being fulfilled still today?

4.   What comfort does Jesus give his disciples about their persecutions? See verses 26–33.

5.   How does the teaching of this chapter compare with the teaching of 5:3–12 and Psalm 46?

6.   Do you think that verse 23 teaches that Jesus would return within the lifetime of his disciples?

7.   What do we find in this passage to lead us to praise, thanksgiving, confession of sin, intercession for others, and petition for ourselves?

For STUDY 10:
Read Matthew 11:2–30 and 25–26 of the commentary.

STUDY 10: Matthew 11:2–30

AIM: To consider our own response to Jesus in the light of the varied responses made by others.

1. Why do you think John sent messengers to Jesus to ask if he really was the Christ?

2. How does the response Jesus makes to John's question deal with his questions, and with ours?

3. What was the response to Jesus made by those whom he calls 'this generation'? See verses 16–19. Do you see this response in others today?

4. Why does Jesus say that cities of his day would receive a more severe judgment than Tyre and Sidon or even Sodom? See verses 20–24.

5. To whom does Jesus give the gracious invitation in this chapter? See verse 28. How have you responded to Jesus?

6. How does taking on the yoke of Jesus provide rest for our souls?

7. What do we find in this passage to lead us to praise, thanksgiving, confession of sin, intercession for others, and petition for ourselves?

For STUDY 11:
Read Matthew 12 and chapters 27–29 of the commentary.

STUDY 11: Matthew 12

AIM: To consider again our own response to Jesus.

1. Why did the Pharisees condemn Jesus' disciples for plucking heads of grain on the Sabbath day?

2. How does the example of David in 1 Samuel 21:1–6 and Hosea 6:6 show that the Pharisees had not truly understood how to keep the Sabbath?

3. Why did the Pharisees explain Jesus' power as coming from Satan and why did Jesus warn them so severely against blasphemy of the Holy Spirit? See verses 22–32.

4. How is Jesus greater than Jonah and greater than Solomon? See verses 38–42. What is the principal sign to be given to the generation of unbelievers? See verse 40.

5. Who is the true family of Jesus and what is the right response to make to him? See verses 46–50.

6. What do we find in this passage to lead us to praise, thanksgiving, confession of sin, intercession for others, and petition for ourselves?

For STUDY 12:

Read Matthew 13:1–52 and chapters 30–32 of the commentary.

STUDY 12: Matthew 13:1–52

AIM: To understand the nature of the kingdom of heaven and to make a right response to it.

1. Parables are often described as 'earthly stories with a heavenly meaning'. Considering the parable in Matthew 13:1–9, and its interpretation in 13:18–23, do you find this a good description of what a parable is?

2. Of the four types of soil described, how many received an unfavourable evaluation and how many a favorable one? What are the elements of a favorable response to the kingdom of heaven?

3. What do the parables of the weeds, the mustard seed, and the leaven teach us about the presence of the kingdom in the world? See verses 24–43.

[314]

4. What do the parables of the hidden treasure and the pearl of great price teach us about the kingdom?

5. One commentator has said that the parables of Jesus were designed 'to make one stabbing truth flash out at a man the moment he heard it'. Does this fit with Jesus' own explanation for why he chose to speak to the crowds in parables? See verses 10–17.

6. What do we find in this passage to lead us to praise, thanksgiving, confession of sin, intercession for others, and petition for ourselves?

For STUDY 13:

Read Matthew 13:53–14:36 and chapters 33–34
of the commentary.

STUDY 13: Matthew 13:53—14:36

AIM: To understand the ministry of Jesus in the light of Old Testament precedents, and what it teaches us about him.

1. Why do you suppose Jesus had no honour in his home town? See verses 13:53–58. For whom is this passage a warning today?

2. Herod's response to Jesus follows immediately upon the response of Nazareth, and Matthew inserts the story of how John the Baptist died at Herod's hand at just this place. What does this juxtaposition teach us about the responses now being made to Jesus?

3. Matthew puts stress on the fact that Jesus moved into 'a desolate place' or wilderness area. See verses 13 and 15. Why would this be important as a setting for what will follow?

4. How do stories of feeding the 'five thousand men, besides women and children' and Jesus' walking on the water echo events from the Old Testament? See Exodus 12:37 and Psalm 77:16–20.

5. Given these links to the Old Testament, how are we to understand the use of 'It is I' by Jesus to identify himself? See verse 27 and Isaiah 41:4, 43:10, 43:25, and 48:12.

6. What do we find in this passage to lead us to praise, thanksgiving, confession of sin, intercession for others, and petition for ourselves?

For STUDY 14:
Read Matthew 15 and chapters 35–36 of the commentary.

STUDY 14: Matthew 15

AIM: To understand what is true defilement in God's eyes and what is not.

1. What is it that defiles a person in the eyes of the Pharisees and scribes? What defiles a person according to Jesus? See verses 1–20.

2. Matthew calls a woman from the region of Tyre and Sidon a 'Canaanite' woman, an anachronistic term for his day. Compare Mark 7:26. What do you think Matthew is suggesting? See 1:5 and Joshua 2 and 6.

3. Why do you think Jesus treated the Canaanite woman with such indifference and used such derogatory words in speaking to her? See verses 23–26.

4. How does the Canaanite woman serve as a contrast to the Pharisees and scribes in the response she makes to Jesus'

harsh words? See verse 28. Do you think she is a model for us today?

5. Does the feeding of the 'four thousand men, besides women and children' in the wilderness teach us the very same lesson as the earlier feeding, or is there something new for us here? See verses 29–31.

6. What do we find in this passage to lead us to praise, thanksgiving, confession of sin, intercession for others, and petition for ourselves?

For STUDY 15:

Read Matthew 16–17 and chapters 37–40 of the commentary.

STUDY 15: Matthew 16–17

AIM: To understand more about who Jesus is and how the cross is central to his life and to ours.

1. What does the alliance between the Pharisees and Sadducees tell us about the responses now being made to Jesus? See Acts 23:8. What is 'the leaven' that they share? See Matthew 16:5–12.

2. Why do you suppose that Jesus chose the time just after Peter's confession to make the first prediction of his death at the hands of the Jewish authorities? See Matthew 16:13–23.

3. Why does Peter find this prediction so contrary to the purposes of God? See Matthew 16:23.

4. What further surprise does Jesus give his disciples on this occasion? See Matthew 16:24–28.

5. How does the Transfiguration account (17:1–13) underscore the importance of 'hearing' Jesus on the part of the disciples? See verse 17:5.

6. The Transfiguration account is placed between two predictions of the suffering and death that await Jesus. See verses 16:21–23 and 17:22–23. What does this juxtaposition of passages tell us?

7. What do we find in this passage to lead us to praise, thanksgiving, confession of sin, intercession for others, and petition for ourselves?

For STUDY 16:

Read Matthew 18 and chapters 41–43 of the commentary.

STUDY 16: Matthew 18

AIM: To understand how the disciples of Christ are to care for one another in the church.

1. What is it about a child which illustrates so well how Christian disciples should view themselves? See verses 1–4.

2. What is the warning given against causing one of Christ's 'little ones' to sin so severe? See verses 5–6. What comfort is there for us in this warning?

3. How do you think most people, both Christian and non-Christian, react to the idea of church discipline and excommunication?

4. How does the juxtaposition of the parable of the lost sheep affect our understanding of verses 15–20? How does James 5:19–20 affect our understanding of church discipline?

5. How do verses 21–35 affect our understanding of verses 15–20?

6. When verses 15–20 are understood in the light of what comes before and after, what does the failure to practise discipline say about our attitude to Christ and to his people?

7. What do we find in this passage to lead us to praise, thanksgiving, confession of sin, intercession for others, and petition for ourselves?

For STUDY 17:

Read Matthew 19 and chapters 44–45 of the commentary.

STUDY 17: Matthew 19

AIM: To understand the state of heart needed to be a follower of Christ.

1. Why did the Pharisees ask Jesus for his interpretation of what the Scriptures taught about divorce? See verse 3. Do you think his view was really important to them?

2. Before we ask about the conditions under which divorce might be granted, what must we understand about God's purpose for marriage? See verses 4–5.

3. Why do you think the hardness of people's hearts became a reason for Scripture to allow for divorce?

4. How do the disciples react to Jesus' teaching on marriage? See verse 10. What does this show about their hearts?

5. How does the action of the disciples to prevent children from coming to Jesus fit with their response to Jesus' teaching on marriage?

6. What does the story of the rich man tell us about the state of heart needed to become a follower of Christ? See verses 22-24.

7. What do we find in this passage to lead us to praise, thanksgiving, confession of sin, intercession for others, and petition for ourselves?

For STUDY 18:
Read Matthew 20:1–28 and chapters 46–47 of the commentary.

STUDY 18: Matthew 20:1–28

AIM: To gain further understanding of the state of heart needed to be a follower of Christ.

1. Why do the labourers in the vineyard who were hired first complain about the wages they have received? What are they resenting about their master? See verse 15.

2. How does this parable link with the story of the rich man? See verses 19:30 and 20:16. What state of heart do we need to accept this feature of God's dealings with the world?

3. While Jesus is more and more focused on the cross before him in Jerusalem (verses 17–19), on what are the disciples focused? See verses 20–24.

4. How must the disciples' hearts be changed if they are to be like their master? See verses 25–28.

5. How is leadership and authority in the church to differ from what is found in the world? See verses 25–28.

6. What do we find in this passage to lead us to praise, thanksgiving, confession of sin, intercession for others, and petition for ourselves?

For STUDY 19:

Read Matthew 20:29–21:46 and chapters 48–50 of
the commentary.

STUDY 19: Matthew 20:29–21:46

AIM: To understand our own response to Jesus in the light
of those who cry out to him for help and those who
reject him.

1. How is the story of the two blind men (20:29–34) linked
with Jesus' entry into Jerusalem (21:1–17)? See verses
20:30–31, 21:9, and 21:15.

2. What does the story of the cleansing of the temple (21:12–17)
teach us about the focus of church life?

3. How does the story of the fig tree (21:18–22) illustrate the
response of the Jewish nation to Jesus, and of his response
to them?

4. How does the parable of the two sons indicate the varied
responses made to Jesus by the sinners of that day and by
the religious authorities? See verses 23–27.

5. In the parable of the tenants, the chief priests and the
Pharisees perceived that Jesus was speaking about them
(verse 45), yet they supplied the condemning verdict to
the story (verse 41). Why do you think they did not fear the
judgment Jesus predicted and turn in repentance, like the
son who first refused to go but later changed his mind
(verse 29)?

6. What do we find in this passage to lead us to praise,
thanksgiving, confession of sin, intercession for others,
and petition for ourselves?

For STUDY 20:

Read Matthew 22 and chapters 51–53 of the commentary.

STUDY 20: Matthew 22

AIM: To see the greatness of Christ in triumph over his opponents and to bow before him as our Lord.

1. Why did those first invited to the wedding feast for the king's son refuse to come? See verses 1–6.

2. How did the king respond to their rejection? Who benefited from this? See verses 7–10.

3. Why do you think the man who had no wedding clothes was cast into the outer darkness? See verses 11–14.

4. How does Jesus confound the Pharisees and the Sadducees in their efforts to entrap him? See verses 15–40.

5. How is the Christ both David's son and David's Lord? See verses 41–45.

6. What does Matthew want us to believe about Jesus from this series of encounters with his opponents? See verse 46.

7. What do we find in this passage to lead us to praise, thanksgiving, confession of sin, intercession for others, and petition for ourselves?

For STUDY 21:

Read Matthew 23 and chapters 54–55 of the commentary.

STUDY 21: Matthew 23

AIM: To know the errors and danger of an outward religion with no inner reality.

1.   What were the fundamental faults that Jesus found in the scribes and the Pharisees? See verses 1–7.

2.   Are there lessons in these verses for ordinary people as well as religious leaders?

3.   What danger does Pharisaic religion pose to others? See verses 13-24.

4.   Jesus repeatedly calls the scribes and Pharisees 'hypocrites' in this passage. See verses 13, 15, 23, 25, 27, and 29. Why is it a hypocritical religion?

5.   What danger is there that in condemning the Pharisees we might become like them?

6.   What is the comfort that we may find in the great lament which Jesus makes over Jerusalem? See verse 37.

7.   What do we find in this passage to lead us to praise, thanksgiving, confession of sin, intercession for others, and petition for ourselves?

For STUDY 22:
Read Matthew 24 and chapters 56–58 of the commentary.

STUDY 22: Matthew 24

AIM: To know our calling until the coming of our Lord Jesus Christ.

1. What did Jesus' departure from the temple following his seven woes of judgment signify? See Ezekiel 8–11.

2. What was assumed in the three questions posed by the disciples to Jesus in verse 3? How might this assumption confuse us about the interpretation of this chapter?

3. In the face of mounting troubles for those who follow Christ, what must we do if we would be saved? See verse 13.

4. Is it ever right to flee from persecution when it comes? See verses 15–22.

5. Why do you think the Father has not revealed to us, or even to his incarnate Son, the time of the Son's return in glory?

6. How will the faithful followers of Christ be known when he returns? See verses 45–50. What is their duty until the end? See verse 14.

7. What do we find in this passage to lead us to praise, thanksgiving, confession of sin, intercession for others, and petition for ourselves?

For STUDY 23:

Read Matthew 25 and chapters 59–61 of the commentary.

STUDY 23: Matthew 25

AIM: To examine our own lives in the light of the final judgment.

1. Why does a wedding serve as a good analogy for the second coming of Christ? See Eph. 5:22–33 and Rev. 21–22.

2. What is the main point being made by the parable of the ten virgins? See verses 1–13.

3. How does the main point of the parable of the talents complement the parable of the ten virgins? See verses 14– 30.

4. What great challenge is given to us in what Jesus says about the servant with just the one talent? See verses 24–30.

5. How does the parable of the final judgment provide a grand conclusion to the lessons of this chapter?

6. If salvation is by grace through faith, apart from works of the law, why does Jesus' teaching about the final judgment say so much about works? See verses 31–46.

7. What do we find in this passage to lead us to praise, thanksgiving, confession of sin, intercession for others, and petition for ourselves?

For STUDY 24:

Read Matthew 26:1–68 and chapters 62–65 of the commentary.

STUDY 24: Matthew 26:1-68

AIM: To discover the deep love our Saviour has for us, the persevering faithfulness he shows in that love, and how the weakness of our flesh reveals that we desperately need that love.

1. What great contrast is brought out by Matthew's placing of the story of Jesus' anointing in between the reports of the plot to kill Jesus and Judas' betrayal? See verses 1–16.

2. How does the account of Jesus' last supper with his disciples show us that God's sovereignty over all that takes place does not eliminate human responsibility for the evil that we do? See verses 17– 25.

3. Matthew's account of the Passover meal includes the little phrase 'with you' in Jesus' words to his disciples. How does this little phrase highlight a theme found in the beginning and the ending of Matthew's Gospel? See Matthew 1:23 and 28:20.

4. Contrast the faithfulness of Christ to his disciples shown in verses 30–56 to the unfaithfulness of the disciples. What comfort is there for us in this contrast?

5. How are the importance of prayer highlighted in verses 30–56 and the danger of the neglect of prayer highlighted in verses 69-75?

6. How does this chapter show us the persevering love of Jesus and the desperate need we have for that love?

7. What do we find in this passage to lead us to praise, thanksgiving, confession of sin, intercession for others, and petition for ourselves?

For STUDY 25:
Read Matthew 26:69–27:61 and chapters 66–68
of the commentary.

STUDY 25: Matthew 26:69–27:61

AIM: To understand the depth of love and devotion given for us in the death of Jesus.

1. Why do you think Pilate delivers an innocent man over to death? See verses 11–26.

2. Why do the crowds ask for Barabbas to be released in place of Jesus? See verses 15–23.

3. To show that Jesus' death was 'according to the Scriptures' Matthew uses many phrases taken from the Old Testament. See chapter 68 in the commentary. Why is this important and how does it strengthen our faith? See 1 Cor. 15:3–4.

4. What can we learn about Jesus' suffering from his cry of dereliction on the cross, 'My God, my God, why have you forsaken me?' See verse 46.

5. What is so remarkable about the manner in which Jesus is buried? See verses 57–61.

6. What do we find in this passage to lead us to praise, thanksgiving, confession of sin, intercession for others, and petition for ourselves?

For STUDY 26:
Read Matthew 27:62–28:20 and chapters 69–70 of the commentary.

STUDY 26: Matthew 27:62–28:20

AIM: To consider how Matthew concludes his gospel and to understand what that teaches us about the Lord's kingdom and our calling in it.

1. Does it seem odd to you that the chief priests and Pharisees make preparations to seal the tomb because of Jesus' predictions of rising on the third day, but the disciples are not expecting it? See verses 27:62–28:10.

2. Why is it important for Matthew to mention Galilee three times in this chapter? See verses 7, 10, and 16.

3. Since the Jewish authorities knew of Jesus' promise to rise from the dead, why do you think that they seek to account

[327]

for the empty tomb with an absurd explanation, even though the soldiers have reported to them the supernatural events that have occurred? See verses 11–15.

4. When the disciples see Jesus on the mountain in Galilee, why do you think some doubted? See verse 17. Do you think believers today also struggle to become settled in faith?

5. Why do you think that Jesus chose to make his first resurrection appearance to the women who came to the tomb? See verses 28:1–10.

6. What impact does the repeated use of the word 'all' (including 'always') make in verses 18–20?

7. What do we find in this passage, and in the whole of Matthew's Gospel, to lead us to praise, thanksgiving, confession of sin, intercession for others, and petition for ourselves?

FOR FURTHER READING

D. A. CARSON, 'Matthew', *The Expositor's Bible Commentary*, Volume 8; Grand Rapids, Michigan: Zondervan Publishing House, 1984.

R. T. FRANCE, *Matthew: Evangelist and Teacher*; Downers Grove, Illinois: InterVarsity Press, 1989.

R. T. FRANCE, *Matthew*, The Tyndale New Testament Commentaries; Leicester, England: Inter-Varsity Press and Grand Rapids, Michigan: William B. Eerdmans Publishing Company, 1985.

LEON MORRIS, *The Gospel According to Matthew*, The Pillar New Testament Commentary; Grand Rapids, Michigan: The William B. Eerdmans Publishing Company, 1992.

THE ESV STUDY BIBLE. Wheaton, Illinois: Crossway Bibles, 2008.

On the doctrine of inspiration, as discussed on pp. xvii–xviii:

B. B. WARFIELD, 'The Biblical Idea of Inspiration', in *The Inspiration and Authority of the Bible*; Phillipsburg, NJ: P & R Publishing, 1948.